John Codman

The round trip by way of Panama through California, Oregon,
Nevada, Utah, Idaho, and Colorado

John Codman

The round trip by way of Panama through California, Oregon, Nevada, Utah, Idaho, and Colorado

ISBN/EAN: 9783337147709

Printed in Europe, USA, Canada, Australia, Japan

Cover: Foto ©Andreas Hilbeck / pixelio.de

More available books at **www.hansebooks.com**

BY WAY OF PANAMA

THROUGH CALIFORNIA, OREGON, NEVADA, UTAH,
IDAHO, AND COLORADO

WITH

NOTES ON RAILROADS, COMMERCE, AGRICULTURE, MINING,
SCENERY, AND PEOPLE

BY

JOHN CODMAN

NEW YORK
G. P. PUTNAM'S SONS
182 FIFTH AVENUE
1879.

To

MY COMPANION IN THESE JOURNEYS, AND IN THE JOURNEY
OF LIFE, THIS MEMENTO OF PLEASANT DAYS IS
AFFECTIONATELY INSCRIBED.

NEW YORK *April,* 1879.

PREFACE.

DESIRING to be on familiar terms with my readers, I have adopted the unconstrained style of a personal narrative, without any affectation of modesty in avoiding the use of personal pronouns.

Lest complaint should be made of anachronisms, and there should be discoveries of ubiquity, the reader is notified that this book is the result of more than one year's experience, brought up as nearly as possible to the conditions of the present day, and combined as continuous.

I wish to point out objects of interest not often "written up." Thus, little is said of large cities, and absolutely nothing of the Yosemite.

The tourist starts upon the Trans-Continental tour with a library of illustrated guide-books and maps, some of which are indispensable. If he goes directly from New York to San Francisco, and thence directly returns, they are all that are necessary.

If, however, he has the leisure and inclination to look at some things not exactly on the line of railroads, he may perhaps profitably make a selection from THE ROUND TRIP.

CONTENTS.

CHAPTER I.

A Winter Trip to California by the Isthmus Route—Leaving New York—At Sea—Nearing the Warm Regions—Social Lines on Shipboard—San Salvador—A Cultured Young Lady—Aspinwall—The Princess Columbus Married—A Duel . . . . Page 1

CHAPTER II.

The Trip Across the Isthmus of Darien—The Commerce of the Isthmus—Surveys for a Canal—Panama Railroad Company—The Terminus on the Pacific Side—Panama—Its Eventful History—Commerce of the City—British Enterprise 9

CHAPTER III.

A Comfortable old Ship—Settling a Feminine Dispute—"The Pacific Agitator"—Ports and Trade of Central America — Acapulco — Arrival at San Francisco 17

CHAPTER IV.

CALIFORNIA.

A FABLE—A REMINISCENCE OF 1848—THE COMPARATIVE PRODUCTION OF GOLD AND SILVER—THE CAREER OF JAMES C. FLOOD, ONE OF THE BONANZA KINGS . . . . Page 27

CHAPTER V.

LEAVING FOR SOUTHERN CALIFORNIA—THE PIOUS AGRICULTURIST—GREAT AND SMALL FARMERS—IRRIGATION—RIDICULE OF FEVER AND AGUE—A CALIFORNIA EDITOR'S HOMESTEAD 32

CHAPTER VI.

THE "CORKSCREW" AND "LOOP"—THE AUTOCRAT OF THE DESERT—BELOW THE LEVEL OF THE SEA—A CRAZY PLAN FOR IRRIGATION—THE CITY OF YUMA—THE ONWARD MARCH OF THE SOUTHERN PACIFIC RAILROAD—FUTURE PROSPECTS OF ARIZONA—THE INDIANS AND THEIR CHIEF . . . 42

CHAPTER VII.

RIVAL TOWNS IN THE SAN BERNARDINO VALLEY—NEWSPAPER ENTERPRISE—PARADISE OF ORANGE TREES—INTELLECTUALITY AND LAZINESS—MORMON AND ROMAN CATHOLIC CIVILIZATIONS—THE MISSION OF SAN GABRIEL AND ITS GOOD WINE 53

CHAPTER VIII.

LOS ANGELOS—DISAPPEARANCE OF THE GREASERS—A KENTUCKIAN'S DISCOVERY OF CONTENTMENT—THE FOUNDER OF THE CALIFORNIA WINE INDUSTRY—STATISTICS OF ORANGE CULTURE 63

CHAPTER IX.

NATURAL DIVISIONS OF CALIFORNIA—ANAHEIM—A THRIFTY
GERMAN SETTLEMENT . . . . Page 68

CHAPTER X.

SANGUINE "SANJAIGANS"—EFFECTS OF THE DROUGHT—SANTA
MONICA—A STEAMSHIP WITH A HISTORY—SAN BUENAVEN-
TURA—THE OJAI VALLEY—MISSIONARY ENTERPRISE . 74

CHAPTER XI.

A STAGE RIDE UP THE CALIFORNIA COAST—THE COACHER'S
YARNS— HOW A CLERGYMAN WAS RE-BAPTIZED — THE
CITY WITH THE PERFECT CLIMATE—A SMALL LANDOWNER
AND HIS TRIFLING POSSESSIONS 79

CHAPTER XII.

THE UPS AND DOWNS OF TRAVEL—THE DEATH OF THE HERDS
—A SAND STORM—SAN LUIS OBISPO—THE SPRINGS OF PASO
DE ROBLES—BATHS OF WATER AND OF EARTH—GERMAN
EXPLANATION OF THE MUD BATHS — HOTEL LIFE IN A
COTTAGE 84

CHAPTER XIII.

END OF THE STAGE-COACH ROMANCE—THE BOUNDARY OF
SOUTHERN CALIFORNIA—MEXICAN GRANTS—APPROACH TO
SANTA CRUZ—ITS EARLY HISTORY—ITS ATTRACTIONS . 94

CHAPTER XIV.

FROM SANTA CRUZ TO SAN JOSE—THE GARDEN OF SANTA
CLARA VALLEY—THE TOWNS OF SAN JOSE AND SANTA

CLARA — ANOTHER MISSION — THE CHURCH AND THE GRAPE-WINE AND BRANDY—THE ENTERPRISE OF GENERAL NAGLEE. . . . . Page 102

CHAPTER XV.

NORTHERN CALIFORNIA—MOUNT SHASTA IN THE DISTANCE—RAILROADS—FARMING ON A LARGE SCALE 111

CHAPTER XVI.

REVIEW OF THE MINING AND AGRICULTURAL INTERESTS OF CALIFORNIA—ALONG THE SACRAMENTO—NAPA—CALISTOGA—THE PETRIFIED FOREST — THE GEYSERS — SAN FRANCISCO 119

CHAPTER XVII.

"THE CHINESE PROBLEM" 126

CHAPTER XVIII.

ALONG THE COAST TO OREGON—DISCOVERY OF THE COLUMBIA RIVER—THE BAR—INDUSTRIES OF OREGON—SALMON FISHERY. 135

CHAPTER XIX.

ASTORIA—PORTLAND—WILLAMETTE VALLEY—SCENERY OF THE COLUMBIA—THE DALLES—INDIAN TROUBLES—OREGON'S OPPORTUNITY—DEPARTURE 145

CHAPTER XX.

FROM CALIFORNIA EASTWARDS—THE MINES AND GARDENS OF GRASS VALLEY—LAKE TAHOE, CARSON AND VIRGINIA CITY—THE SINKS OF THE HUMBOLDT—THE GREAT AMERICAN DESERT—ARRIVAL AT SALT LAKE CITY 158

CHAPTER XXI.

Sunset at Salt Lake—The Mormon Jerusalem—The Assembly of the Saints—The Late Brigham Young—The Close of the Conference—Society in Utah . . Page 169

CHAPTER XXII.

Out into the Country—The Great Salt Lake—Mormon and Gentile Towns—Elections—Ophir Camp—Successful Business Men 178

CHAPTER XXIII.

Camp Floyd Ruled by a Bishop and the Bishop Ruled by his Wife—William Hickman—Lehi and the Bishop who Ruled his Wives and his Diocese—The Garden of Isaac Goodwin 189

CHAPTER XXIV.

Sorghum—Luzerne—The American Fork Canon . . 202

CHAPTER XXV.

Provo—Factory and Co-operative Store—The Two Mormon Sects—The Childless Bishop and his Nine Fortunate Brothers 207

CHAPTER XXVI.

The Journey to the South—The Hotel at Payson—Our Landlady's Choice—Mormon and Gentile Amenities—Hospitalities of the Bishops—Mount Nebo—Energetic Conduct of a Bishop's Wife—San Pete Valley—War, the Consequence of Miss Ward's Obstinacy—A Monogamous Mormon Town—Reflections of Mrs. Price—The Coal Mines 213

CHAPTER XXVII.

TOWNS AND VILLAGES IN THE SAN PETE VALLEY—GERMAN PREACHING—PROVIDING TABERNACLES FOR DISEMBODIED SPIRITS — BRIGHAM YOUNG'S JOURNEY — THE MOUNTAIN MEADOW MASSACRE—LIFE AND CHARACTER OF THE APOSTLE GEORGE A. SMITH . . . . Page 223

CHAPTER XXVIII.

IMPRESSIONS OF TRAVEL IN UTAH UPON THE FEMALE MIND—THE STORM IN CLEAR CREEK CANON—COVE FORT—THE UTE INDIANS—ANGUTSEEDS AND KANOSH—ON THE WAY TO THE NORTH—FILLMORE—SCIPIO—LOST ON THE DESERT—THE TINTEC MINES—RETURN TO SALT LAKE CITY. . . . 235

CHAPTER XXIX.

IDAHO—SODA SPRINGS—NATURAL CURIOSITIES—THE UTAH AND NORTHERN RAILROAD—A JUMPING TOWN—THE BANNOCK INDIANS—POLICY OF THE GOVERNMENT 254

CHAPTER XXX.

TRAVELS AMONG THE MORMONS—THE PROLIFIC PATRIARCH— THE LEGEND OF BEAR LAKE—BROTHER COOK AND HIS FAMILY—VICARIOUS BAPTISM—A MORMON COURT—A PROSPEROUS CONVERT—BLACKSMITH'S FORK CANON—RETURN TO THE LINE OF THE UNION PACIFIC 268

CHAPTER XXXI.

THE UNION PACIFIC RAILROAD—THE ROCKY MOUNTAINS— EASY-GOING EMIGRANTS — GREELEY, ON THE ROAD TO DENVER 282

CHAPTER XXXII.

THE CITY OF DENVER—SUNDAY—CLIMATE—RAILROADS—EN-
THUSIASTIC MCALLISTER—COLORADO SPRINGS—COLORADO
CITY — MANITOU — "GARDEN OF THE GODS" AND CAN-
ONS . . . . Page 286

CHAPTER XXXIII.

ASCENT OF PIKE'S PEAK—THE HERMIT OF THE MOUNTAIN—
THE SIGNAL STATION—A HUNTING EXPEDITION—ON THE
DENVER AND RIO GRANDE RAILROAD 297

CHAPTER XXXIV.

PUEBLO—THE DENVER AND RIO GRANDE, AND THE ATCHISON,
TOPEKA AND SANTA FE RAILROADS—CANON CITY—THE
GRAND CANON OF THE ARKANSAS—DENVER AGAIN—COLO-
RADO CENTRAL RAILROAD—IDAHO SPRINGS—GEORGETOWN—
GENERAL GRANT'S DRIVE—RETURN TO THE LINE OF THE
UNION PACIFIC 307

CHAPTER XXXV.

CHEYENNE—PROJECTED RAILROAD TO THE BLACK HILLS—
THE GREAT CATTLE RANGE—LIFE OF THE RANCHMAN—
SUGGESTIONS TO YOUNG MEN—NEBRASKA—OMAHA—THE
BRIDGE ACROSS THE MISSOURI—RAILROADS TO CHICAGO—
THE CHICAGO AND NORTH-WEST—A DINNER IN THE
HOTEL-CAR—CONTRAST OF MINING AND AGRICULTURE—
CONCLUSION 320

THE ROUND TRIP.

A WINTER TRIP TO CALIFORNIA BY THE ISTHMUS ROUTE—
LEAVING NEW YORK—AT SEA—NEARING THE WARM
REGIONS—SOCIAL LINES ON SHIPBOARD—SAN SALVADOR
—A CULTURED YOUNG LADY—ASPINWALL—THE PRINCESS
COLUMBUS MARRIED—A DUEL.

THERE is not a great degree of self-sacrifice in bidding one's native land adieu when the cold March winds are whistling around the corners of city blocks, and the streets are ankle deep in snow and slush.

Cheerless as were the skies overhead, their cheerlessness did not pervade our hearts, and there were few among the passengers of the "Colon" who were not willing to say good-by to their friends on the wharf, pitying rather than envying those who remained behind. The "Colon" is one of the new iron screw steamships of the Pacific Mail Steamship Company, complete in all her appointments, and ably commanded by Captain Griffin, who has had a long experience in the service. Before she had reached the Hook and discharged the pilot there were ominous signs of a gale—dark masses of clouds heaving up in the northeast, and soon spreading themselves like palls over the heavens. Then came the rushing of the blast, bringing with it driving hail and snow, covering the decks. The good ship plunged into the south-west sea that fought in crested ranks against the advancing waves from the north-east; the red light on the port and the green light on the starboard side glared into the gloom, eyes of red and green shot across our foamy track, stared at us for an instant as they passed, and we were alone upon the deep. For us the whole world became concentrated in the cabins covered by the small area of our decks.

For three days the north-east gale lasted and drove us across the gloomy waters of the gulf stream down to calm and serene regions in the balmy air of the tropics.

As many who had been snugly stowed away in their state-rooms came out to breathe the fresh air on deck, we began to know each other. Heretofore the passengers had thought more of themselves than of society. Now, some of the ladies who had only occasionally appeared in very simple attire, the grace of which was heightened by the looseness of their floating locks, considered it necessary to "do up their hair" and to pull back their flowing robes in such a manner as to make the ascent of the companion-way more difficult. Fashion resumed its sway in our little world. We were introduced over again to some of those we did not recognize in their disguise, and long before we arrived, the eighty cabin passengers had divided themselves into coteries and sets, to the best of their ability, after the fashion of people in larger communities. It is astonishing how quickly women take the measure of each other. Men who belong to them, and who are not able to make such nice distinctions, are soon made aware that they will transgress by an innocent recognition of "that woman," who has been tabooed upon suspicion! Oh, yes! there is a West End and a Fifth Avenue on board of a steamer. She has her South End and her Bowery. Big worlds move and little worlds move, and ants of various degrees crawl around upon them all.

Many people prefer, as we have done, to make the trip to San Francisco by steamer and over the isthmus rather than by rail, especially when for them there is no novelty in the overland road. In summer the inducements of the route are not so great, but for those who have the time to spare it cannot be more pleasantly and healthfully employed at this season.

There is something inexpressibly luxurious in escaping from the clasp of dreary winter, without even a day of intervening spring, and falling into the soft arms of summer repose. Overcoats and sealskin jackets drop off as if by magic, and each passenger comes out from his chrysalis in a new dress.

It was almost sad to witness the calm delight of some invalids who had left home with the fond hope that health would come to them on the wings of the mild zephyrs of the South, and from the ozone of the sea air. Alas! how often they are disappointed! But this is not apparent to them at the outset, and they flatter themselves—and the well meant but feigned encouragement of friends aids in the deception—that they are realizing their fond expectations, while to strangers who look on with quiet sympathy, the hectic flush, the glassy eye and hollow cough tell the story of inevitable decline and death. The favorable appearances caused by milder weather are evanescent; and, as the flower that for a day turns its grateful face to the sun and dies at night from the heat it has courted, the consumptive becomes enervated by what at first seems a genial warmth, until

sooner than if he had remained at home he falls a victim to a
a false hope. Too often the physician, fearful that the patient
may die on his hands, thoughtlessly recommends the trial of a
warmer climate, when change of any kind comes too late, whereas,
in the outset, he should have advised a person of delicate lungs
to hasten to the mountains of Colorado or Montana.

On the 21st day of March, four days from New York, we
passed the island of San Salvador, or Watkins Island, as it is
now called, with disgraceful disregard of the renowned discoverer,
who gave its original name. ·

Well might Columbus have hailed this low islet on that
eventful morning when it met him, in advance of a new continent, as the "Holy Savior" from the threatened mutiny
of his crew. While cities of the old world have contended
for the honor of his birth, and those of the old world and the
new have in turn served as places of his burial, this island com-
memorates the most important event of his life, and is the earliest landmark of American history. It would be a fitting tribute
to his memory, and, moreover, serve as a guide to passing navigators, if the American republics would raise upon its highest
mound a high and enduring monument in his honor.

"Dear me," exclaimed a young lady, as we were running
close under its lee, "so that is the island discovered by Columbus!" "Yes, ma'am," replied a nautical gentleman at her
side, "and that large house on the height is the one first occupied by him. He was married to the Indian princess in that
church at the foot of the hill."

"Oh, how lovely—how romantic it must have been! I am so
glad you told me!"

"Why, did you never read that in your geography, or history
of America?"

"Geography? No! I never had one, and histories are vulgar. You know they are all written in English. I believe they do teach them, however, at the primary schools in Boston. I never heard Emerson or Weiss talk about such things. Oh, don't you think that Emerson is splendid? How he takes one out of one's self, and lifts the soul into the blue empyrean of the universe, to revel in the realms of psychological investigation!"

Passing through the channel that separates Cuba from St. Domingo we were reminded of one of the most humiliating events in our national history—the capture of the "Virginius" and the unpardonable submissiveness of the United States government. The cheek of every American should blush with shame and indignation when he remembers how in the autumn of 1874 that little blockade-runner, for she was neither more nor less, commanded by an American citizen and under the American flag, unarmed and without the intention of her captain or crew to participate in active hostilities, was captured outside of the prescribed distance from the Cuban shore by a Spanish gunboat, brought into a Cuban port, and her captain and crew shot down without a trial affording opportunity for defense. After the deed was done our government remonstrated, we used diplomacy, months passed on and we obtained possession of a useless old hulk for future adjudication, and purposely allowed her to sink off Cape Hatteras to avoid further trouble with "a friendly power."

After a run of three days through the Caribbean Sea, we approached the end of our voyage on the Atlantic side. On Sunday, the eighth day from New York, land at Navy Bay hove in sight, and at an early hour in the afternoon we made the port of Aspinwall.

With what infinite delight did the first comers to the tropics land on this shore, skirted with palms and bananas! Lolling negroes, chattering monkeys, croaking papagayas, piles of cocoanuts, plantains, oranges and pineapples, thatched shanties, stagnant ditches, clouds of mosquitos—all greeted us at once and welcomed our ship's company to the Isthmus of Panama.

Aspinwall is the American, and Colon the Spanish name for this miserable collection of huts, containing a few hundred inhabitants. The Panama Railroad Company own all the buildings fit for dwellings and the docks, excepting that of the Pacific Mail Steamship Company. A church where English service is held, is the only public edifice.

Near by is a monument—of no especial attractiveness—erected to Aspinwall, Chauncey and Stephens, the founders of the Panama Railroad. Not far from it is a bronze statue of Columbus, of greater artistic merit, deserving a site where it might be better seen and appreciated. It was a present from the Empress Eugenie to this little town, because it bore the name of the immortal discoverer. For want of a firm foundation—difficult to find in this miasmatic swamp—it is blocked up with a few stones upon the morass. Here it serves the convenience of washerwomen, who hang their clothes upon the arms and legs of Columbus and those of the Indian princess who, bending before him, represents the continent on which he lays his hand.

"So that is the princess Columbus married," exclaimed Miss Culture, of Boston. "What a disgraceful position! I would not stoop to any man in that way, even if he had a continent to settle upon me."

"The dower was in the other direction; she gave the continent to him," I replied.

"More shame to her, then. She should be represented as standing thus"—straightening herself to the utmost of her little

A WINTER TRIP TO CALIFORNIA. 7

height—" and he should have been at her feet. Woman did not understand her true position in those days." Well, she has a realizing sense of it now!

On the passage there had arisen a fierce dispute between a testy ex-Confederate major, of Baltimore, and a usually quiet young gentleman of San Francisco, regarding the pre-eminence of their respective cities. This resulted in a challenge on the part of the military hero, which was promptly accepted by the civilian, and an appointment made for a meeting, to take place as soon as practicable after arrival. To do the major justice, he was no coward. Preparing for a result, possibly fatal to himself, with a steady hand he drew and signed his will, and gave directions that in such case his body should be embalmed and sent to his relatives.

A little party left the steamer late in the afternoon, and proceeded to the outskirts of the village, where, in a beautiful spot under the shade of palms, the ground was selected and measured. Standing fifteen paces apart, the antagonists discharged their pistols simultaneously, without effect. At the second fire, the Californian brought his left hand to his forehead, and the red current was seen to flow from between his fingers as he fell into the arms of his second.

The major was now beside himself, actuated equally by a feeling of remorse and a regard for personal safety. Like Richard, he would have given his kingdom for a horse—nay, if he had possessed a kingdom, he would have given it for a mule —on which to escape into the wilderness.

But the ship's surgeon, who was on the ground, upon examining the wound, pronounced it only a concussion of the os frontis and a slight abrasion of the epidermis, suggestive of no serious consequences; and as all the requirements of honor had been satisfied, everybody returned to the ship in a happy frame of mind.

The doctor placed a patch upon the forehead of the Californian, which disfigured him somewhat on his appearance at dinner; and the major did not discover, until the next day, when the plaster fell off, that there had been no wound, because there had been no bullets in the pistols, and no blood had been shed, because a sponge, saturated with red ink, had been used for the occasion.

CHAPTER II.

THE TRIP ACROSS THE ISTHMUS OF DARIEN—THE COMMERCE OF THE ISTHMUS—SURVEYS FOR A CANAL—PANAMA RAILROAD COMPANY—THE TERMINUS ON THE PACIFIC SIDE—PANAMA—ITS EVENTFUL HISTORY—COMMERCE OF THE CITY—BRITISH ENTERPRISE.

NOTWITHSTANDING the insignificant appearance of Panama, its commercial importance cannot be overestimated. The Isthmus of Darien holds two keys in its hands: one unlocking the commerce of the world on the Pacific side, and the other opening it upon the Atlantic. Eight lines of steamships keep their vessels loading and unloading at the wharves, and millions of treasure and merchandise are in almost daily transit. On the week of our arrival 80,000 bags—over 10,000,000 pounds—of coffee were shipped from Aspinwall, and this product is but a small part of its commerce.

The country about produces little comparatively, yet a weekly shipment of 600 tons of bananas is not a trifling operation. All the trade is now carried over the Panama Railroad, whose construction has multiplied it a thousand-fold.

The Panama Railroad and the Pacific Mail Steamship Company have been our great commercial missionaries in these latter days, already rivalling in their work the steam and railroad communication with the East by way of Suez. Should the road be succeeded by a canal, the victory would be complete. The sand might then be allowed to fill up the work of M. Lesseps, as ages ago it filled it after his predecessor under the Pharaohs, had accomplished a similar undertaking.

It is now freely admitted that a canal across the isthmus of Darien is practicable, and the only question is one of expense. Two hundred million dollars are required; and the great republic that could spend $4,000,000,000 in a civil war, nearly one-half of which was, in one way or another, stolen by contractors and officials, hesitates about this comparatively paltry sum! If the work is ever accomplished, it will be done by British capital, for the interest of British commerce that, with our concurrence of indifference, now dominates the globe. How mortifying is our commercial decadence! While we quarrel about the personal claims of candidates for the Presidency and the small politics of the day, we do nothing for our commerce but fetter it with new shackles. All the attention we have given to our everchanging tariffs with a view to "protection," has had the effect of protecting England and Germany in making them the carriers of the ocean. We argue that man can rise only by being made free, and that commerce can rise only by having its freedom taken away. This western continent is ours by the law of nature and the opportunity of neighborhood, and we reject the boon which Providence brings to our doors.

England is our great rival, and Germany is becoming a rival not to be despised. Both these nations encourage their manufactures, not by protecting mill-owners in order to keep out the goods of foreign nations; not by protecting ship-builders in order that other people who can build cheaper ships may steal our carrying trade, but they protect their subjects with the surest protection—that of liberty: liberty to buy and sell every thing, merchandise and ships included, in the most favorable markets of their own selection.

Still, in spite of the neglect of our government, steamships and railroads are introducing our manufactures on the west coast of North and South America, while England is bringing by far the greater quantity of cheaper goods in cheaper ships. Our necessity in competition is to diminish the cost of both. Reduce our tariff so that the operatives of Lowell can live at the same expense as those of Manchester, and repeal at once the odious registry laws, so that Americans need no longer be the only subjects—and I use the word intentionally—on earth who cannot own a steamship without paying one or two Delaware ship-builders whatever they see fit to demand for whatever kind of a ship they see fit to supply, and then we shall be on equal terms with England. This done, if the canal is constructed, we shall have the commerce and the carrying trade not only of the west coast of America, but of the world, in our hands.

The late explorations for a canal across the Isthmus of Darien have been no improvements upon that made by our distinguished fellow-citizen, the late William Wheelwright, whose enterprises contributed so much to the prosperity of the South American republics.

About the year 1825, Mr. Wheelwright ascended the Chagres River and took an informal survey of the isthmus, with a view of making a canal, or rather of demonstrating that the project was feasible. He selected almost the identical route now occupied by the railroad, tracing a line, the greatest elevation of which was a little over 200 feet. Lloyd Falmark, Gavella,

Courtines, and the various exploring expeditions authorized by the governments of England, France, and the United States, have succeeded no better, and if ever the project is carried out, it will doubtless be on the line of the first survey, unless the Nicaraguan scheme should be adopted.

In the mean time, the Panama Railroad Company is in assured possession, and will maintain its power for many years to come. Its profits are very large notwithstanding the enormous taxation to which it is obliged to submit to meet the exactions of the government of New Granada.

The greatest difficulty attending all enterprises in these regions rises from the instability of the administrations. The company made a bargain with the rulers who happened to be uppermost at the time, and received a concession, upon the condition of paying $250,000 annually; but in various ways, such as free transportation of troops, munitions, etc., the road is made to pay the government a sum equal to $1000 per day, a severe subtraction from its receipts.

It is the custom of the steamship company to forward its passengers and fast freight immediately by railroad to Panama, in time to meet the connecting steamer—the balance of the cargo being more leisurely carried over, to be shipped in the succeeding one.

Our rate of progress was not rapid, nor did we regret its slowness. Amidst tropical verdure and jungles surely breathing miasma in the rainy season, and along the banks of the Chagres, now almost dry, we wound at the rate of twelve miles an hour, the whole distance being forty-eight miles to the terminus on the Pacific. A few wretched villages, inhabited by half, quarter and other fractional breeds of the Indian, negro and Spanish races, skirted the road. We occasionally stopped to take water for the engine and fruit for ourselves, in which novelty many indulged freely, and fortunately without inconvenience ; but the practice is not to be commended.

Mr. Mozly, the superintendent of the road, was on board the train, and was never weary in answering the questions, for which he had ready replies, as they had doubtless been often proposed to him before. Nevertheless, our obligations were as great as if he had been catechised for the first time. He is the agent of the Panama Railroad and the Pacific Mail Steamship Company, these corporations being connected with each other in some way mysterious to the uninitiated, but doubtless satisfactory to those most interested.

Totally different is the appearance of the ancient city of Panama from the mushroom town of Aspinwall. It is built of stone and brick, in distinction from adobe and palm-leaf thatch. Shorn of its former splendor and wealth, now squalid and poor, it still presents an appearance of solidity defying the total extinction which a tempest might bring upon the other town in an hour.

The streets are paved—if huge, irregular bowlders may be styled pavements—the houses are of a thickness intended to ward off the intense heat, and churches, abundant in all Spanish towns as in the city of Brooklyn itself, although many of them are dilapidated and despoiled of their former glory, remain in sufficient preservation to make them worthy of notice.

For us, the building of greatest architectural merit was the Grand Hotel, where we were pleasantly located for two days awaiting the readiness of the "China" to receive us on board. The weather was far from oppressive, and the time passed very agreeably in walks by day about the town and in evening strolls upon the Alameda, a long promenade built upon the seawall, against which the waves came tumbling over long reaches of coral reefs.

The present city, dwindled from its former prosperity to a town of 10,000 inhabitants, is more than 200 years old, and yet is young compared with its predecessor. Old Panama, vestiges of which may still be seen overgrown with jungle, now the abode of serpents and wild beasts, was founded in 1518. It was the earliest possession of Spain on the shores of the western continent, and at the time of its destruction contained more than 7,000 houses, 2,000 of them built in the style of regal palaces, of the finest stone and the variegated woods so abundantly produced in this country. The walls of these sumptuous residences were adorned with costly paintings; statuary imported from Italy graced their courts surrounded by gardens of rare exotics, and the streets, tastefully laid out, were shaded with palms. It contained numerous monasteries and convents, and its churches exceeded in magnificence those of the old world. All this was produced by an abundance of silver and gold, dug not only from the earth, but chiefly stolen from the natives reduced to slavery by their cruel taskmasters.

The day of retribution came. The greedy eyes of the buccaneers were attracted to Panama, the stories of whose wealth had reached their ears. As the Indians had been the game of the Spaniards, so in their turn the conquerors became the prey of the English freebooters. After a terrible battle, old Panama fell into the hands of Morgan and his ruthless horde, on the 27th of January, 1671. It was at once sacked and destroyed, the plunderers securing an immense booty, although the Spaniards had fortunately taken the precaution to place the valuable ornaments of the churches on board a vessel, which eluded the pursuit of the invaders.

When Morgan took up his march to return across the isthmus, his train consisted of 175 mules packed with treasure, and 600 prisoners, men and women. Those who could not afford to pay the ransom demanded, were transported to Jamaica and sold as slaves. So totally was the city razed to the ground that the present and more favorable site, six miles further up the bay, was chosen for a new location.

This, too, being attacked by the buccaneers from sea and land, at times suffered severely. Then came the separation from Spain, involving repeated capture, until at last a nominal independence was secured. which makes Panama, like all Spanish republics, the occasional theatre of riot and revolution, and will chain the wheels of progress so long as the chariot of liberty is drawn on its uncertain track by ignorance and superstition.

The railroad terminating at Panama, where the water is too shallow to allow large vessels to approach the wharf, a steamboat and lighters are required to transport passengers and freight over a distance of three miles to the roadstead at Flamenco Island.

This, although a source of profit to the road of more than $50,000 annually, is by no means a satisfactory arrangement for the passengers and owners of merchandise. It is to be hoped that the company will soon see the advantages of complying with the terms of their charter, and completing the road to a more convenient terminus, for as the means of saving no little time and expense, it will eventually contribute more profit than the comparatively slight gains from lighterage at present.

The harbor is more secure than that of Aspinwall, where violent northers frequently oblige steamers to put to sea. In the smooth waters of Panama such an emergency seldom arises.

Here centres the traffic of the whole west coast of North and South America, most of it coming from the north in steamers of the Pacific Mail Company, and from the south in those of the British Pacific Steam Navigation Company.

This service of fifty-six well appointed steamers, sending its semi-monthly ships from England through the straits of Magellan, and thence distributing traffic from ports in various connections of its own to the isthmus of Panama, owes its origin to the same energetic American whose name has been mentioned in connection with the first survey of the Panama route for a canal.

In 1842, unable to obtain capital at home, Mr. Wheelwright formed this company in England, and brought out the first steamers, the "Peru" and the "Chile," that ever ploughed the waters of the Pacific.

Here is another instance of British enterprise in grasping trade which we failed to secure for ourselves when the means lay in our power. We are a loud mouthed people. We talk of what we have done in carrying out the "Monroe doctrine" by excluding foreign governments from our continent, while at the same time we surrender into their hands our commerce—a greater power than is wielded by the scepters of their kings. The commerce of the Central American States, Mexico and South America, has more than doubled within the past three years. Forty-five thousand tons of sugar were shipped last season from Peru, all for the English market. Being of a high grade it is virtually prohibited by our tariff.

The coast line of the British Steam Navigation Company receives a subsidy of £1,800. Their ships costing one-third less than ours, this bonus secures to them an absolute monopoly.

CHAPTER III.

A COMFORTABLE OLD SHIP—SETTLING A FEMININE DISPUTE—
"THE PACIFIC AGITATOR"—PORTS AND TRADE OF CEN-
TRAL AMERICA—ACAPULCO—ARRIVAL AT SAN FRANCISCO.

However ill-adapted to compete with more modern steamers in profitable business, the China was certainly a luxurious home for passengers. She possessed every requisite excepting speed, and fastidious must he have been who could find fault with the ample accommodations, well spread table, attentive service, and especially with the courteous captain who supervised all these comforts.

No travellers can so well understand the requisites of patience and adaptability in a packet commander as those who have been placed in the position themselves. When in the early days of California gold hunting steamers were smaller and vastly over-crowded with all sorts and conditions of men, these qualities were of the most intrinsic value, but notwithstanding their best exercise, frequently of little avail. A ship was often a pandemonium of drunkenness and riot, from her departure until her arrival. Our captain had passed through all this experience, so that he was abundantly qualified to superintend the more civilized company now under his care.

His was a calm philosophy, that settled a dispute between two elderly ladies who occupied the same stateroom. On a night when the weather was intensely hot, one of them, and our sympathies were certainly with her, desired that the window should remain open. The other wished to have it closed.

"I must have it open!" exclaimed the first.

"I will have it shut!" cried her room mate.

The altercation at length became so violent that it attracted the attention of the steward, who vainly attempted to quell the tumult.

"I shall die if that window is shut!" vociferated the occupant of the lower berth. "I shall die if it is open!" screamed the lady overhead.

"Well, ladies," said the patient fellow, who had no patience equal to the emergency, "I'll report to Captain Cobb, and see what he says."

This he did accordingly, and he returned with the decision, which, to my mind, equals the judgment of Solomon in the case of disputed maternity.

"Ladies," said he. knocking at the door, "the captain says I'm to open the port, so that the one who is to die with it open may die as soon as possible, and afterward I'm to shut it, so that the other will die, and then, ye see, you can't either of you dispute any more about it."

With an exceptionally long voyage of twenty-three days still before us, we cast about in our minds every expedient to make it pass agreeably. Anticipating a pleasing variety in the frequent stoppages on the way, having congenial society and a well-stocked library, our only want seemed to be news from the outer world. This we resolved to fabricate for ourselves.

We established a newspaper styled the *Pacific Agitator*. It is true we had no printing press. The old Athenians had none, and yet there must have been a public reading room at the Areopagus, "for all the Athenians and strangers which were there spent their time in nothing else but either to tell or to hear some new thing." How they could discover new things in any other way than by reading newspapers, we of this generation cannot understand. It is certain that their journals were not printed, but there were industrious scribes at Athens, and such, too, there were on board the China.

This is the modest editorial of the *Agitator*: "The *Pacific Agitator* is the outgrowth of a feeling of ennui inseparable from a long voyage at sea. It is a pioneer effort, and will doubtless disclose many errors more or less serious, but which indulgent readers will pardon, both because of the brief period between the conception and execution of the plan, and the inexperience of those who control its destinies. The *Agitator* will be issued from time to time during the trip to San Francisco, and will treat of current topics, society gossip, light literature, together with commercial matters of interest to the passengers. The editors solicit contributions, with the assurance to those volunteering their aid, that their effusions will not be treated with the contemptuous indifference usually bestowed by classic editors. We have no waste basket; we can't afford it at present. Our exchanges are exceedingly limited, and this journal will probably contain more original matter to the square inch than can be found in any newspaper on the Pacific slope."

Our telegraphic reports were received by "submarine tubular," and were necessarily imaginative. A considerable space was devoted to advertisements, the amusement column announcing very creditable performances of Ethiopian minstrels and theatrical entertainments. Various items of a local character, in which care was taken to avoid personal offense, were pleasing contributions, and the illustrations were by no means of an inferior order.

This being the "coffee season," comprising nearly five months of active trade, it was expected that we should call at several small ports in the Central American States to receive cargo. The delay was an unexpected pleasure rather than a troublesome inconvenience.

We must confess that the oldest part of the continent was the least known and the most new to us. I am not ashamed to admit that I was ignorant, in common with so many of my countrymen at the North, of the political status and the resources of the countries lying between Mexico and South America. We have a general impression that the isthmus of Panama and its neighborhood is peopled by a set of half-breeds, whose principal business it is to quarrel with each other and with themselves—and in this we are, in the main, correct. But the opportunities of our voyage somewhat enlightened us respecting their nationalities and their commercial importance.

Panama is the capital of a State of the same name, forming part of the confederation of New Grenada, or as it is sometimes called, the United States of Colombia. These comprise an area of three hundred and fifty thousand square miles, and contain two million seven hundred thousand inhabitants. Its chief exports are gold, silver, coffee, cocoa, hides, tobacco, quinine, india rubber and straw hats, valued at from fifteen to twenty million dollars annually, and this trade naturally, as it grows, calls for a corresponding amount of imports from Europe and America in exchange.

Although, by means of the Panama Railroad and the Pacific Mail steamship line, some of the profits are secured to the United States, most of them are in English hands, and the carriage is by British steamers. Trade is nominally free, there being no import or export duties, but the freedom of trade like the freedom of the people, is far from being real. The merchant pays no impost at the custom house, but when the government has need of money he is politely waited upon and requested to make a loan, which the government forgets to repay.

This, in addition to the local taxes, makes free trade in Panama somewhat more expensive and uncertain than our tariff at home. We know precisely how much we have to pay for the enrichment of our manufacturing monopolists. The merchants in these regions can never calculate upon the demands that may be made upon them. It makes us somewhat contented with our own system, when we see others imposed upon to an infinitely greater degree.

Leaving Panama, we skirt along the coast until, in the 83d degree of west longitude, we reach the boundary lines of the Central American republics. There is no confederation here, each of the five States—Costa Rica, Nicaragua, San Salvador, Guatemala, and Honduras (the latter being entirely on the Atlantic coast)—governing themselves, and raising revolutions at their pleasure. In all of them, until lately, there have been various and excessive tariffs, deranging commerce even more by their inequality than by their enormity. But three years ago Barrios, the Dictator of Guatemala, the most powerful and advanced of all these States, overcame San Salvador and Honduras, his border neighbors, by force of arms, and by treaty obliged them both to conform their tariffs to those of Guatemala. Although the duties amount to somewhat over 50 per cent. and, in some instances, to 100 per cent. *ad valorem*, established rates render trade more secure, and offer better inducements for the merchants to remain.

It is thought that San Salvador and Honduras will be united with Guatemala, and that they will eventually bring Nicaragua and Costa Rica into their confederation. A good government being impossible for any of these States, a strong government is next in order. Self-government appears an impossibility for the Spanish race.

The condition of affairs might have been very different on the Isthmus of Darien had success attended the Scottish Expedition of 1699.

While Drake, Morgan, and other buccaneers had been intent upon invasion for the purpose of plunder, the honest Scots came to buy the ground from the aborigines, and, settling among them, endeavored to teach them the religion of Christ and the arts of peace. They numbered about four thousand in all, and were well fitted out with provisions and the tools of husbandry necessary to success. But internal dissensions, first incited by fanatics among them, who insisted upon a government founded on church polity, with the jealousy of the Spaniards, and the same feeling on the part of their own countrymen connected with the East India Company, who ridiculously imagined their rights interfered with, soon brought the new colony to grief, and caused the final abandonment of the scheme.

Had every thing gone well, the Anglo-Saxon race, instead of the Latin, might now have peopled the isthmus, and we should have been able to solve the problem of the demoralization of Europeans in the tropics. We should have known if this is attributable to the fault of particular races, or to the physical weakness of mankind in general, when transported to uncongenial climes.

Our good ship, as intimated, makes no pretensions to speed She starts upon her course at the rate of eight knots per hour, having on board 700 tons of coal, 800 tons of cargo, and 80 cabin passengers, 100 steerage passengers, and a crew of 120 men, 100 of whom are Chinese. These men are excellent firemen, cooks, and waiters, and although not equal to Europeans in point of seamanship, answer all the requirements of a steamship in this respect. They are orderly and generally obedient. When they are otherwise, it is only necessary to tie them together with their tails, and mutiny is instantly quelled by a threat of cutting off these hair pennants. Their wages are about half those that white men demand, and the same ratio holds good for their food.

Our first stop was at Puntas Arenas, the chief seaport of Costa Rica, which we reached on the 31st of March, two days after leaving Panama. It has one of the best harbors on the coast. As for the town, the enchantment lent by distance was quite lost when, on landing, we were nearly stifled with the heat, and saw nothing but a few huts and their wretched inhabitants. Of this town, and of the others at which we touched, it is sufficient to say that Aspinwall is a favorable specimen. There are about six hundred people in the village, a few of whom are employed in carrying coffee to the wharf and lightering it to the ship, while the others are actively engaged looking on. Here we remained two days, and received on board 9,150 bags of coffee; and proceeded to our next port of Libertad, on the coast of San Salvador. This is an open roadstead, and although a strong iron wharf projects far out into the sea, the surf rolls in unceasingly, causing the boats to toss and surge in a style that renders loading, and even landing of passengers, difficult, and at times dangerous. Receiving here 900 bags, we next called at San Jose, a port of Guatemala, about the same size as Libertad, both smaller in population than Puntas Arenas, but all of commercial value as ports of entry to their respective republics. Here we received 2,500 bags, and sailed on the 5th of April, having completed all our business with the Central American States. Fortunately, the Americans have control of the carrying trade of these more northern republics, although the percentage of merchandise imported is in favor of Great Britain.

A Spanish merchant, who took passage with us at San Jose, says that this is, in great measure, owing to the readiness of the English to comply with the wishes of buyers by packing goods, according to their desire, for mule carriage; whereas the New York or San Francisco merchants tell them to take the large bales and boxes and pack them to suit themselves. "Our people," he naively remarked, "do not like so much trouble. They prefer other people should take it for them."

When we consider that the population of all this region numbers three millions, who have so much to give us in return in coffee, indigo, and other products—coffee alone amounting to 25,000 tons annually—we surely should endeavor to secure such a valuable trade. There is no limit to the production of coffee in the Central American States.

We made no stop at any of the Nicaraguan ports, but kept on our way to Acapulco, where we arrived on the 9th of April, for coaling purposes.

This is a town of modern decadence from ancient commercial prosperity. Like Panama, it has the remains of architectural splendor gone to even greater decay. Its port must have been formed by some volcanic freak of upheaval and explosion into its present commodious basin. In its safe and land-locked harbor, a hundred ships may ride quietly at their moorings in its smooth waters, while tempests rage and seas lash the shores without.

The Spaniards discovered it at an early date of their conquest, and put it to a practical use. Being only 180 miles southwest from the City of Mexico, which conducted its business with Spain from Vera Cruz, Acapulco became the depot of Spanish trade with the Manila colonies. Here were fitted out the galleons which often became such valuable prizes for the buccaneers, but more frequently carried their treasures of silver safely to the Indies, and brought in return silks and spices, to be transported overland to Vera Cruz. When they arrived, the Mexican merchants assembled at great fairs, that were held for competition, and business must have been infinitely more active than at present. Now, a Pacific Mail steamer occasionally calls to receive her coal, while her passengers do a little shopping for oranges and bananas.

In the rainy season, the high hills, sloping down to the bay on all sides, are covered with verdure. In the ravines we could see cultivated estancias and groves of trees, whose abundant yield supplied the market with delicious fruit. Having every thing so liberally bestowed upon them by nature, the people have no necessity to labor to support existence. Lying upon the ground or swinging in hammocks, they doze through days and nights all merged together in their estimate and employment of time. Too lazy to be vicious, too ignorant to be responsible, their future cannot be one of punishment or reward. We can imagine nothing in reserve for them but annihilation.

Leaving Acapulco, we soon steered in a more northerly direction, coming into a cooler atmosphere, and though generally at a greater distance from the land, higher peaks became visible, and sometimes the smoke of volcanoes ascending from their craters. The whole shore assumed a wilder and more desolate aspect, and for the remaining ten days of the passage there was little or no verdure to attract the eye. We had left the tropics. When within four hundred miles of our port, a fierce northwester, culminating in a gale unexpected on an ocean supposed to be always pacific, materially impeded the China's progress. At last, however, on the twenty-third day from Panama, and thirty-fifth from New York, the Golden Gate was before her, and on the morning of the 21st of April she anchored in the splendid bay of San Francisco.

In this account of the voyage, I have endeavored to give some commercial information, which, it is hoped, may prove of value. All that we need, and all that we ask from our Government, is the freedom in trade that is accorded to other nations, so that every American citizen may stand upon equal terms with their subjects. Our own energy can accomplish the the rest. This investigation has been the chief *pièce de résistance* of the narrative—the little *entremêts* of the trip, made up of the episodes of daily life, serve to garnish it, so that the whole may be digested as a palatable meal. I have desired, withal, to show what resources may make a passage enjoyable, and can hold a a company of eighty people in a bond of union strong enough to overcome the little distinctions of society, born of exclusiveness, but driven out of existence by mutual forbearance and good will. We all agreed, and I hope my readers will be of the same mind, that there is a pleasant variety in coming to San Francisco, *via* Panama.

CHAPTER IV.

CALIFORNIA.

A FABLE—A REMINISCENCE OF 1848—THE COMPARATIVE PRODUCTION OF GOLD AND SILVER—THE CAREER OF JAMES C. FLOOD, ONE OF THE BONANZA KINGS.

THE hungry Seyd Ibrahim drew his bow, and his successful shaft brought down a great bird to his feet. Ravenous for food, he tore open his prey, and to his astonishment discovered a sparkling diamond in its maw. "Now, God be praised!" he exclaimed, as he threw the bird away, "for we are rich!" "Can we eat the diamond?" asked the practical Zulima. Ibrahim's senses returned to him, and the fortunate pair first made a hearty meal, and then, recovering their strength, were able to go to the bazaar with the jewel, which but for the food that accompanied it would have been of no more value than a stone.

When California came into our possession we craved it for the advantage it might bring, not only as an extension of our boundary, but as a field for pasturage and agriculture, and for its forests of timber. Its mineral wealth did not enter into consideration, for it was undiscovered. As Ibrahim opened his bird, so we forthwith began to open the country, and as he discovered his jewel, we became crazy over our unexpected gold. The hoe was abandoned for the pick. The cattle were allowed to range at their pleasure, the woodman ceased to penetrate the wilderness, ships were deserted to rot in the bay, and every body cried " now God be praised, for we are rich ! "

Although not "a forty-niner," I have my reminiscences of those days. I happened to be at Manila in the spring of 1848, having arrived there by way of the Cape of Good Hope. Just then came into port the first ship that had succeeded in getting away from San Francisco—the Rhone. She brought the news of the gold discoveries, and fired the colony with the same intense desire that inflamed the Spaniards of the sixteenth century. The fever extended to China and down the coast to the Straits, where it met the flow of news rolling in from the East, and thus the whole world was made to feel the tidal wave.

The captain of the Rhone told us that he was obliged to pay his sailors two hundred dollars a month to induce them to leave San Francisco. " I took off my hat then to Jack," said he. " Meeting an old shellback on the beach, I asked him if he did not want a voyage." " Where's yer ship?" he asked in the most independent style. " There she is," I replied, meekly pointing to the vessel in the roads. " Here, what'll you take for your old craft?" asked Jack as he pulled a handful of nuggets from his pocket, " I'll buy her of you ! "

John A. Sutter was the hero of a revolution in civilization. The first discoverer of the gold at the " Mill Race " is yet living, and his fate is an example of those who in adding to the wealth of nations have impoverished themselves. He has still his unaudited claims before the government for supplies furnished the army in the early days when by his means the infant settlement was preserved from Indian depredations. If the matter ever reaches a Congressional Committee, it is quite possible that it will be rejected on the same ground with the French claims— that the claimants are all dead, and if he is not dead, he ought to be, for he is very old. It is worthy of remark that a member of Congress is never too old to get his mileage and pay.

It is now only thirty-one years since Sutter's men brought him a handful of glittering sand found in the mill sluice, and from that day till the close of 1878, the product of gold and silver has been one thousand five hundred and eighty nine millions from the Pacific Slope. It is a common mistake to suppose that the production is regularly increasing.

From an interesting table of statistics compiled by the editor of the San Francisco *Commercial Herald*, it appears that the greatest yield was in 1853, namely, sixty-eight millions. In 1875 it was the smallest since 1848, namely, seventeen million seven hundred thousand.

But I believe with Zulima that the flesh of the bird is of more value than the diamond it had swallowed, and intend to show how the wealth of California is to be found in its soil rather than under its mountains and in its gulches.

One day we called upon James C. Flood. Who has not heard of the raid of Flood & O'Brien on the Bank of California and the tragic death of Ralston consequent upon that time of excitement?

I asked Mr. Flood if all this was true.

"All was a lie," he said. "Ralston was a good fellow; he died, I don't know how—well, the coroner's jury gave its verdict, but I tell you this: I did not drive him to it. He owed me a great deal of money, and only two days before his death he told me he was in trouble, and asked me not to present a check of his for $200,000 which I held. I kept my word, and when I heard of the run on the bank, although I knew it would go down, I did not call for my money. He was my friend. Some newspapers are not my friends, for they lie about me."

Mr. Flood is a representative miner, I mean of the successful class. The bar-room loafer, the convict, the suicide represents an infinitely larger constituency.

This fortunate gentleman is somewhat over fifty years of age, of robust appearance and pleasing address. He was ready to answer all our questions, and, moreover, volunteered some incidents of his personal history, which I reproduce in brief; for people like to hear how a "self-made man" made himself out of nothing into a golden image of the value of twenty-five millions of dollars.

"I came out here," he said, "in 1849. I was a coachmaker by trade, and readily adapted myself to the business of a carpenter, at which I earned sixteen dollars a day. But I had the gold fever like all the rest, and so I struck out for the mines. Well, we had a rough time that winter. It was as much as we could do to dig ourselves out of the snow without digging much gold. But I stuck to it and I made three thousand dollars. I thought I was rich, and so I went home and took my family out west, where I bought a farm. I soon found that three thousand dollars was not a fortune. Accordingly we sold out, packed up and came here again. I went into business, was successful at first, then went under owing $4,000. I earned that money and paid up. From one thing to another I got into the Hale and Norcross mine, and that gave me my first big start. I've been in the mining business ever since. I never bought a share of stock that I did not pay for and take away. I never sold a share short. Mining is a risk, any way, but it is a risk almost always the wrong way to people who speculate on margins. You ask me about the Bonanzas. Well, I believe in them; but you need not pin your faith on me. I've a right to do what I like with my own money. I've got a comfortable home for my little family, and so I spend what I don't want for marketing and clothes in Bonanzas. As to these mining boards, I don't care if the Stock Exchange closes to-morrow and there is never another share bought or sold. If the mines fail, why then I'll take the money I've got out of them and set the timber on fire, and that will be the end. No, don't go, I'm not busy—I'm never busy now. I was busy when I had to scull round to get five dollars. Now I can afford to pay my clerks and talk with my friends." In this style he ran on for an hour or two, and then our own business called us away, for we do not possess twenty-five millions of dollars, and cannot afford to pay clerks for collecting our money.

CHAPTER V.

LEAVING FOR SOUTHERN CALIFORNIA—THE PIOUS AGRICULTURIST—GREAT AND SMALL FARMERS—IRRIGATION—RIDICULE OF FEVER AND AGUE—A CALIFORNIA EDITOR'S HOMESTEAD.

ON the 19th May, crossing the ferry to Oakland, we took a palace car at 4:30 P.M., bound on a trip over the Southern Pacific Railroad. It may be premised that this road, which had been gradually extending for the last five years until it had reached Yuma, in the territory of Arizona, a distance of seven hundred and fifteen miles, is the conception and work of Governor Stanford and his associates, who built the Central Pacific and various other lines in the state, and whose surplus capital is always expended in public works of this character. They are regarded as the monopolists of California by some who consider themselves oppressed. I do not suppose that such people could be convinced of their error unless the rails should be taken up, the grades destroyed, and travel again performed by wagons and pack mules. Doubtless these few gentlemen have made princely fortunes by the success of the Central Pacific, which would not have been built but for their energy and perseverance. They have developed the resources of Nature, and Nature has rewarded them for their outlay. Their present enterprise is of a similar character. They are again planting ties and rails, the seeds of another fortune, if the enormous outlay is successful. I do not believe that their harvest will be a failure, but should it prove so, will the men who envy their past profits repay them for their future losses? Not so. Capital takes its risk, and in either case is entitled to its results.

All days are delightful here. We are in love with the climate excepting when we have a lover's quarrel, and the weather gives us a cold shoulder as the northwesters whistle through the streets of San Francisco. But these little "spats" are soon over, and the gentle zephyrs woo us again as they did on this charming afternoon. We were drawn for miles through gardens and orchards, passing the country-seats of the wealthy and the more modest dwellings of less pretension in the display of grassy lawns and smoothly rolled driveways, but whose taste was equally shown in the ornamental culture of roses and other flowers of sweet perfume everywhere abounding. When we see the vines twining about a poor man's house, and shade trees planted by his line of road, we place a higher estimate on his character than on that of his neighbor who in his bare walls is mean to himself, to those around him, and to posterity. Where there were contrivances for artificial watering everything was green and luxuriant, but as we emerged into the open country the unusual dryness of the previous winter showed its impress upon the soil.

" I don't know if Providence does it accidentally or on purpose," said one of the inhabitants, "but the rain is beneficial to the soil and not hurtful to man ; when it comes it is generally in the night, and I think that would be a good arrangement everywhere, as people would get all the advantage without being put to inconvenience."

At the East the fields assume their most exquisite verdure in May and June. Here they were putting off their green dress and clothing themselves like autumn. The grain was fast ripening, and was nearly ready for the sickle. It is cut when ours is scarcely out of the ground. It needs no barns or storehouses. It lies where it grew until it suits the convenience of the farmer to thresh it and carry it to market. He knows that no rain will fall, for he can trust Providence, who in summer, as in winter, arranges every thing for the good of the Californian. " The Lord did seem to go back on us this year," said the old farmer, "for we shall have only a small crop; but he is making up for it," added the pious man, " by letting 'em get into a war in Europe, so that the price of wheat is likely to be doubled. He does all things well!"

Gradually our speed was diminished as we ascended the grade surmounting the " Coast range," that little extra backbone running from north to south through this part of the State, and dividing the last slope to the Pacific from the great valley of San Joaquin and its southern continuations. In the dry season the water slope fares better than that inclining to the valleys, for the mists distilled from the sea lend it their gentle influence in almost every month of the year. There are the prolific vegetable gardens of the thrifty Italians and Chinese who supply the daily San Francisco market. They are in a small line of business compared with the rancheros of many thousand acres, but they manage by hard toil to gather in a sure harvest of dollars in return for their light truck. If the receipts of the " Italian market" could be estimated, they would be found to swell to an enormous amount, divided among these small farmers, who are independent of the large landholders.

The land of the interior, where irrigation is a necessity, naturally falls into the possession of those who are able to improve it. The farmer of moderate means is obliged either to take up his quarter section in a district where, in a dry season, his crop may be a total loss, or to avail himself at higher prices of land reclaimed by capitalists. It is cheaper for him to acquire by the last method a small property of forty acres than to be the owner of three times the area free of cost. To say nothing of the comparatively small productions from land dependent solely upon rain in ordinary seasons, experience has demonstrated that they are absolute failures in three years out of ten. Unfortunately the year 1877 was one of them. Some large proprietors and many small landholders on the uplands became bankrupt, but all farmers of either class whose soil was irrigated profited by the misfortunes of their neighbors.

We descend rapidly from the Coast Range elevation to the San Joaquin Valley. This is one of the greatest agricultural districts of California, a plateau including the Tulare and the Kern Valleys, geographically appertaining to it, three hundred miles in length, and an average of thirty-five in width, not comprising the bench hills mounting on either side to the coast and Sierra Nevada ranges. If Providence would contrive every thing to suit Californians it would make every man a millionaire without labor, and every stock gambler among them a successful operator.

Unfortunately for this people, however, nature has left a little something for them to do. They have a magnificent climate, an atmosphere of elastic health, gold and silver mines, and rich soil capable of producing the utmost that Mother Earth can bestow. For the gold and silver the Californian has always been willing to dig, but he has asked of the soil to yield its increase with the smallest demand upon him for labor. He has not ploughed the land, but he has scratched the dirt, carelessly dropped his seed, expecting an abundant crop, which in this way he sometimes gets; and then he is not satisfied, for he is apt to make the field do its own work afterward as a "volunteer." Eastern farmers come out here and lecture the Calfornian. They tell him he is exhausting the ground by repeated sowing of wheat. He says he knows that, but land is plenty, and when it is exhausted he will go for more. They tell him to plough deeper for a moister soil. He says that is all nonsense. It may be necessary in Massachusetts, but it is not so here. It takes too much time and labor. In short, he will receive no lesson from any thing but a good square ruinous drought. That is the lesson he has had, and he has resolved to profit by it.

Here, now, is this beautiful far-famed San Joaquin Valley, seven years out of ten nodding its myriads of wheaten heads in the breeze, ready to fall before his hand, and to be garnered for the market—now a scorched and desolate plain. Providence did not send down its rain, nor has it made a sufficiency of streams to gush from the canons on either side and fertilize the valley. The Californian must do it himself, and when he finds he must do a thing he does it with a will.

A variety of plans for irrigation are now contemplated, but they all look to watering this immense tract of land by taking supplies from the Kern and Tulare Lakes at the southern end of the valley, and carrying them down to the north, diffusing their life-giving influences over the whole surface. That this will be done within two or three years there can be little doubt, and then the annual yield of the State, instead of 700,000 or 800,000 tons, will be something incalculable. Then California will show its true wealth, and its mining will be scarcely worth considering. Out of its population of 750,000, not more than

150,000 engage in agriculture. There are more people working in the mines of Nevada than are cultivating the ground of California, and California is larger than all New England, New York, New Jersey, and Pennsylvania, possessing more arable land, if reclaimed and irrigated, than all of them combined.

During the night, we passed through the property of Messrs. Muller and Lux, the most extensive real estate owners in the valley. Here is a farm seventy-three miles in length by twenty in width. If a poor man owned one hundred and sixty acres of it, it would be worth nothing to him, as part of it is swamp land about Lake Tulare that he could not drain, and part of it a desert sand, that he could not irrigate. But to these capitalists it is valuable, because they can cause the two unproductive parts to fructify each other by means of canals. At present, while engaged in this enterprise, they content themselves with raising a few thousand acres of alfalfa, and with the pasturage of their eighty-five thousand head of cattle and forty thousand sheep! One single straight fence on their property is seventy-three miles long.

Now, this has the appearance of "gobbling up land." But when the small number of inhabitants and the vast area of territory in the State are considered, and especially when the result of this speculation is inevitably division after improvement preparatory to cultivation, it will be seen that the gobbling is for the general good. Consulting the early history of New York and New England, we find that the territory was ceded by the Crown in patents to a few individuals. Property there has been divided and sub-divided, until one hundred acres is considered a large farm. So in the future it will be here.

We travelled as far as Lathrop, eighty-three miles on the Central Pacific. At this point the Southern Pacific branches off in a southerly direction, passing Merced fifty-seven miles further on our way. This is the railroad terminus of the best route to the Yosemite. Tourists here take the stage for the two remaining days of that journey. When we took the excursion five years ago, part of the travel was done on horseback or on foot, and I imagine that the present more comfortable mode of locomotion has not added to enjoyment. A little hardship gives a zest to pleasure. If any one entertains the intention of making this trip, he can readily follow us to Merced. Here he may part from our company until he has made the Yosemite excursion. He should go into the valley after visiting the big trees at Mariposa, remain there a week to get some small idea of its incomparable grandeur and beauty, returning by way of Coultersville. In this way the Yosemite and Southern Californian journeys may be combined to the greatest advantage.

At five o'clock on the morning after the departure from San Francisco, we left the train at Bakersfield, a small town three hundred miles distant on the road. It was a pueblo of the old Mexicans, and after the cession of the country to the United States, was squatted upon by "pikes," a set of poor whites from Pike County, Missouri, and a few negroes, whom they brought with the intention of maintaining the domestic institution. Here was a rare chance for a miscegenous production of humanity by the admixture of these immigrants with the "greasers" and the Indians. The result of the experiment was that the new-born population possessed about one-fourth part of manhood. I do not know why the Pikes should have selected this spot, unless because of its swampy proclivities to fever and ague, their favorite disease. Gradually a better immigration from the North ousted them, drained the marshes, and made it a comparatively healthy and thriving little town. There is still enough of the fever left in August and September to satisfy the few original settlers, but for those who do not supplement "the shakes" with bad whiskey, there is little danger now to be apprehended from malaria. "It never was much anyway," said one of the Pikes; "all a feller had to do was to take sixty grains of quinine when the fit came on, and then take forty grains of calomel to work that off; afterward he wanted to get about nine ounces of iron into his blood to strengthen himself up, and then he was all right. D——n the shakes; I ain't afraid of 'em!"

We drove first to the residence of Mr. Chester, the editor of the *Southern Californian*. Mr. Chester resides in a pretty country house, a mile from the village, where he has a little farm of seven hundred and fifty acres, all in a high state of cultivation. In his small garden were ten acres of grapes. He does not trouble himself to pick them, but sells them on the vines to the fruit dealers for $1,000 per annum. Then, there is an orchard of peaches, another of cherries—trees bearing in three years after planting the pits. Did he expect us to believe it? Yet it was not more wonderful than many other things. He did not care for his garden or his orchards, but he thought no little of his wheat, turning out forty bushels to the acre, and two crops at that, one of them a volunteer. But his chief delight was his alfalfa, ten tons to the acre, worth $18 per ton, and five annual crops; four hundred acres were in alfalfa. From one lot of one hundred and twenty acres he realized last year $6,000. Beside his wheat and alfalfa, he has one hundred and twenty acres in barley, yielding sixty bushels to the acre. These are products of a "small farm," and I imagine the profits exceed those of the *Southern Californian*, although it is an exceedingly well-conducted journal, edited by Mr. Chester, with the sole view of furthering the agricultural interests of the country.

We drove on four miles, to one of the ranches of Messrs. Haggin & Carr. These gentlemen own one hundred and forty thousand acres in the San Joaquin Valley, thirty thousand of which they have already irrigated and prepared for cultivation. On this property they have expended $650,000, digging one hundred and fifty miles of canals. It is divided into several ranches, the one we were to visit containing six thousand acres. Driving two miles from the residence of Mr. Chester, we entered the domain of the "Bellevue" ranch. Two thousand acres were taken in last year. At present, there are only four thousand under full cultivation. The force employed consists of one hundred and fifty-five whites and ninety Chinamen, who receive on an average one dollar per diem and their food. Three hundred mules and horses are kept at work, eight thousand head of cattle are on the place, a flock of twenty-two thousand sheep occupying the uncultivated range. We drove through alternate lots of wheat, barley, and alfalfa for three miles before reaching the house. One of the proprietors received us courteously, and entertained us at luncheon. Alfalfa, too, was his pride and delight. Every living creature on the ranch, excepting man, feeds on alfalfa. The hogs, as well as the horses, mules, and cattle, live on it when green, and fatten on it when dry. Its roots strike more than six feet into the soil, and it never requires replanting unless the ground is broken up. While every year there are five crops of alfalfa, there are two only of wheat and barley! The income of such products is, of course, very great; but as yet the expenses are enormous, for it is the intention to reclaim the whole one hundred and forty thousand acres, and then the property will be for sale "in small lots to suit purchasers." In the meantime, the expenses exceed one thousand dollars per day; so that the balance can hardly be in favor of profit.

Pleased and instructed by our visit to the Bellevue ranch, we returned to dine with Mr. and Mrs. Chester, whose cheerful entertainment pleasantly closed the day. One little episode preceding dinner diverted us. Hearing two or three reports from a gun not far from the house, our hostess quietly assured us by saying that a man was shooting chickens. "When we want turkeys or chickens for dinner," she said, "we always shoot them, for there are hundreds of them all over the place—they live on the alfalfa." We returned at a late hour to the "Arlington Hotel," to be in readiness for an early start in the morning. Our sleep was pleasant, for in our dreams we were cradled in a ten thousand acre lot of alfalfa.

CHAPTER VI.

The "Corkscrew" and "Loop"—The Autocrat of the Desert—Below the Level of the Sea—A Crazy Plan for Irrigation—The City of Yuma—The Onward March of the Southern Pacific Railroad—Future Prospects of Arizona—The Indians and their Chief.

We again took the Southern Pacific train, reaching Caliente just as the rising sun darted his rays through the rugged peaks of the Sierras, among which we were about to climb a steep grade of one hundred and sixteen feet to the mile. Skilful engineers, after a study of three years to ascertain the most practicable route, at length made this selection. It is here that a spur of the Sierras, straying from the great chain, sweeps over to join the coast range, closing upon the valleys stretching from the Sacramento to the South.

On the plains we speak of the line of a railroad. Here it is appropriately termed the "corkscrew," and beyond it is the "loop." The "corkscrew" section winds around the sides of the mountain exactly as its name indicates, affording passing and recurring views at all points of the compass. The "loop" is a still more wonderful exhibition of engineering ingenuity. First, the road runs through a tunnel, then bridges an abyss, and finally crosses over itself, seemingly tying a bow-knot with its iron straps. By these skilful devices, it is brought to an elevation of three thousand five hundred and forty-nine feet above the plains. This is the Tehachapé Pass, by which Fremont first crossed the mountain ridge between northern and southern California.

The slow progression added to our enjoyment. On reaching the summit, the engine was allowed to take its ease, as pushed by the train without effort, it rapidly slid down the southern incline. This pass, with the desert beyond, forms the barrier between the grain-producing plains of the north, and the fruit-bearing valleys of the south,—for such is the general, although not universal distinction to be made.

We were now on a desert utterly barren, a sea of sand without sufficient nourishment for a predatory grasshopper. One hundred miles of road is laid over it. The desert has a capital. States, territories and countries sometimes quarrel about their capitals, but there was no opposition in the desert district to Mojave. It has its railroad station, its county court, its church, its hotel, its business quarter, all in one house, the landlord being city government, judge, parson and everybody. The autocrat said that Mojave was already a place of considerable business as a mining depot, and "there is plenty of room for it to increase," he added, as he waved his hand around the circle of the sandy horizon. "Water is handy," he said. "Tain't more'n twenty miles off, and provisions are getting plenty since we've got the railroad. Before that we had to haul them a hundred miles."

We breakfasted at Mojave, expecting under the circumstances to be charged an exorbitant price for our meal, which was a very good one, and were agreeably surprised at the moderate charge of seventy-five cents. That hermit of the desert is actuated by generous impulses, or he is sadly ignorant of his opportunity.

Still journeying over the long reaches of sand, ribbed occasionally with reefs of rocks, we came to the tunnel under another cross range of hills. This excavation is more than a mile in length, and is shored with timber like a snow-shed. Boring the mountains for the last time—for we have passed through many tunnels on the way—we leave them and the Mojave desert behind, and look down upon the vineyards and orange groves of the southern valleys, where peeping through its vines and its orchards, we see the lovely Pueblo de Nuestra Señora de los Angeles. We will surely abide there a while on our return, but now let us finish our journey "to the front," as the Californians call it, to Yuma, in Arizona.

We have yet before us two hundred and forty-five miles on the Southern Pacific road. From three o'clock in the afternoon until dark, we run through the valleys of Los Angeles and San Bernardino until the Gorgonio Pass is reached. This district thus far is easily watered and naturally productive, but extensive irrigation is required. That desirable improvement has been accomplished, a flume bringing water from a distance sufficient to supply ten thousand acres. This wooden canal, called a V from its shape, also brings logs and railroad ties, shooting them fourteen miles in half an hour. A man said that he had made the trip in a three foot boat, but he "felt like a hog in a trough riding to the devil, and did not care to try it again."

The change was sudden from the green grass, the grain and the semi-tropical fruit trees of the valley. Our pathway was one of strong contrasts. Cultivation and desolation succeed each other continually, and we have again the desert before us, "the desert" *par excellence*, if excellence means excelling all abominations. But first we mount its arid wastes through the picturesque Gorgonio Cañon. Moonlight lent its weird enchantment to the shadowy outlines of distant mountains dimly seen beyond the dark rocks through which the road was cut. The cold winds reached us from their snowy summits. " Cold is it? " asked the brakeman. "Ye'll be begging for half a breath of it before morning."

We realized this when we descended into what might be called "the valley of the shadow of death"—if there could be a shadow there. There is no object on this vast area, one thousand miles long, and from one to two hundred miles wide, capable of making a shadow. In the deserts of Africa there are oases with their shady palms and wells of living water; here there is nothing but stunted sage brush and straggling spears of yellow grass. For miles not even these are to be seen; nothing, absolutely nothing, but an everlasting waste of sand, bounded by the horizon or the bases of distant mountains, whose blue outlines have so often mocked the hopes of weary travellers doomed to perish for want of the water in their sight.

This is the great American Sahara, which, although mostly in the limits of California, is called the "Colorado Desert," and has become familiar to the public through the proposition of Dr. Wozencraft. That enthusiastic gentleman has long been endeavoring to persuade Congress to give the company he represents a right to turn the Colorado River into the desert for the purpose of irrigating a few million acres, and making them profitable as farming lands. I have not heard a single individual who has crossed this plain characterize this scheme as anything but insane, and now that we have seen it, I am fully of that opinion.

The valley was unmistakably at one time a bay of the sea, and if the experiment would not result in the destruction of the railroad, it could not be put to a better use than to make it revert to the original owner. This could be accomplished easily by cutting a canal only a few miles from the coast and letting in the Pacific Ocean, which is higher than the plain. Our track actually descended before reaching Yuma, to a depth of two hundred and fifty-three feet below the sea level, and we have some marine shells picked up from the sand.

There are stories told of a wreck that was found here not long ago, to prove that this was once a navigable sea. But such apocryphal legends are needless. In this case fact can sustain itself without the aid of fancy. The indications furnished by the shells and other outward appearances are made still more conclusive by the extraordinary depression of the ground, and by the fact that the water brought up from the low bottoms is salt.

On the higher grade water has not yet been reached. At one station where we were delayed, men were boring an artesian well. They had perforated one hundred and eighty-five feet of sand, as dry at that depth as at the surface.

One glance at Dr. Wozencraft's scheme should be sufficient to condemn it. The Colorado River, a stream whose importance has been greatly exaggerated, is not an eighth of a mile wide where it is crossed at Yuma, and is so shallow that it is only navigable for stern-wheel boats drawing less than two feet. Still, it is too valuable for purposes of navigation to be taken out of its bed. But supposing it turned on to this desert, it would be lost in almost the first acre of sand. The Mississippi would not wander far before it would be literally sucked in, as Congress would be metaphorically, if it should give its sanction to such an absurdity.

The Southern Pacific Railroad, from its point of leaving from the Central Pacific, has already been extended six hundred and thirty-two miles, to Yuma. When it is considered that about one-fourth of the distance is accomplished over an absolutely irreclaimable desert, where local traffic is reversed—the trains carrying tanks of water for distribution at the stations—the question naturally arises, on what sources does the road depend for its profits? An enterprise so vast, undertaken by men of such known ability, must have had its foundation in sound calculation.

We must remember that they have first their individual interests at stake. These are located in California and centred in San Francisco; consequently, whatever is for the benefit of the State and its capital redounds to their own profit. It is clearly not for their advantage that any road from the East should find its terminus at San Diego, the extreme south of the State. Perhaps they would not care to have any other communication with the Atlantic coast than that afforded by their own profitable Central Pacific, but as they are aware that a parallel road in a more southern latitude is inevitable, they have determined to control its terminus and its traffic—in short, to bring the trade of the South to San Francisco, and to manage it in such a way that the new road shall be an advantage rather than a detriment to the old one.

To accomplish this result it pays to traverse an unproductive desert. But this is not all. It is safe to predict the success of the Southern Pacific even if it should not reach any connection with the East. This is assured by the increasing importance of Arizona as a mining region. It is the purpose of this railroad company to secure the whole trade of Arizona for San Francisco before any eastern communication is opened. When that takes place it will join their road, and it will be too late to turn the stream of traffic from its western course.

These considerations, with others of minor importance, furnish a sufficient answer to the question so frequently proposed: "How can men be such fools as to build a railroad across the desert?" I am sure that we never should have thought it worth our while to visit Yuma by crossing it on mule-back, or by the still slower route of steamers around Cape St. Lucas, up the Gulf of California and the Colorado River, the usual way of getting here in twenty days' time, until this railroad was built. Now the same end is accomplished, if no stops are made, in thirty-six hours. What such rapid transit will do for Arizona, what impetus it will give to trade, what influx of population, what general prosperity to the territory, are all certainties of the immediate future.

We reached the terminus of the line at seven o'clock in the morning, there being a mile of road yet to be constructed to the river bank. On this two or three hundred Chinamen were busily at work, and it was to be finished the next day to the river. I shall have something more to say about Chinamen by and by, but will only observe just now that railroads are very strong pro-Chinese arguments. It would have been impossible to build this road without their labor.

The Colorado having since been spanned by a bridge, the road is now being extended along the banks of the Gila. Half way between Yuma and the Maricopa Wells, in the heart of a great desert, two thousand men are busy laying rails at the rate of two miles per day, pressing on we know not where. The present objective point is Maricopa Wells, 160 miles east of Fort Yuma, and 408 miles from Los Angeles. As Maricopa Wells is a mere watering spot in the great desert of Arizona, we assume that the work is to be pushed further eastward, at first to Tucson, and then, perhaps, to the Gulf of Mexico, thus forming another transcontinental railroad.

Two opposition wagons were ready to transport the passengers for the remaining mile. "Git in here!" yelled our driver; "that darned cuss wants to skin you. He charges five dollars and I'll take you for three, if I do lose money by it." So we went with this self-sacrificing man and contributed to his poverty.

Fort Yuma has a garrison of fifty or sixty soldiers, under command of Colonel Dunn, to whom, as well as to Major Ernest, we were indebted for kind attentions. It is situated on the California side of the Colorado, which is crossed by ferry to the city of Yuma.

The city of Yuma—no pen can portray it; no photography can reproduce it; no painting can by coloring represent the sandy desert of its wide streets, the irregular blocks and scattered houses, the lazy Mexicans lolling about the grog-shops, and gazing wistfully at their contents; the glare of the burning sun; the total absence of trees, shrubs, grass, or any green thing to vary the monotony of sand and dust. This is Yuma, the thriving city, with its wealthy merchants, its newspaper, its hotels, its court house, and probably its churches—although we did not happen to see or hear of them. This is Yuma, with its two thousand inhabitants, the frontier settlement on the west of Arizona, situated at the confluence of the Gila and the Colorado, one hundred and fifty miles from the sea by the course of the latter river, and one hundred miles in a direct line. By and by, when it increases in wealth and importance, as its opportunities indicate that it will, a more refined taste will change its present forbidding aspect. A few thousand dollars will pay for abundant irrigation, avenues of trees will supersede the shadeless streets, elegant houses rise upon the ruins of wretched abobes, and churches and schools will take the place of saloons and gambling dens. The poor Indians and the Mexican "greasers" will be drowned out by the coming wave of civilization, and in ten years from this time, whoever may read this description will say that it could not have been true of beautiful Yuma.

The earliest occupation by the Spaniards of what is now Arizona, was in 1769, and the first American settlement was made in 1853. Until the recent discovery of silver no progress was made, and it was valued only as a military post. The whole territory now contains about thirty-five thousand whites, beside the Mexican and Indian population, amounting in round numbers to fifteen thousand more. The mining excitement is drawing reinforcements so rapidly that estimates are good only for to-day. Fabulous stories are told of the new bonanzas. There is a perfect mining furor among these people, who talk of the Comstock lodes of Nevada as "played-out pockets," and hold with the utmost sincerity to the faith that Arizona will be the greatest silver-producing district of the world. There is abundant proof that this mineral was known to exist here one hundred years ago, when mines were worked by Spaniards. It is also shown by exhumations from the mounds that the Aztecs, and probably races anterior to them, possessed the same knowledge and used it for their advantage. However great the amount of silver they may have produced in those early days, it fades into insignificance compared with what may be turned out by modern science and machinery.

Do not be induced by any thing I have said to abandon a profession or trade that affords a decent subsistence and emigrate to Arizona to hunt for silver. Mining is a lottery in which more blanks are drawn than prizes. There are always plenty of fools, however, who will take tickets in it. Successful or not, they must all be fed. So the safest and best thing you can do, if, for health or a living, you wish to pass your days in the purest atmosphere of the continent, is to take up farming land in Arizona. This can be found in abundance in many parts of the territory, although every thing around Yuma is a desert. Thus you may have the benefit of mining without its attendant risk. Still there is an excitement in "prospecting" that attracts many good and useful citizens to the territory. They like the pursuit, whether they succeed or not, and they will either become rich and acquire interests in real estate, or they will lose all they have, and will not be able to get away. So both classes will remain, and, their families increasing, Arizona will doubtless soon be admitted as a State to the Union, and the Indians will disappear, as their race has always passed away before advancing civilization.

The principal tribes, most of whom are on reservations, are the Mojaves, the Maricopas, the Apaches, the Navajos and the Yumas. Of the last there were about fifteen hundred loitering around the town. They are a quiet, inoffensive set of beings now, though in times past warlike and ferocious. The men are tall and finely formed, and the women, when not disfigured by tattooing, are not remarkably repulsive. They are all fond of dress, that is, as far as they dress. In distinction from the habits of civilized life the men are much more vain of their personal appearance than the women. They like to wear gaudy colored jackets and vests. Both sexes content themselves with the avoidance of absolute indecency, and all are literally *sans culottes*. The men wear long strips of bright calico attached to their belts, trailing behind them to the ground as they march along, with the feeling of a Broadway beau fresh from the hands of his tailor.

Visiting their camp, two miles from town, we called upon Pasqual, the chief of the tribe, a man apparently eighty years old. He sat upon his haunches, looking stolidly on as one of his wives was bruising mesquit beans in a rude mortar. The Yumas live chiefly on this bean, a sort of locust growing wild and abundant in the river bottoms. They also plant corn, squashes and melons, which they dry and preserve for winter use. These articles constitute their diet, excepting an occasional rabbit or fish. They do not care to go upon a reservation, but are quite satisfied with their present mode of life.

When Major Ernest came forward and addressed the chief, the old man arose from his humiliating posture and assumed at once his natural dignity of mien. He shook hands in the most condescending manner, and uttered a few unintelligible words of welcome. "He has been a great rascal," said the Major, to his face, "a brave man, too, for he gave us lots of fighting before he came in and surrendered. Now he is quiet as a kitten. We can rely upon his word that he will give us no more trouble." The bright eyes of the old chief gleamed with satisfaction, for he seemed to know that something flattering was said about him. He grunted approval at the end of the Major's little speech, and shaking us again cordially by the hand, intimated that the audience was at an end, and we left him standing barelegged in front of his hut with an air of self-possession equal to that of a field-marshal or an emperor.

CHAPTER VII.

RIVAL TOWNS IN THE SAN BERNARDINO VALLEY—NEWSPAPER ENTERPRISE—PARADISE OF ORANGE TREES—INTELLECTUALITY AND LAZINESS—MORMON AND ROMAN CATHOLIC CIVILIZATIONS—THE MISSION OF SAN GABRIEL AND ITS GOOD WINE.

Beauty and deformity are alike intensified by contrast. The green carpets of the Swiss valleys owe their coloring to the rugged crags and eternal snows of the Alps above them, and those high surroundings seem more desolate when we turn from the verdant fields to look upon them than if they stood alone in the scope of our vision. Perhaps we have thus exaggerated the desolation of Yuma and the Colorado desert, and now on returning to the garden of Southern California, it may have acquired for our eyes new features of loveliness. Still, we have the best intentions to be honest to Nature in describing her lights and shadows.

On our return from Arizona we alight at a small railway station called Colton. This city has five houses, a stable, a church and a printing office. Civilization has triumphed lately over the old custom of forming settlements in this part of the country. The prime necessity was once the grog shop—

now it is the press. The very first thing to be done in these days is to establish a local newspaper. Once it marched in to supply the demands of the people ; now the people are expected to come at the call of the newspaper. To discover the age of a town we need but to glance at the head of the newspaper columns. Thus the Colton *Semi-Tropic*, published every Saturday by Scipio Craig—for that is the name of the editor—leads us to infer from its "Vol. 1, No. 31," that the town is thirty-one weeks of age. This may not be exact to a day, but appearances indicate that it is a fair ground for estimate. We called upon Mr. Craig. Having written his leader and made up his paper and his form with the assistance of a little boy, he was busy working off his issue of May 26 with a hand press. It is intensely local, for the map of San Bernardino county, of which Colton is the capital, is stereotyped over a large space. There is a corner for politics—and the editor is politic himself, for he wants settlers, be they Democrats or Republicans ; there is also a summary of telegraphic news. But the animus, the strength, the true meaning of the *Semi-Tropic* is, "Come hither, ye immigrants! This is the most favored spot in creation."

It is on the line of the Southern Pacific Railroad, which might, if it had been so disposed, have run through the old town of San Bernardino, where there are four thousand inhabitants, or through the newer settlement of Riverside, of greater promise. But it did neither. Railroads have selfish ways. They study their own interests as individual men study theirs. Railroads own land upon their borders, and care more for them than for the lands of others.

San Bernardino is four miles north and Riverside is eight miles south of Colton. I asked one of the oldest inhabitants about these towns. He shook his head; he "didn't like to say any thing agin his neighbors, but they have fever and ague considerable in San Bernardino, and the water ain't fit to drink at Riverside. Hows'ever, as I said, I don't like to say any thing agin 'em, some folks like them kind o' things—I don't; that's all."

As this impartial critic left us to form our own opinions we set out to see for ourselves, on some capital ponies, which carried us forty miles over the ground that day with ease. There is no difficulty in procuring good horses at reasonable prices in all the towns of Southern California. You may buy them for twenty-five dollars, or you may hire them for a few shillings.

We first took a survey of Riverside. Crossing the river Santa Ana by a ford, we followed its banks under the guidance of Mr. Evans, the president of a land company formed for the purpose of colonizing the district. Eight miles above the town, two canals are opened from the river sufficient to irrigate twenty-five thousand acres of the property. Operations were begun only six years ago. Within that time—a newspaper, of course, being the precursor—a town of little gardens has been built in the centre of the rancho. Four hundred thousand dollars have been expended on canals and roads. An avenue one hundred and thirty feet wide and eleven miles long, with triple rows of eucalyptus and magnolia trees, has been laid out, and the land on each side, with abundant water privileges, cut up into forty-acre farms. Ten thousand acres have already been sold.

"I shall make it a paradise!" exclaimed Mr. Evans, with justifiable enthusiam.

Truly Adam and Eve never walked under such an avenue as this will be, and they never saw such orange groves as grow on its borders, or apples would not have tempted them. Think of ten thousand acres planted almost exclusively with orange trees, and the remaining fifteen thousand to be cultivated in the same way. Many of the Riverside colonists are "eddicated, intellectooal cusses," as an envious San Bernardino farmer termed them. Many of them are invalids, who have a little property, so that they are not obliged to work with their own hands; most of them are a combination of ill-health, intellectuality, and comfortable circumstances. Orange culture is eminently adapted to their condition and circumstances. They can sit on the verandas of their pretty cottages—the refined essences of abstract existences—inhaling the pure air of the equal climate, reading novels or abstruse works of philosophy, according to their mental activity, from day to day, and waiting from year to year for their oranges to grow. Extremes meet. This is the sort of farming agreeable alike to literati and lazzaroni.

After a long ride about Riverside and its environs, we returned to lunch at Colton, and in the afternoon rode over to San Bernardino.

There is something romantic about the settlement of this town—one of the earliest occupied by Americans in the State. When the Mormons were driven out of Illinois, their astute leader sent a colony to settle in California, preparatory to a general exodus of his people. Their reports of the richness of the soil led him wisely to infer that the country was altogether too good for his purpose, as the "Gentiles" would soon drive the "Saints" away again. He accordingly selected the alkaline deserts of Utah, little dreaming, prophet though he was, that the railroad would soon be on his track, and that the roses grown by his indomitable perseverance on that forbidden soil would be plucked by Gentile hands. Most of the California colony were recalled, and obedient to the mandate of their leader, the reluctant band marched across the Sierras to the land of promise—such promise as it gave when compared to the beauty and abundance they were forced to abandon! The Israelites escaped from Egyptian bondage to establish themselves in a land flowing with milk and honey. These colonists, after long persecutions, having found a refuge in this paradise of the earth, voluntarily subjected themselves to new toil and privation in the barren wastes of Deseret. They left the garden that nature had planted for them to conquer from nature a bare subsistence. Now that men speak all manner of evil concerning the Mormons, let this instance of self-devotion and religious faith, fanatical but sincere, be placed to their credit, as it will assuredly be by the Great Judge of all motives and actions.

A few of the Latter-day Saints were permitted to remain in California. Two of them, Amasa Lyman and Charles C. Rich, came here before 1850, and acquired the title of San Bernardino, with eight square leagues of land and fifteen thousand head of cattle. Three hundred persons formed a settlement, and laid out the streets from north to south and from east to west, one hundred and thirty-two feet wide; brought in irrigated canals, planted avenues of trees, divided the town into garden lots, and established every thing on the scale of villages now seen in Utah, but with far greater beauty, for climate and soil beneficently aided, instead of opposing, their efforts. The town is now thirty years old—a very ancient one for California—and by far the prettiest place we had yet seen. The trees have grown to a maturity that sixty years would not have given in the East. Each street is a boulevard; and every house, if we except the few assigned to business purposes, is covered with creepers and nestled in full-grown orchards and vineyards.

We talked with two of the old Mormon settlers. They said that, with all the beauty around them, and all the comfort and luxury afforded by the teeming abundance of the soil, some of their number, sorrowing for their kindred and their religious associations, like those who wept by the rivers of Babylon, had gone over the mountains to Utah; and now, in a population of four thousand, not more than one hundred and fifty of the saints were left. Their fellow townsmen speak of them as quiet, inoffensive people, who have no disposition to make themselves obnoxious by practices distasteful to the sentiments of the community. They belong to the "Josephite" branch of the church, in opposition to the Brighamites.

The old Spaniards were accustomed to christen their discoveries and settlements with the names of saints upon whose protection they relied. When they reached this vale of verdant fields and rosy bowers in the spring of the year 1769, they rightly judged that no saint was entitled to the honor of being its defender, and so, with a combination of piety and gallantry, when they had founded their town, they christened it and its valley "Our Lady of the Angels." If in the wild luxuriance of nature, with these grand mountains in the background and the blue Pacific rippling on its shores, the picture seemed to them so beautiful, how much more worthy of its name would they have thought it, could they have seen its gardens adorned by cultivation and its surrounding plains made pastures for herds and flocks! Heretical as the present occupants may be, they have only modified its title for an economy of words. For them the valley and the town are still Los Angeles—"The Angels."

We are all more familiar with the conquests of Peru and of Mexico than with the progress made by the invaders to the North, resulting in the subjugation of the natives of California, because it was slow and gradual, lacking that dashing effrontery which Pizarro and Cortez displayed in conquering new worlds at a blow. By other means Spain gained her foothold on the more northern coast of America. For one hundred and fifty years after the conquest she vainly attempted to extend her dominions in this direction by military force, and then turned over the enterprise to religious zeal, commissioning the Franciscan Fathers to obtain possession of the peninsula of Lower California. They accomplished this successfully, and seventy-nine years afterward pushed on to the region now known as Southern California, where the line is drawn between Mexico and the United States.

In 1769, two small vessels, fitted out by the missionary friars, reached San Diego, and simultaneously there came by land a small detachment of men, driving before them two hundred head of cattle, and as many horses, sheep, and hogs, to stock the country they intended to occupy.

These Catholic priests were practical missionaries. Their doctrine was, that religion meant civilization and its attendant benefits, as well as the mere adoption of certain articles of faith. Until they were superseded by military robbers, their influence over the Indians was, on the whole, for their temporal good, though they doubtless attached more importance to the salvation of their souls. They subdued them by a policy for the most part of kindness, while they conquered new territories for Spain without shedding blood. Their methods of conversion were not in all respects justifiable. Their appeals were not always founded on reason; sometimes the *argumentum ad hominem* was literally a lasso thrown over the head of the victim, by which he was captured and brought into the mission grounds to be baptized.

The Church has always been accused of reducing men to

slavery of the mind. Here the tyranny was chiefly exercised over the body, for the Indians had not much mental nature to overcome. The dazzling ceremonial of worship, the lighted tapers and fragrant incense, were enough to subdue what little intellect they possessed; their bone and muscle were made serviceable in building monasteries, cultivating vineyards and herding cattle. A quasi religion and a quasi civilization thus gained foothold together in California. They were the shadows of coming events now realized and enjoyed by us.

Trees of bigotry were planted on the Atlantic and on the Pacific shores. They were of different stocks, but they have both been grafted with scions that have borne a better fruit. As New England celebrates her anniversary of December 22d in memory of 1620, so California should make a gala day of the 1st of May in gratitude to her pilgrim fathers of 1769. They established their first mission where they landed in San Diego, there beginning their efforts for the conversion of their heathen neighbors to a civilization which, with these, as with all other savages. must result in extermination, not attributable to religions, Catholic. or Protestant, but to the advent and colonization of a superior race.

From San Diego they advanced to the north and to the interior, driving their increasing herds before them, corralling Indians, building monasteries and possessing themselves of the land. Of the twenty-one mission churches founded by them, most remain in some state of preservation—that at Santa Barbara being nearly perfect. Some of them are occupied by a few Franciscan brothers, who flit about the spacious cloisters like ghostly images of their predecessors, the great territories surrounding them having long since been secularized.

The fathers enjoyed their highest prosperity in the early part of this century. It is said that the Mission of San Miguel in 1821 owned nearly one hundred thousand head of cattle, fifty thousand sheep, and thousands of horses and mules, and the prosperity of this mission corresponded with the rest. So much for their stock; as for the land, they owned it all. Mexican independence, declared the year afterward, was a severe blow to this ecclesiastical hierarchy. Military adventurers despoiled them of their wealth, gradually reducing their property and influence, until in 1840 the government took possession of their vast estates, and five years afterward sold them to the highest bidders. Hence came the "Mexican grants," which, being allowed when the country was ceded to the United States, have been sold to enterprising Yankees, and are now their colossal monopolies.

A few miles from Los Angeles is the famous mission of San Gabriel. The church, one hundred and six years old, one of the earliest built after the landing of the Franciscans at San Diego, is in excellent preservation, though time-stained and mossgrown with age. The mission no longer serves for the conversion of Indians. They have disappeared entirely, or left the dregs of their blood to wander in a slow current through the veins of Mexican "greasers." A few of these half-castes still remain to prostrate themselves before the altar and to remind the sad Franciscan brothers of their order's sway, when clouds of natives flocked to the standard of the Cross, and willing slaves stocked their larders with provisions and their cellars with wine. Now they look about them and behold the stranger and the heretic gathering the fruits of their labors. The people of Los Angeles are indebted to those old fathers, not only for their land, but for its most valuable productions. They brought with them from Mexico the orange and the vine. The mission grounds now contain trees one hundred years old, and the mission grape, from which most of the wine of this district is made, has been the most profitable product of the soil. From the bottle of its pure juice before us, we drink to the memory of the Friars of the Order of San Francisco.

CHAPTER VIII.

Los Angeles—Disappearance of the Greasers—A Kentuckian's Discovery of Contentment—The Founder of the California Wine Industry—Statistics of Orange Culture.

The city of Los Angeles is in a condition of renaissance. It is throwing off its old caterpillar Spanish nature, and coming out to soar on the gay wings of its new existence. It is already so changed that there are few traces of the Mexican element which formed its total population thirty years ago. In a score and a half of years it has grown from a slow pueblo of adobes, to a thriving city of business streets and costly dwellings. The old inhabitants who remain are driven into a cluster of little hovels and vendas with Spanish signs, where patois Castilian may be heard, brown señoras seen, and the aroma of garlic scented. The disappearance of the "greasers" is a more curious study than that of the Indians. They were, and they are not; nobody has murdered them; they have died of no epidemic; they have not emigrated, and there has been no impediment to their birth. What has become of them no one knows, they have only faded out of sight.

Los Angeles is now an American city of eighteen thousand

inhabitants, prosperous and gaining in population and wealth, having already reached the fourth rank in the State. It is not strictly a sea-port, although it is connected with the ocean by two railroads, one extending twenty miles to Wilmington, and the other reaching Santa Monica by a shorter route. These make it the favorite headquarters for invalids, who generally find the air of the city agreeable; but if they desire a change they obtain it in an hour at the sea-shore. The temperature is remarkably even for the whole year, mostly averaging between sixty and seventy degrees Fahrenheit, seldom exceeding the latter. Many persons of delicate constitution, incapacitated for work in the Eastern States, coming here merely for their health, regain it to such a degree that they are able to engage in business or farming. Of such persons and their families, no inconsiderable part of this population is composed. After remaining a short time on compulsion, they fix their abodes for the remainder of their lives from choice. When you ask them if they never intend to return to their old homes, they invariably reply: "Yes, I should like to go back—for a visit."

Mr. Bliss, a Kentuckian, told us that he came out prospecting, not for silver or gold, but for a home. He tried all sorts of homes for a while, living in cities and on ranches, and was finally tempted to purchase his present dwelling, about a mile from the centre of the city. This was a forty-acre lot, having on it an adobe house which he made exceedingly pretty by adding another story. His grounds were already planted with twenty-two acres of vines, and one hundred and seventy-five orange trees in full bearing, besides young orchards and vineyards rapidly maturing; and all the rest not occupied as a beautiful flower garden, was laid down to alfalfa. I would not thus notice the estate of a private gentleman who so kindly entertained us, without his permission; and I mention this instance mainly to illustrate the comforts of life that may be acquired by those of moderate means whose health or inclination leads them to search for the desirable habitations easily attainable here. Mr. Bliss purchased the place for $18,000, and has expended on his house, stable and other outfits $7,000 more, so that it cost him altogether, about $25,000.

Now let us see what this farm or garden—as one may choose to call it—will yield in an ordinarily productive year, leaving out of account the incipient orchards, whose profit is in the future, and supposing the space they occupy to be planted with alfalfa:

```
32 acres of grapes, as sold on the vines..........  ..............$2,200
 3 acres, containing 175 orange trees, the oranges selling for $20 a tree. 3,500
 2 acres occupied by house, stable and flower garden................  ——
13 acres of alfalfa...................................... 1,300
                                                         _____
    Total.....................  ........................ $7,000
```

The labor employed is little, as the oranges and grapes are sold on the trees and vines. All the weeding, pruning and mowing can be done by two Chinamen at an expense of seven hundred dollars a year. It must be remembered that this value of the crop will be greatly enhanced when the young orange groves and vineyards come to maturity. It may be said that every one has not the capital wherewith to purchase an already productive estate. Very true; but youth is capital, and young men can afford to await its development. Land as good as this can be bought for fifty dollars an acre or less, and in ten years will be as productive. In the mean time, patient economy in raising wheat and vegetables and the product of the wonderful alfalfa will support life, and the sure hope of the future will give it a zest.

It may be that the business of orange culture will be overdone—this is a matter to be considered; but the grape can never be overproduced. It never has been since the time that Noah came forth from the ark to give it his earliest attention. One of the greatest advantages our country will derive from California is the increasing manufacture of pure wine, which introduced among the people will overcome their taste for poisonous whiskey, and make them as temperate as the peasantry of Southern France and Italy. Most of the California wine has heretofore been made from the Mission grape, introduced at their advent by the Franciscan Friars. Latterly the white Muscat has received more favor.

The name of the man who first showed the capabilities of California as a wine-producing State, and whose children have seen his efforts crowned with success, was Haraszthy, a Hungarian refugee, who came here not many years ago. I remember hearing him in New York speak enthusiastically of his plans for California, and I remember how, in common with others, I regarded his schemes as wild and visionary. But he persevered until he gained the confidence of the Legislature of California, who sent him back to Europe to procure the choicest vines of all its wine-producing countries. How he succeeded on his mission the hillsides and valleys of the State from Sacramento to San Diego attest. Millions of vines every year entwine their wreaths to crown his memory, and to keep it green and fruitful like themselves.

We drove through the "Mission fruit belt" eight miles from the city. After reaching it the road for miles was a perpetual boulevard of orange trees—sometimes a forest of them—or of lemons, limes, walnuts, almonds and olives. Where they were not, the fields for hundreds of acres on each side were covered with clustering vines just forming their blossoms into grapes

The most extensive orchards and vineyards were those of Messrs. Rose, Titus, Kewen and Baldwin, whose acres are to be counted by thousands. Beside these, the small proprietors possess their hundreds and the cottagers their tens. All the trees and vines are not yet fully grown, but an idea may be formed of their present productiveness when it is remembered that last year Southern California sent to market two million seven hundred thousand oranges, three hundred and fifty thousand lemons, and one hundred and twenty-eight thousand limes, most of them coming from Los Angelos and its immediate neighborhood. Of the grapes I have no statistics, as most of them are pressed into wine on the spot. The culture of oranges is attracting the greatest attention.

The Southern Californian has "orange on the brain." He dreams of oranges at night, and they are his realities by day. Will the thing be overdone? Let us see. There is one nursery containing five hundred thousand slips destined to be trees; there are many more perhaps not so large. A tree reaches perfection in fifteen years. In fifteen years, if one hundred thousand acres are planted—and that is an exceedingly moderate estimate—with sixty-four trees to the acre, there will be six million four hundred thousand trees. Each tree averaging one thousand oranges, there will be six thousand four hundred million oranges. We will suppose that in fifteen years from this time the population of the United States shall reach sixty millions, and that these people are all able to buy oranges and cannot get them from any source but California. There will be one hundred and six oranges and two-thirds of an orange for each man, woman and child in the country.

CHAPTER IX.

NATURAL DIVISIONS OF CALIFORNIA—ANAHEIM—A THRIFTY
GERMAN SETTLEMENT.

California is cosmopolitan in its inhabitants and universal in its productions. As its people come from every part of the world there is too great a variety for sharp divisions in religion, or social life. Their quarrels would be many-sided, so they have wisely concluded not to occupy their time in fighting, but to settle down into an *olla podrida* of good-fellowship. The plants and cereals get on in the same amicable manner—the orange trees forming avenues through the wheat-fields, and the vine growing lovingly by the side of shocks of Indian corn. Climate, however, has drawn a line through the State. It does not disturb the friendly relations of mankind and of nature, but it gives a greater preponderance of different classes to different latitudes. Thus Northern California is for the most part settled by northern men, robust and enterprising farmers and miners. They have taken possession of the lands best suited to their character—lands where corn and wheat best thrive, and rocky hills where gold abounds. On the contrary, Southern California is more often the home of the less active southerners, who hail from the lower Middle and Gulf States, or from France and Italy.

They become ranchmen or fruit-growers, their indolent habits leading them to prefer the care of herds and the culture of the grape and semi-tropical fruits to the harder toil of the husbandman and the gold-hunter. Here the atmosphere and soil kindly respond to their more modest requirements, and yield a sufficient reward for lighter labor.

It is true that northern and southern men, as well as wheat and vines, gold and orange trees, are to be found everywhere, but latitude draws a general line between them, notwithstanding their universal harmony. It seemed to us that there was not the same haste to be rich among the people of Los Angeles that we found in San Francisco. We saw no excited crowds turning the street corners into stock exchanges; there was little talk of Consolidated Virginia, California and Sierra Nevada; but people were mildly excited about cattle and sheep, vines and orange trees. There must be something fascinating in having beautiful things grow up around one's home, promising such splendid results for so small an outlay. There is Mr. Wolfskill, in the outskirts of the town, whose father planted an orchard and vineyard now producing annually thirty thousand dollars for his son, who has merely to look on from year to year as the golden treasures fall into his lap, and the wine flows out in a rich stream.

Not far from the city we found the "Indiana Colony," so named, perhaps, from the fact that the State of Indiana is the one least represented. Here are several thousand acres laid out as orange plantations, and two or three dozen cottages awaiting the shade trees growing up to beautify them. Some of the residents expressed their doubts of rapidly acquiring a fortune, but all agreed that the neighborhood was well adapted to persons suffering from bronchial or pulmonary ailments.

The land in these valleys is watered chiefly by the Los Angeles and Santa Ana rivers, two queer little streams that play " hide and seek " from their sources until they are lost in the Pacific. It is supposed that they are continuations of the Humboldt and other waters, which disappear far beyond the Sierras, and after undermining them, gush forth in salient fountains on the western slope. Thence they course down the plains, sometimes on the surface, then sinking again but easily followed in their tracks, and with a little digging brought to light. The Santa Ana serves the purpose of abundant irrigation at Riverside, as we have already seen, and then comes forth to be likewise employed at Anaheim. This is an exceedingly pretty town of two thousand five hundred inhabitants, and has a history as romantic as fiction.

Twenty-one years ago some Germans who had drifted to San Francisco in search of gold became dissatisfied with their adventure, and, longing for the vineyards of the Rhine, would gladly have returned to their old homes. While they were considering this step it occurred to some of them that, as they could not conveniently get back to Germany, they might in a manner bring Germany to California. They had heard of the adaptation of land in the South to the culture of the grape, and of its success in the hands of the old Franciscan monks. Accordingly, with a spirit of enterprise which was creditable to their new idea, and with a concentration of capital and labor attesting their mutual confidence, they dispatched an agent to Los Angeles to survey and purchase for them a tract of land. This agent, Mr. Hansen, was a practical engineer, who is still living to enjoy the satisfaction of witnessing the happiness to which he so largely contributed. Armed with full authority and a fund subscribed by fifty of his countrymen, he came to the desert plain now occupied by Anaheim, took up the apparently valueless land at small cost, dug a canal seven miles long from the Santa Ana, and divided the area of eleven hundred and sixty-six acres into fifty private lots of twenty acres each, reserving the rest for schools and other public buildings. Before any distribution was made he turned irrigating canals on every lot, set out rows of willows or cottonwood trees around them, and planted eight acres of each with vines. When three years had elapsed, and not before, the purchasers were called to take possession.

The distribution was made by lot, according to value—some paying more and some less, all in just proportion. At the end of three years every stockholder had paid on an average twelve hundred dollars, including assessments, and when the property was divided there was a surplus to each of one hundred and twenty dollars, and they had their land nearly half planted with thrifty vines and all irrigated and fenced. There was nothing for them to do but to go to work, and this they did energetically, in brotherly co-operation. Many of them are still on the spot, having raised their families around them, built school-houses and churches, a theatre, dance house and *Weingarten*, and now they are the happiest people in one of the loveliest towns we ever beheld.

The history of Anaheim is not unlike that of San Bernardino, both having been started by a bond of fellowship productive of good results. Each of these villages, so tastefully laid out by their founders, so well cultivated and improved, blooms like a little Eden of happiness and repose. As we walked through the shaded streets of Anaheim, passing the cottages adorned by trailing vines and flowers, and in the evening caught the chorus of German songs, we seemed to be carried back to the Fatherland, where we had often witnessed similar scenes. But how greatly was the Fatherland improved upon by the absence of poverty and the presence of comforts in this new home on the banks of the Ana, so happily named the Ana Heim!

Such agreeable surroundings could not fail to attract others to the town and its environs, where nearly three thousand people are now domesticated. The German purchase formed only a small part of the extensive "Stearn's Ranches," originally comprising one hundred and forty thousand acres, of which sixty-five thousand have been already sold and tenanted.

While at Los Angeles I received the following note from the agent who has this extensive property in charge:

"DEAR SIR: As I understand that you are travelling through Southern California, and, of course, desire to see the best, as you have already seen much of the worst part of it, I invite you to visit Anaheim; and if you will give me time I will take great pleasure in showing you the surrounding country, which, in this dry season, presents a marked contrast to what you have seen during your journey, excepting where the land was irrigated. We have greater advantages for irrigation than any other part of California, and we have, in addition, thousands of acres of land always moist and covered with perpetual verdure, pastures that require no irrigation and never fail. I wish to show you that, instead of the dry, hot country that we are supposed to have, you will find a fertile soil with an abundance of water, a mild, genial, temperate climate never either hot or cold, and a remarkable growth of vegetation, such as is seen nowhere else. Yours truly,

"WM. R. OLDEN."

It affords us great pleasure to bear witness that Mr. Olden has not by any means exaggerated the advantages of this region; moreover, he gave us the opportunity of much enjoyment and an experience of the most agreeable hospitality.

Anaheim lies twenty-seven miles in a south-easterly direction from Los Angeles, and is only thirteen miles from the seacoast. Its climate is somewhat cooler than that of its neighbor in the summer, as the sea breeze always prevails in the afternoon. Satisfactory as this condition is to most persons, those having weak lungs should give the preference to the interior, unless they are willing to risk an occasional cold as an offset to a constant tonic. The best advice to invalids is not to settle down anywhere. They are often inclined to do so, and they should always have a policeman after them ordering them to "move on."

CHAPTER X.

SANGUINE "SANJAIGANS"—EFFECTS OF THE DROUGHT—SANTA MONICA—A STEAMSHIP WITH A HISTORY—SAN BUENAVENTURA—THE OJAI VALLEY—MISSIONARY ENTERPRISE.

Had time permitted, we might advantageously have extended our tour beyond Anaheim one hundred and ten miles to San Diego, the last city of Southern California on the Pacific coast; No journal is absolutely complete that does not comprise a reference to this point, not only connected with the earliest history of the State, but one that purposes to be a rival of San Francisco so soon as railroad communication from the East is perfected.

"That time is fast coming," said a visionary " Sanjaigan." "We have the finest harbor on the coast." (By the bye I have heard that remark at every open roadstead between San Pedro and San Francisco.) "We shall draw all the travel from the East on a road not blocked with snow, and we shall of course have all the trade with China by way of the Sandwich Islands. In ten years, sir, San Francisco will be nowhere." All the San Diego people whom we met looked upon Tom Scott and Jay Gould as their good angels. Scott would be sure to bring them a road from Texas, and Gould would continue the " Utah Southern " through the Gorgonio Pass to their town, thus connecting

New York, the present greatest city on the Atlantic, with San Diego, the future greatest city on the Pacific.

Before turning our faces to the North it may not be amiss to refer once more to the chief agricultural resources of Southern California, compressing the trustworthy information obtained into the smallest possible space. I have already described the vineyards and orange groves, but those are by no means all that the farmer depends upon. Indeed they are yet in their incipient stages.

The old Mexicans relied for subsistence almost entirely upon their flocks and herds, and these are still the most productive sources of revenue to the rancheros. The unusually dry season had made sad havoc among the cattle and sheep. The same cause operated disastrously on the corn, barley and wheat of the uplands. Of these nine-tenths were lost. The oranges, limes, figs, lemons, olives, almonds, walnuts and grapes, being mostly cultivated on irrigated land were in their usual abundance, and the cereals grown on similar ground were more profitable because of the general famine. The conclusion is that no man who is not willing to take his chances in a lottery should invest in cattle or sheep, or in land that cannot be irrigated as occasion requires.

Sixteen miles from Los Angelos is the charming wateringplace of Santa Monica. As the village forms part of a large ranche, the proprietors, of whom Senator Jones of Nevada is chief, have laid it out with a view to make it attractive, and thus to benefit the rest of their property. Is has been called the "Long Branch of California," and is far superior to its namesake in every natural resource. The town, consisting at present of a large comfortable hotel and its adjacent saloons, billiard rooms and stables, beside a few private cottages, stands on a high bluff in the bight of a bay lined from point to point by a hard, wide sand beach. The breakers seldom dash and roar as they do on the Long Branch of the Atlantic, but the milder Pacific sends them in to curl in long festoons of green water, and to beat their time of softer music on the shore. Along the bluff for two miles there extends a straight race course, for running horses, on which not unfrequently may be witnessed such skilful horsemanship in chasing and lassoing as would astonish our eastern park equestrians. The temperature of Santa Monica is very equable, and the daily sea breeze renders it a most agreeable spot. The company's steamers touch here three times a week in their trips from San Francisco to San Diego, and on their return.

We left Santa Monica at 6 o'clock of the afternoon on the old steamer Senator, a ship that had been recently rebuilt and put in excellent condition. This little craft of one thousand tons has a history. She has probably earned more money than any vessel ever known. It was a daring but successful adventure to send her from New York through the Straits of Magellan in 1848. When she reached San Francisco thousands of men were there, and hundreds daily arriving, who had no means of ascending the Sacramento River on their way to the placer mines. The Senator, the first steamer that had ever floated on those waters, was immediately placed upon the route. Her owners were able to fix the rates of passage and freight at any sum they pleased. Day after day and month after month for the first year this bonanza boat gathered in not unfrequently fifty thousand dollars for the trip of a few hours' time. This monopoly could not last forever; one rival after another appeared on the Sacramento to claim a share of the spoils, and finally the railroad settled their pretensions by taking the trade for itself. The race-horse who in his youth has won the stakes, in his age draws the wagon; so the Senator took her place in the Coast Line, with newer but not better ships than her staunch old self. The ancient "forty-niners" patronize her for association's sake. "Yes, sir," said one of them whom we met in her cabin, "this blessed old barkey carried me on my first trip to the mines. She has earned money enough in gold to sink her to her guards, God bless her!" A Californian never loses his respect for any person or any thing that has "made money."

After a run of six hours, we left the steamer at Buenaventura, preferring, for the sake of seeing the country, to take the stage for the remainder of the route. San Buenaventura richly deserves its whole name. Its former owners found time to pronounce it in full, but the present proprietors, whose time is money, have dropped the San altogether, and in common speech cut off half the remainder; with them it is Ventura. By and by it will be Tura, and that will do better for men in too great a hurry to adopt the present pronunciation.

Call it what they please, it is a lovely little town. Before it rolls the broad ocean; behind it is the Coast Range, through which runs the lovely Valley of the Ojai, on whose slopes are the old Spanish ranches, now divided into smaller farms, where grain and fruit are raised in the greatest abundance. For the tourist and the seeker of health, the Ojai has great attractions. It is far enough from the sea to escape its rough winds, and near enough for its air to be tempered by them as they pass over the intervening country. For the agriculturist no better soil can be found. The recent discoveries of petroleum in this neighborhood have given a new importance to Buenaventura, and brought it into notice as a commercial port.

Those glorious old pioneer fanatics, the Franciscan monks, who had already settled San Diego and Los Angeles, sailed along the coast, and landed here in 1782, founding the mission now standing in good preservation. They at once began their double work of converting the natives and cultivating the soil, and soon acquired a controlling influence over the Indians. Twenty years afterward the convent records classify the aborigines—some as "gentiles, wild Indians," who refuse to be domesticated; others, "converted Indians, good Indians, Indians fit to die." Of such who were living in the village about the mission, there were then nine hundred and thirty-eight.

The success attending farming was equal to that of conversion. In 1825, the mission owned more than seventy thousand head of cattle, horses, and sheep, beside orchards, vineyards, and church property, and one hundred and fifty thousand dollars in cash. Now, that is making missionary enterprise a profitable undertaking in the hands of good managers. Herein those old Catholic *padres* have certainly shown more financial wisdom than any of the Protestant societies have evinced in their operations which call for constant outlay. Doubtless the secret of their conversions might be found in the greater adaptability of their forms and ceremonies to the character of the Indians; but their worldly wisdom was acquired by a more thorough education and a closer study of nature at large, as well as of human nature, than is now required for the outfit of a missionary to the heathen.

CHAPTER XI.

A STAGE RIDE UP THE CALIFORNIA COAST—THE COACHER'S YARNS—HOW A CLERGYMAN WAS RE-BAPTIZED—THE CITY WITH THE PERFECT CLIMATE—A SMALL LANDOWNER AND HIS TRIFLING POSSESSIONS.

Our thanks to you, Messrs. Flint, Bixby & Co! We regard you as the representatives of a method of locomotion fast becoming obsolete, but kept alive by you for the benefit of those who travel to see all that can be seen. Here the old stage-coach still lives. No iron horse snorts defiance to its prancing leaders, or runs through cuts and holes in the mountains to shut the light of day and the wild magnificence of nature from our sight. Long may it be before his track is laid over these vast solitudes of sierras and plains! It is not a wish agreeable to speculators in town lots and real estate. We speak only for ourselves and for those who may follow in our wake.

At Newhall, a point on the Southern Pacific Railroad where it crosses the Mojave Desert, this stage line begins and runs in a north-west direction fifty miles to Buenaventura. Thence it continues along the sea-shore thirty miles to Santa Barbara, and thence two hundred and twenty-two miles further to Soledad. We took the coach at Buenaventura. Nearly the whole distance to Santa Barbara was accomplished on the beach, the tide being fortunately at low ebb. The politeness of our fellow-passengers gave us seats upon the box with the driver, whose ceaseless yarns of border life divided our attention with the ceaseless roar of the breakers. He related, with great satisfaction, an exploit of himself and six comrades in coralling eighty-five Indians who had committed some depredations on a settlement. The redskins were surprised on a small island, and, as they attempted to leave, were shot from the shore of the lake, falling one by one until none were left alive. This happened twenty years ago, about the time of the Mountain Meadow Massacre. We have all heard of that, but "who had heard this story before?" I asked him. "Like enough, nobody out East," he replied. "Perhaps they never heard of our killing about as many rattlesnakes one morning, either?"

It was a lovely day as we drove over the smooth surface of the beach, fanned by the light breeze, and inhaling the pure air of the sea. "Sometimes it isn't this way, though," said the driver; "I was coming along here once at high water, when it was blowing fresh. At such times I generally wait for the tide to go down, but there was a parson inside, and he was in a big hurry. He wanted me to drive on. Now that suited me, for I hate parsons; so I let the cattle go, and, just as I expected, a big sea come in and went clean through the coach, landing a pile of kelp on top. You should have seen that minister when we got by the point! I don't know what denomination he started in on, but he wasn't a Free-Will Baptist when he got out."

Long before we reached Santa Barbara, the town looked down upon us from the north cape of the bay, where it is spread out on the southern slope of the hills, completely sheltered from the cold winds of the coast. Probably more letters are written to the Eastern press from Santa Barbara than from all the cities and towns of California combined. It has come to be regarded as the chief health resort of the State, and I am not sure that it does not merit some of the praise that has been passed upon it. As to its climate, its advocates go too far in claiming for it perfection. We have never yet found a perfect climate suited to all conditions of health and disease, and I do not believe that such an atmosphere exists below the level of Heaven. In many respects San Bernardino, Los Angeles and Anaheim are superior to Santa Barbara, Santa Monica and Buenaventura. The former are at a distance, greater or smaller, from the sea coast; all far enough not to be affected by its rough winds. As to the latter, for those who can stand the sea air, there is probably little choice to be made, if climate alone is considered. But Santa Barbara being voted the home of consumptives, every thing has been done to make it home-like and attractive. The hotels are all comfortable, and some of them luxurious. Their prices, as well as those of the many boarding-houses, are graded to meet requirements of wealth, competence and slender means. Three poor men can live on the money one rich man pays, hotel prices running from one to three dollars a day, and board by the month being still more reasonable. There are churches of almost every denomination, common schools, and a high school called a college. Many people of leisure and culture being domesticated here, there is no want of society and its attendants of parties, clubs, lectures, and libraries. The winter is the best season for health, and for all these adjuncts to its maintenance.

At the time of our stay, the few days were termed "exceptional." We meet a great many of these "exceptionals" everywhere. Every morning a chilling fog arose from the sea and shrouded the town in a veil of mist till nearly mid-day. They said it never did so before, and never would do so again. The weather is a pet of these Santa Barbarians, but like other household pets, children and dogs, it does not always "show off well" before strangers. There are many pretty drives and rides in the neighborhood, and good carriages and saddle horses may be obtained on moderate terms.

Colonel W. W. Hollister, who is well known on this coast as a political economist as well as a wealthy ranchero, invited us to pass a day at his farm of three thousand six hundred acres, a favorite part of his estate of nearly one hundred thousand. Beside these, I may add, he owns one hundred and fifty-seven thousand more in partnership with Mr. Dibblee. In 1870 these gentlemen sold twenty thousand acres for three hundred and seventy thousand dollars, part of a Mexican grant purchased by them for almost nothing. In 1874 the crops of this twenty thousand acres sold for one million five hundred thousand dollars. As we picnicked in a dell shaded by a forest of live oaks arching their branches over our heads and forming an immense arbor, the colonel sat on a stump and related the story of his early life.

"I started with eight thousand sheep from Ohio," he said, "in 1853. By loss and robbery in various ways they were reduced to eight hundred when I arrived here. We were fourteen months on the way. When I struck the place where my house stands yonder, I sat down to rest while the sheep were grazing, and looking around at the beautiful prospect I resolved to settle here. I took up a section, and as my sheep increased and I got money, I bought out Mexican grants. Well, I don't know," he continued reflectively twirling his walking-stick, "somehow I grew rich ; I couldn't help it. The sheep and the cattle would have young ones ; I couldn't help that, could I ? The Greasers wanted to sell out cheap ; I couldn't help buying, could I ? Whose fault is it ? They say I'm a land-grabber. Well, wouldn't they grab if they could ? I bought the land at market prices, and I'll sell it at market prices now, in lots, small or large. Well, well," he added, after another thoughtful twirl, as his eye brightened with satisfaction, "my cattle and my sheep are dying off for want of grass this year ; nobody offers to pay me for my loss, but I'm glad it will make some people happy."

We bade the hospitable philosopher good-by, expressing our sympathy for him in his misfortunes ; and, after riding through the grounds of Mr. Cooper and Mr. Stowe, planted alike with vines and fruit trees, returned to our hotel from a charming excursion of thirty-five miles.

CHAPTER XII.

THE UPS AND DOWNS OF TRAVEL—THE DEATH OF THE HERDS—A SAND STORM—SAN LUIS OBISPO—THE SPRINGS OF PASO DE ROBLES—BATHS OF WATER AND OF EARTH—GERMAN EXPLANATION OF THE MUD BATHS—HOTEL LIFE IN A COTTAGE.

Securing outside seats on the coach, we left Santa Barbara at four o'clock in the morning. If day was breaking we knew it not, for it must have been breaking far above the dense fog that enveloped us in a wet blanket and dampened the enthusiasm with which we had looked forward to a journey across the mountains. Driving ten miles over a level grade, we began to ascend by a winding road until the highest elevation was reached. By actual measurement we discovered that the fog was eighteen hundred feet thick, and that was all the discovery to compensate for our disappointment in losing the view of the plains, and islands dotting the sea.

The driver jocosely remarked that it was a "pleasant morning—pleasant, I mean, by contrast; for coming down this mountain in a fog or on a dark night, on the full run round these short turns to make time, when I can't see my whip handle, why it ain't pleasant."

Occasionally, as we caught a glimpse of precipices overhanging unknown abysses when our wheels were a foot or two from the edge of a narrow path, we realized the comparative danger, and were willing to admit that by contrast the daylight was cheerful and bright.

"Here, ma'am," said the driver to my wife, with a view of allaying her apprehensions, "here's the place where my two leaders slipped off last winter and went down. The passengers jumped out lively and cut the traces and saved the wheelers and the coach, but the leaders were killed. Now I never knew the same thing to happen twice on the same spot." Coming to another sharp turn, he advised her to "hold on tight, but you needn't be so particular as if you was coming down; here's where poor Tom Buddington fell off the box and rolled down two hundred feet. The agent blamed me for being behind time that morning, but we had to stop to pick up his body and fetch him in."

Surmounting the ridge at last, we had a little experience of a down-hill rush around corners for three miles, until we arrived at the breakfast station. This shanty was in charge of an Irish lady, who obligingly "shooed" the pigs out of the banquet hall during our meal, which consisted of fried bacon to look at, and some excellent roasted potatoes to eat. By time that we were ready to start on our second stage the fog gathered itself in great folds, mounted aloft in clouds to be dispersed by the sun, and the bright day reigned supreme. The down grade, though not so long as the ascent, was in many places quite as steep, and, like it, circled round projecting crags, and was cut through notches in the side-hills. Then we descended, perhaps a thousand feet, until we reached the plateau of a park nearly one hundred miles in length, and ten miles in breadth.

You may have seen the parks planted with white-oaks on some of the large English estates, adorned as they are by every device of artistic taste; but you would confess, on driving over this park of nature, that they resembled it only in miniature, as a hundred acres bear comparison with a hundred miles, and as a hundred of their noble trees counted against thousands upon thousands of these nobler live oaks. No forester could have set them out at more proper distance with a view to effect; no skill in pruning could have made them more graceful, and no cultivation could give to the English oaks the everlasting verdure of this pride of California.

We were left to imagine what the landscape would be in ordinary seasons, when beneath their overhanging branches is spread a carpet as green as their leaves; and when, instead of the few lean straggling cattle and sheep, tens of thousands of herds and flocks may be seen grazing upon the rich abundance. Now, all was parched and barren, scarcely a spear of grass was to be seen, and numbers of the poor beasts had literally starved to death.

I do not know what these inoffensive creatures have done to suffer thus. Can anybody explain this mystery of Providence? Man is punished—we understand that in a degree; theologians attribute it to sin, either of our own or of Adam. But what had these beasts or their progenitors to do with that? Lord Dundreary has been laughed at as a fool; but when he says of another matter as he would say of this—"It is one of those things that no fellow can find out"—he shows himself as wise as any of us who attempt to reason upon it.

Before the pasturage failed altogether, many of the herds and flocks were driven away; but now they could find nothing to eat while on their journey. It was imperative, therefore, to slaughter them. A man near Santa Barbara had been compelled to sacrifice forty thousand sheep to save their skins. Another shipped three hundred by steamer to San Francisco. He showed us his account sales: Net proceeds of three hundred sheep, three dollars and thirty cents—a little more than one cent each. We passed through a ranche belonging to Mr. Pierce, eighteen miles long and eight miles wide. Generally there is at this season more than a foot of grass over it all, and it is well stocked with cattle and sheep. This year he could not cut a ton of hay on the whole of it. A few of his animals had been driven off, while most of them had been lost.

By the side of the road the land is portioned out in these enormous estates, there being very few small proprietors. One only remains in the hands of the Old Catholic Missions, and that is managed in the interest of the "Sisters of Our Lady of Gaudalupe," who devote its proceeds to educating children of the poor.

We reached Bell's ranche for dinner after a drive of sixty miles, not having met a single human being on the road. The ground squirrels might have been counted by thousands. They are the only animals that get a decent subsistence, as the acorns were as abundant as ever. Several deer ran across our track, and quails trotted along as familiarly as chickens, all seeming to be tamed by hunger.

Approaching Gaudelupe, near the sea, the country was fenced in more for cultivation, but this, like the pasturage, was a failure. A few farmers had succeeded in raising a scanty crop of corn, but a new plague had come to ruin them. For three days the sand from the shore had been blown over the fields by a heavy gale, completely covering the crops. It was still blowing, and sadly incommoded travellers.

It blew into our eyes and nostrils so that we could hardly see or breathe. It rolled up in large drifts like snow, frequently bringing the coach to a standstill and obliging all the passengers to descend and wade behind. This disagreeable visitation of nature detained us two hours, so that we arrived at San Luis Obispo only at one o'clock in the morning, after making one hundred and fifteen miles steady travel in twenty-one hours.

San Luis Obispo has recently been connected with the shore by a narrow-gauge railroad to Port Hartford through a cañon nine miles long, and thus becomes another claimant for future supremacy as a commercial mart.

Our opportunities for investigation were limited, as after a rest of only five hours we were called to breakfast and to resume our places on the coach. We went through an experience like to that of the previous morning on leaving Santa Barbara. The ascent, however, was not so long or so steep, and the clear weather made it enjoyable, affording a magnificent view of the valley and the western slope. We reached the highest level in two hours and rapidly descended into another immense park of live oaks. Winding through this beautiful grove for twenty miles after reaching the plateau, we came to Paso de Robles, one of the best-known watering-places of California.

The law of compensation holds good for the Californian throughout. His winters of rain are succeeded by cloudless summers; his occasional short crops are followed by years of abundant harvests, and after the depression of his mining stocks there is a rebound to a "booming market." Almost the only local disease to which he is subject is rheumatism. It requires but little medical knowledge to understand how a climate unfavorable to free action of the skin should tend to this distressing malady. It certainly prevails to an extent unknown in the Eastern States, and persons affected by it there should not attempt to better their condition by coming here. But nature has furnished an offset to this misery of her favorite children in an abundance of mineral springs, most of which are especially adapted to the prevailing disease. Nobody has dyspepsia. If it is brought here it is cured by the air. Therefore chalybeate waters are not required, while sulphur springs are found in all parts of the State.

Notwithstanding its difficulty of access, this hot spring of Paso de Robles is one of the most renowned and greatly frequented. We reached the place by a stage journey of one hundred and forty-two miles from Santa Barbara, and one may come by a direct line of railroad and eighty miles of coaching from San Francisco; but the readiest approach is by steamer to San Luis Obispo, thence over the mountain by a romantic road twenty-seven miles long. Its situation is indicated by its name, the "Pass of the Oaks," where the vast park is narrowed between the ridges of mountains on both sides, and the scattered live-oaks have drawn together in a grove of evergreen arbors. Do not understand by the word "grove" a few trees in a clump; there are thousands within sight under whose branches we may walk for miles. Among them is the hotel with its surrounding cottages. When we reflect that everything in the way of materials and furniture was dragged over the mountains for so many miles, we cannot withhold our admiration of the energy that has accomplished so much. The hotel would not be discreditable to Saratoga, and the cottages are pretty little boxes scattered about the grounds under the oaks, most of them with a parlor and two bedrooms to accommodate individuals or families. Near by is one of larger dimensions elaborately furnished, built by the late William C. Ralston, for his own use, but never occupied, as it was hardly finished at his untimely death. It is now leased by the proprietors of the hotel, who have established a novelty in hotel life. They have a first and second class price for rooms and table, the former paying eighteen and the latter twelve dollars per week. Thus the facilities of bathing are offered to many who cannot meet the higher charges. Another novelty is that the baths are free. This boon may be readily afforded, as Nature kindly aids in the act of benevolence by furnishing subterranean fuel for heating the water. The temperature of the great springs, gushing out from a fountain twelve feet square, is from 105 to 110 degrees Fahrenheit.

Among my readers there may be chemists, physicians, invalids and hypochondriacs. As all who compose these various classes are supposed to be interested in this most celebrated of the California springs, I give the analysis, one in many respects indicating the general character of mineral waters in this region.

MAIN HOT SULPHUR SPRING. (Temperature 110° F.)

One imperial gallon contains—

Sulphureted hydrogen gas	4.55
Free carbonic acid gas	10.50
Sulphate of lime	3.21
Sulphate of potassa	.88
Sulphate of soda (Glauber's salts)	7.85
Peroxide of iron	.36
Alumina	.22
Silica	.44
Bi-carbonate of magnesia	.92
Bi-carbonate of soda	50.74
Chloride of sodium (common salt)	27.18
Iodide and bromides, traces only.	
Organic matter	1.64
Total solid contents per gallon	93.44

All mineral springs have histories. If they have none that are authentic they have some invented for them. Carlsbad in Bohemia owes its importance to the cure of a sick hound belonging to the Emperor Charlemagne, followed by the cure of the dog's master. Kissingen, Baden Baden, Vichy, Aix en Savoie and all the rest, according to the guide-books, "date from a high antiquity," and so this hot spring of Paso de Robles, most like that of Aix in its taste and temperature, "was used and highly valued by the old mission priests eighty years ago, and before that much frequented by the Indians," according to the information that accompanies our bill of fare.

I do not doubt that in many cases the waters are efficacious, nor that in others they injure by injudicious use. One of the chief adjuncts of European spas is lacking here, and the want is a common one at American bathing resorts, namely, proper medical advice. The reverse may be carried to an absurd extent, as in Germany, where a whole town of five or ten thousand inhabitants is absolutely under the control of a board of physicians who dictate the diet of the hotels and restaurants, stand by the "quellen" to see that their patients do not drink one gill too much or too little of the water, and prescribe baths of an exact degree of heat. But this extreme is safer than the practice prevailing here of placing no restrictions on the quantity of water taken or the heat and duration of baths. Every man is "a law unto himself," rivalling every other man in his ability to soak and to be soaked. Time being always money, rheumatism is not supposed to wait for it, but its ejection from the citadel is carried on so vigorously that the citadel is more likely than its tenant to succumb.

We have here a reproduction of a monstrous German absurdity, the mud bath. At best it is a filthy invention, but at

Franzenbad, where we first saw it, the nastiness of the thing was somewhat qualified. For each patient fresh mud was shovelled into a tub, so that he might be sure that the dirt in which he chose to wallow was that of the earth alone. Do you know the philosophy of the mud bath? I never understood it until the information was imparted by a Franzenbad doctor. "How does it cure?" I asked. "Vell, you see," he replied, "dere is seven million littel pooahs in the hooman shkin. De mineral of the mood goes into dem, and de disease comes out." "But how is that?" I ventured to observe. "If the mineral goes into the pores and the disease comes out, one would think they would meet half way in the cuticle." "Oh, you don't understand," answered the doctor after a little deliberation as to how this natural objection should be met. "Don't you notify yourself that half of seven million is three million five hoonderd towsand? In one tree million five hoonderd towsand dere is room for de mineral to get in, and in de oder dere is room for de disease to get out!" Now that is an explanation of the *modus operandi* of the mud bath as clear as the mud itself. So much for the European "mood bad" as practised with a decency superior to the habits of pigs.

The mud bath of Paso de Robles is a sulphur spring not unlike the one used for general bathing and drinking purposes. Into this a sufficiency of dirt is thrown, and renewed once every week to make a hot mush. Will it be credited? There are "ladies' days" and "gentlemen's days" alternating, when a dozen or twenty people at a time go down to the hole and plant themselves up to their chins in this horrid mixture, simultaneously expelling and absorbing disease through their seven million pores!

Notwithstanding all, cures are effected at Paso de Robles

in spite of carelessness in water-drinking and bathing, and the detestable mud baths. The pure air, delightful scenery, freedom from care, horseback exercise and good table more than counterbalance these pernicious practices. Here we passed several days in the most independent style of hotel life, with a lovely little cottage for our " own hired house," opening its doors and windows for the refreshing air of the night, and by day *recubans sub tegmine* " *querci* " more widespreading, green and impervious to the rays of the sun than the beech tree of the original text.

CHAPTER XIII.

END OF THE STAGE-COACH ROMANCE—THE BOUNDARY OF SOUTHERN CALIFORNIA—MEXICAN GRANTS—APPROACH TO SANTA CRUZ—ITS EARLY HISTORY—ITS ATTRACTIONS.

The romance of the stage-coach was by this time nearly dispelled. We looked forward with modified enthusiasm to eighty miles of travel on one of the hottest days of this " exceptional " season to bring us to a railroad station. During this toil of pleasure, however, we reflected that others suffered more, and pitied poor Colonel Kane, who is obliged, by the force of circumstances of his own making, to "coach it" day after day over the same road, which time and habit must have made uninteresting. At all events, the charm of novelty was not exhausted, while the Colonel must sometimes feel like his brother whip of the White Mountains, whose stolidity was the wonder of the fashionable young ladies on his box. " How can you drive along as you do," they exclaimed, " without being enraptured with the beauties of nature on every hand?" "Well, I'm kind of used to it," he replied. "I wish I could see something new, and then like enough I'd gawk 'round same as you do now."

There had come to be a weariness in this everlasting park

of live-oaks; the ascent and descent of the mountains from repetition had grown tame. Rolling over the foot-hills we came to dine at Pleito, a small relay station on the fifteen-thousand-acre ranch of Mr. Pimberton, an English gentleman, whose mansion, built in old country style, gives the wild park of nature a striking likeness to the ornamented landscapes of Britain. Only two or three thousand acres were cultivated, and fortunately, as the land is low, the crops of barley were not a total loss. No grain was saved this year, all of it having been cut for hay to feed the starving cattle.

In the evening we reached the small village of Soledad, passing the night at an adobe inn, thankful that our drive of two hundred and sixty miles was at last accomplished, resolving to recommend others to go over the same route, but to take it in smaller instalments.

A branch of the Southern Pacific Railroad begins at Soledad and runs through the Salinas Valley for its especial benefit in carrying its grain to San Francisco. Uusually this product is abundant beyond the demand for domestic use. "Last year," said the conductor, "we hauled more than forty thousand tons of barley; this year not a single bushel." This was one of the many tales of the famine.

Following the bed of the Salinas River, we crossed it where it is usually passed by a ferry. Now, there was only a tiny stream three or four yards in width and a foot in depth. But drawing toward its point of discharge into the Bay of Monterey, the moisture of the sea air began to affect vegetation, and by the time the station of Pajaro, beyond Salinas, was reached, we were in a land of comparative plenty, leaving behind the saddest reminiscences of an otherwise pleasant journey through Southern California. That district terminates about here, and with it the desolation of its generally fruitful fields. This is the dividing line of Southern California in distinction from the more northern part of the State. The term should not be confounded with "Lower" California, the country bounded on the north by San Diego, and still under Mexican rule. The annexation of that territory to the Union is not far distant, and is already contemplated by land speculators.

On the passage from Panama the steamer landed a large party of Mexicanized Americans at Cape St. Lucas, whose avowed object it was to survey the most valuable lands of Lower California, and obtain grants from the government of Mexico, which, in its present condition of poverty, and with its uncertain future, is ready to sell them for trifling amounts. After buying up the whole peninsula for a few thousand dollars, these enterprising gentlemen propose to colonize it at once, and, waiting their opportunity to join some revolutionary faction, obtain independence in that way. After this, admission to the Union will not be difficult, and the land-jobbing operation will in the end prove a certain success. It will merely be a speculation somewhat more extensive than those commonly undertaken throughout the State by gentlemen who are content to "grab" only one or two hundred thousand acres. "Grabbing" is a common practice, as may be inferred from frequent notices of the ranches and the rancheros. When men of large capital take advantage of the "desert land" law, and avail themselves of land otherwise unproductive for the purpose of extensive irrigation, they are the benefactors of the community. But when, as too often is the case, they keep the Mexican grants which they have purchased for the sole purpose of pasturage, where the land is adapted to grain and fruit, they can be regarded only as opposed to the best interests of the State. The surest method of bringing them to the adoption of a liberal policy, is to force them to it by taxing arable and grazing land at the same valuation.

The wretched little village called Pajaro, where the narrow-gauge road to Santa Cruz connects with the main line, is remarkable for nothing except the number of its grog shops and the grasping disposition of the landlord of a very bad inn. After waiting two hours at this miserable den we were transferred to the Santa Cruz train. The narrow-gauge road, twenty-two miles long, was built by a few enterprising gentlemen with a view of benefiting their large landed interests, while it gives to Santa Cruz a circuitous communication with the capital. When the more direct line now coming from San José is completed, the value of the present road will be greatly lessened; but tourists and pleasure seekers will always enjoy the wonderfully picturesque scenery along its track. Climbing a grade one hundred and thirty-six feet to the mile, spanning ravines on trestle-work ninety-five feet in height, twisting through cañons of enormous redwoods, turning precipices that overhang the sea, it winds along the northern side of the Bay of Monterey, affording a grand and comprehensive view. The engineer who planned it must have been a poet. Mr. Aptos is one of its owners, and he has perpetuated his name by christening a charmingly romantic glen, where he has built a large and costly hotel. This house stands in a grove of tall redwoods, almost rivalling those of Mariposa in size, and before it the ocean rolls in, dashing spray nearly to its doors. Other stations like this are situated at points selected by a judicious and refined taste, making the route to Santa Cruz as inviting as the city itself is attractive.

The Rev. Dr. Willey, one of the Protestant pioneers of 1849, and Father Adam, who occupies the old mission established by his predecessors in 1791, have been indefatigable in searching the ancient monastic records bearing upon the discovery and settlement of Santa Cruz. From them we learn that this part of the coast was known to the Spaniards as early as the year 1602, when Viscayno landed on the site of the present town and gave a glowing description of the Bay of Monterey, on which it stands, and of the surrounding country. In those days the world was too large, and there were not enough people to make available all the discoveries rapidly following the advent of Columbus. So this region remained neglected until two centuries had elapsed. Then the missionaries, who had landed at San Diego in 1769, followed up their adventures along the coast, establishing themselves here in 1791.

Fathers Salagar and Lopez arrived on the 25th day of September in that year. Practical old fathers were they. The record which Father Adam produces says nothing of the tracts they brought for distribution, but it enumerates thirty cows, ten yoke of oxen, fourteen bulls, twenty steers, nine horses and seven mules. That was a missionary outfit in 1791. "And so they begin their work ; they teach such Indians as they can collect how to make *adobes*, and, as fast as they can, the arts of civilized life. They teach the men the use of tools, and they teach the women to weave." In three years the large church was built, its ruins only now standing, not long ago shattered by an earthquake. Vineyards were planted, cattle increased on the ranges, and Santa Cruz lived and thrived as a Spanish settlement, although its population did not become large until its occupancy by our countrymen at the close of the Mexican war. Then occurred that rapid change we have noted in all the old *pueblos* of California. The Anglo-Saxon race poured in with its industries, enterprise and taste, and the people's wealth increased, until Santa Cruz, the mission station selected first for natural beauties, has become a city of six thousand permanent inhabitants, and the favorite resort of sojourners from all parts of the country. It is but a few hours distant by steam from San Francisco, and as the time will soon be less by rail, its rapid increase and prosperity are assured.

Nature has scooped out with dainty hand a charming valley, in which is nestled this pretty little city, sheltered from the rough touch of the sea breeze that blows over the ridge and tempers the air with the breath of healthful elasticity. The range of the thermometer for the year is remarkably equal. There are no extremes of heat and cold, the humidity is sufficient to keep vegetation green without having an injurious effect upon health, and it is not surprising that so many invalids, to whom a modified sea air is agreeable, have made it their home. The citizens are not niggardly of their land. Here and there in the main street is a block of stores and warehouses, but the dwellings are detached. Doubtless the inhabitants are fond of society, for picnics and excursions to the glens, the wooded hills and the shore seem to be their chief occupation. But they are still more fond of the companionship of the trees, the flowers and the vines that surround every house. Their gardens are their homes, of which the cottages form the smallest part. No man seems to have been allowed to build his house or to lay out his grounds in any way that does not produce a pleasing effect.

With all their temptations to pleasure and indolence, the picnics, the riding and the bathing, in which so many persons appear to be occupied, there is no want of energy and attention to business. Santa Cruz is a town of many industries. The powder works are very extensive. Obtaining saltpetre at a cheap rate of freight from the west coast of South America, they manufacture this article at a large profit. Last year its sales amounted to nearly half a million dollars. The dairies are their pride, for they send one hundred thousand dollars' worth of butter annually to San Francisco. They export a great deal of lime. The back hills being heavily timbered with redwood, great quantities are reduced to lumber, not only for home use, but to ship to other places on the coast. The grape is in high cultivation, and excellent wine is made in large quantities. Mr. Jarvis, one of the principal growers, took us through his establishment and offered—please let it be understood, at various times—glasses of his port, sherry, muscatel, angelica, hock and brandy. His wines readily command from one dollar to one dollar and fifty cents per gallon, and his brandy three dollars and fifty cents. One of his vineyards covers seventy-five acres, and produces three hundred tons of grapes. Extensive as is the wine product of California, Mr. Jarvis thinks it is only in its infancy. He has a correct view of its development when he says that everybody is in too much haste. He has been for years engaged in reaching after perfection, and has not yet arrived at it. "Every man should plant for his own children," he observed, with more wisdom and regard for posterity than is often displayed in this selfish age. "If we all do that, in the next generation California will be the vineyard of the world."

A short narrow-gauge railroad has been recently built, chiefly for the purpose of bringing lumber down from the forests, while it serves admirably for purposes of recreation. It is only eight miles long, but they are such eight miles as are rarely travelled. In less than a quarter of an hour we began mounting a grade of one hundred and twenty-six feet to the mile, through a dense forest of redwood. We arrived at the station of the "Big Trees," where was a forest compared with which the pines of the eastern mountains are dwarfs. Leaving the train and walking under their shade for a quarter of a mile, we came to the veritable giants of the forest. The great *sequoias* of Mariposa are indeed somewhat larger than these, but it is a long distance to them; and if seeing big trees be the only object of one's search, it may be fairly counted that the difference in size is not enough to counterbalance the length of the journey. Ordinary sight-seeing can be more easily gratified by coming to Santa Cruz and making the trip on this little railroad.

Is it not enough to look upon these slightly inferior giants, one of which is two hundred and seventy-eight feet high, sixty feet in circumference, and hollowed out at the base and occupied as a house, with dimensions of sixteen feet by twenty? This is the largest of them, although there are many not much smaller. To a casual observer the difference between these trees and those of Mariposa and Calaveras is not apparent; but it is asserted that the latter are the true *sequoia*, and these a different variety of redwood. The trees here are shorter lived; one of them, on being cut down, showed by its rings that it had flourished only two thousand eight hundred years, while an ancient rival in Calaveras scored three thousand two hundred and fifty-two years, during which it had grown to the height of two hundred and ninety-six feet. It is to be hoped that the public spirit of Santa Cruz will keep this noble forest intact and secure from the ruthless woodman's axe until it has time to attain to the size and age of its competitors.

CHAPTER XIV.

FROM SANTA CRUZ TO SAN JOSÉ—THE GARDEN OF SANTA CLARA VALLEY—THE TOWNS OF SAN JOSÉ AND SANTA CLARA — ANOTHER MISSION — THE CHURCH AND THE GRAPE-WINE AND BRANDY—THE ENTERPRISE OF GENERAL NAGLEE.

We left Santa Cruz on a hot summer morning in an open wagon, uncomfortable from the heat and the dust while toiling slowly up the mountain. That is now forgotten; but we shall never forget the view from the summit, which on one side commanded the ocean, and on the other the lovely Santa Clara Valley —a fruit garden, and, as its people boast, the most beautiful one of California. There it lay before us, a garden of one and a quarter million acres, fifty-two miles long, thirty-four miles wide, variegated with grass-covered undulating hills, orchards, vineyards and yellow fields of grain, spotted all over with the ever-present great live-oaks that, from this height, seemed like little green bushes no higher than the heads of wheat among which they were scattered. The noble six-horse team had brought the last strain upon their muscles to reach the summit, and then, obedient to the crack of the whip in the hands of a skilful driver, darted down the mountain, whirling round steep corners and flying through a cloud of dust as if they enjoyed the sport and were laughing inside their blinders at the terrified passengers behind them. The cultivated plains were soon reached, and long avenues of trees lined the way to the capital of the county, the first capital of the State before San Francisco robbed it of its rank. San José has lost its political importance, but the refinement and easy luxury for which its people are conspicuous amply compensate for the loss of a noisy rabble of office-hunting demagogues; and its nearness to the great commercial centre has given it many advantages beside those of its natural opportunities.

The towns of San José and Santa Clara may be considered as one. They are connected by a long avenue of willows, planted by the missionary settlers in 1799. This wide street of three miles, called the Alameda, is shaded by triple rows of willow, poplar, and eucalyptus trees, whose variety of foliage has a most pleasing effect. The houses, with a good taste that is very general, are at a little distance from the road and partly concealed from it by a perennial shrubbery. It presents a gay scene in the afternoon, when ladies and gentlemen gallop at full speed with a display of daring horsemanship that excites our admiration.

San José, and its suburb Santa Clara, embracing each other as they meet under their Alameda, have twenty thousand inhabitants, and those of the whole valley number somewhat more than thirty thousand. The lazy Mexicans, sparsely scattered over it previous to the American occupation of 1849, devoted no attention to its cultivation, hardly raising an acre of wheat, and allowing the whole of its area to be grown over with wild grass for the pasturage of their cattle.

The wants of those people are few. Wherever the Spanish ranchero is to be found, he avoids, as much as possible, the contact of what we deem civilization. He cares not for books, for society, or even for fruits or bread, his body being as insufficiently nourished as his mind. He never plants a shade tree, and if one happens to grow near to his adobe house he cuts it down as the easiest attainable fuel. *Carne seca*, his dried meat, which he prefers to fresh beef, and black beans, the only vegetable he plants, compose his whole diet. With this food, little clothing, a good saddle and a good horse, his existence is complete and all his wants are satisfied. The old Catholic padres succeeded in domesticating and converting the Indians, but their influence upon these greasers was of little account. The missionaries alone gave their attention to building, manufactures, farming and vineyards, invariably selecting such favored spots as the Santa Clara Valley for the scenes of their operations. When Vancouver landed at San Francisco, in 1792, and made an excursion into this part of the country, he was astonished and delighted at the progress the Franciscans had made. Their establishments were unfortunately secularized when Mexico as unfortunately obtained her independence, and no further progress was made until this territory was ceded to the United States. Then the soil of the valley was struck by the wand of a magician. The magic of freedom, intelligence and enterprise gave it a new life, and robed it with the beautiful garments which now cover the nakedness of thirty years ago.

Already the assessed value of its real estate exceeds thirty-one million dollars, the farming land commanding the highest prices on account of its nearness to San Francisco, which is supplied with vegetables and fruit.

We drove out to the old mission, whose great possessions have now dwindled down to a parish church and thirty acres of land. It is under the charge of Father Cassidy, who received us courteously, and entertained us with histories of the olden times when his predecessors flourished in their abundance, dispensing unlimited hospitality which he modestly emulated as he offered us a bottle of wine of his own manufacture from the vines they had planted. The good father, beside all his parochial duties, attends personally to his vineyard, and it is his chief satisfaction to furnish for the sacramental use of Catholic and Protestant alike the pure juice of the grape, which he provides at the moderate cost of fifty cents per gallon. It is an excellent red wine, bearing transportation, and quite as good as the French claret, costing one dollar per bottle. Father Cassidy says that the old missionaries understood the true theory of vine culture. and practised it successfully by planting their vineyards on side-hills instead of upon levels—the latter mode now commonly adopted increasing the crop, but producing more watery grapes. Certainly this active priest combines much practical knowledge with his clerical duties, entitling him to respect in a double sense as "a laborer in the vineyard." The old church and cloisters of the monastery were built of adobe, and notwithstanding the six feet thickness of the walls, an earthquake had tumbled a part to the ground and shaken the whole pile, so that it was riven by gaping seams. The crumbling nature of the material and its dingy color, prematurely gave the ruins an appearance of age equal to that of stone after the lapse of many hundred years. General Naglee, of San José, has devoted twenty years to the selection and culture of the most desirable varieties of the French and German wine grapes, and to experiments in the manufacture of brandy. His abundant means enable him to study the problem at his leisure, without regard to immediate profits, for his only desire is that the community shall benefit by his labor. His grounds are a mile distant from the centre of the town, and he is generally at home, taking pleasure in receiving his many friends, and in explaining his processes to those who desire to be informed.

After driving over his grounds of forty acres, one-third of them planted with foreign grapes, he introduced us to his manufacturing establishment, where are the presses and the distilling apparatus. Four immense vats were capable of containing 16,000 gallons each, and nine others of 4,000 each, gave capacity for 100,000 gallons of wine, and 20,000 gallons of brandy vintage. General Naglee preserves but little wine, his chief object being to make the purest and best brandy in the world at whatever cost of time and money. Very few people know how brandy is made ; very few know what brandy is, and, if truth were told, in our day there is very little brandy. Probably 999 gallons out of every 1,000 that are sold as brandy are a vile compound of whiskey, distilled spirits, and chemical abominations. This is equally true of wines.

Now, if one thing is palpable without demonstration, it is that the stomach craves stimulants, and these it will have either of food or drink. The Bengalee and the Malay fortify themselves with pepper and curry, the Dutchman uses schnapps for the same purpose, and the Scotch and Irish have a pure whiskey ; the Englishman has his beer and porter, the Frenchman, the Spaniard and the Italian their wine, the Chinese his tea and the Turk his coffee. Either of these articles of food and drink used to excess is as injurious as the gluttony of plum-pudding or drinking too much water. As I never suffered from indulgence in any stimulant, but have acquired a life long dyspepsia by aqueous intemperance at a hydropathic establishment, I hope I shall not be misunderstood in advocating with earnestness the culture of the grape, for the benefit not only of California, but of the people at large, so that the truest temperance may prevail through the land. I would not say any thing to encourage the general use of distilled liquors; but no one except a fanatic will deny that they are sometimes necessary, and that they are agreeable luxuries. At any rate, the fact is patent that they will be drunk, and therefore it is the more desirable that a pure article should take the place of the villanous compounds by which dram-drinkers are poisoned.

General Naglee justly esteems himself a philanthropist in devoting himself to this special object. His brandy is of two classes, the inferior made after the process of most European manufacture, which consists in distilling the dregs of mashed grapes that have been used for wine. This he sells as fast as it is produced. Fortunately he is a gentleman of great wealth, or he could not afford the costly experiment of producing brandy of the higher grade. This is made by using only the finest French and German grapes, and separating the juice between the pulp and the skin without any pressure to bring out the deleterious essential oils which they contain, and thus the very purest juice of the grape is fermented and distilled into the choicest liquor. As yet he has not sold any, 60,000 gallons being in store, some of it in the cellar ten years.

In distilling brandy from wine, the process results in saving only twenty gallons out of a hundred. When all the vats are filled with one hundred thousand gallons, the residue is consequently twenty thousand gallons of pure spirit. This is stored in immense casks, each labelled with revenue stamps, certifying that ninety cents per gallon has been paid to the government.

By the exertions of the State Vinicultural Society, the law has been so far modified that no excise is now paid on brandy until it has been made three years. An important amount of interest is thus saved. It would be curious to compute, if any one cares to make more figures than I do, the cost of this ten years' old brandy that we tasted, supposing that at the outset, including the tax, it cost the manufacturer $3 per gallon, and that money has commanded here all the time the annual interest of twelve per centum, with an addition of twelve per cent. for leakage and evaporation. Let this be compounded, and the conclusion will be reached that the experiment is too expensive to be productive of any thing but self-satisfaction to General Naglee, and of gratitude from those enjoying his hospitality and profiting by his outlay.

Temperance people and prohibitionists may settle the wine question among themselves as far as it bears upon the morals of the community of which they have assumed the charge. There are, however, some people who do not choose to be subject to their dictation. They may be pleased to know what progress has been made by California in the production of the grape.

From the most trustworthy sources at hand, it is established that in the whole State not less than 50.000 acres are planted with vines, numbering from 40,000,000 to 45,000,000, and averaging from 700 to 1,000 vines per acre. In the southern and interior counties the yield is more plentiful, each acre producing, on the average, six tons of grapes, while in the coast counties four tons is considered a fair crop. From one ton of grapes 130 to 140 gallons of wine are pressed. Last year 8,000,000 gallons were produced, but the vine capacity this year is estimated at 10,000,000. Most of the wines have heretofore been made from the old "Mission grape." The exact history of this prolific vine is lost in the antiquity of one hundred years. This only is certain, that it was introduced by the Franciscans with their religion as a part of their civilization. It is worthy of reflection that religious teachers have been the men to whom the world is most indebted for good wine, from the "first preacher of righteousness," down. It has been remarked, as a matter of history, reflecting great credit upon the Catholic clergy, that they first produced to perfection the grapes from which are manufactured the wines of Johannisberg, Steinberg, Hockheim, Clos-Vougeot, l'Hospice, Chambertin, Chateau Yquem, St. Julien, and various other celebrated brands, and that the first champagne was made by a priest.

We know that the first vines of California were planted at St. Gabriel in 1771, but it is not settled if this was done with roots or cuttings imported from Spain or Mexico. General Vallejo, who has given no little attention to the subject, says that the Fathers first attempted to make wine from the common wild grape of the country, but not succeeding in this, they raised them from the seeds of imported raisins. From these the white and blue varieties were both produced, but the former was abandoned, while the latter was adopted and cultivated at all the mission establishments. Since the advent of Americans, many other varieties have been introduced. Colonel Haraszthy, who alone imported two hundred and fifty distinct varieties, gave them all a fair trial, selecting from them, as adapted to various parts of the State, forty or fifty of the best. These are not all used for wine. Many are especially devoted to brandy, table use and raisins. I have no data for these two latter products, but it is known that one hundred and fifty thousand gallons of brandy are annually distilled, large and increasing quantities of raisins are cured, and beside the grapes eaten in the State, many cars are laden with them in the season for distribution from San Francisco to New York.

A very intelligent gentleman remarked, to my surprise, that as the mining interest of California had been superseded by cereals, so they will before many years be neglected, and the specialties of the State be fruit and wine. It is possible that he may be right, although the day is more distant than his prophecy indicated. For grain production, this soil is inexhaustible, but by means of careless farming is rapidly impoverished, while the air and sunlight, which have more to do with the culture of the vine than the ground, have life-giving influences that can never die. Let the California farmer take warning from this prediction. Let him do something more for his soil than to comb it. It needs care as his good horses need grooming, or he will run it to death. He will realize this one of these days when he calls on Oregon for bread.

San Francisco is reached in two hours from San José, by the railroad passing through the beautiful suburbs of Menlo Park, Belmont, and San Mateo. Scattered over them are the country residences of those who can spare time from business to enjoy the luxury of ease, and to dispense the sumptuous hospitality for which so many of them have a merited reputation. The environs have been often described, and are well known to every stranger who visits the city.

CHAPTER XV.

NORTHERN CALIFORNIA—MOUNT SHASTA IN THE DISTANCE—
RAILROADS—FARMING ON A LARGE SCALE.

We came north to get a nearer view of Mount Shasta ; it seems but ten miles distant—a pyramid of snow from its peak to the pine trees that spread their branches at its base. It seems so near ; and yet we might reflect that the apparent base would have a far different color in this temperature of 100 degrees, if it were not merely a part of the summit, for Shasta is one hundred miles away. So clearly defined are its lines in the sky, that at Marysville, ninety miles further south, it is often visible in a favorable atmosphere. Difficult as the region about Shasta is in its approaches, the romantic scenery, cool atmosphere, mineral springs, and hunting and fishing, annually bring many visitors to Sessions—a favorite wateringplace of Californians who can afford to leave their business for a long vacation. Tourists unwilling to go away with only the satisfaction to be obtained from the charmingly deceptive view of Shasta at a distance, have only to follow up the Oregon Railroad forty miles further to Redding, and then take the stagecoach for seventy miles to their destination

Eastern people have but a small conception of the railroad enterprises of California. They are content with the knowledge that there is a direct route from New York to San Francisco, but know little of its connections with the many domestic tenders from which so much of its trade is derived. The railroads stretch out their iron arms to grasp every section of the State.

The Northern Pacific runs eighty miles along the coast to Healdsburg, on its way to Oregon. A narrow gauge is looking in the same direction. The California Pacific has reached Williams, one hundred and twenty-one miles to the north, and the Oregon branch, on which we arrive at Red Bluffs, distant two hundred and seventeen miles from San Francisco, goes on forty miles further to Redding, and is bound to extend beyond the Oregon line. All these roads have lateral branches. Wherever there is a valley for wheat to grow or a forest for timber to be felled, a train of cars stands in waiting to bring produce and lumber to market for shipping or home consumption.

We came to Vallejo in two hours by steamer, leaving San Francisco at an early hour of the morning, and passing the time —which seemed only too short—in gazing at the surroundings of the wonderful bay, which is equalled only by that of Rio de Janeiro, and, like it, surrounded by mountains whose verdant slopes reach to the shore. Saucelito lay smiling under a high cliff, and San Rafael coyly hid itself away in its dreamy valley of shade, its church spires peeping up through the shrubbery to tell where it might be found. Vallejo, fondly expected by its founder (for whom it is called) to become the capital of the State, refuses to be comforted for its disappointment, and will not put on any beautiful garments. A plain, matter-of-fact suburb, it serves, in connection with Mare Island, as a naval depot, beside deriving some little importance as a point of railroad debarkation. The train rolled into the country through a forest of fruit trees; and then, with the exception of little towns and villages on the road, it ran through one far-spread field of wheat.

There were trees and vines in plenty, but their abundance was lost in the immensity of the grain. It was the time of harvest, and here plenty rewarded the toil of the husbandman, and sleek cattle and sheep followed in the train of the reapers to revel in pastures left for their use.

Stopping at "Knight's Landing," we called on Mr. Reed, and were told that he was busy in the field. There he was found in a two-thousand-acre lot, superintending his force of thirty men, his steam engine, headers, wagons, mules, thresher and separator, all working harmoniously together, gathering in the crop; and this was a small outfit compared with that of Mr. Boggs, at Princeton, with whom we passed two days, entertained most agreeably in a princely farmer's mansion. There, in a six-thousand-acre field, machinery was multiplied as one hundred acres each day was harvested, and the stream of wheat rolled into bags at the rate of twelve bushels per minute. Not contented with farming, Mr. Boggs gives his attention to raising some of the finest horses in the State. He owns one hundred thousand acres in California, and fifty thousand in Oregon. Most of it is pasturage, for he raises not more than one hundred and fifty thousand bushels of wheat. He has a few thousand cattle, he could not recollect the exact number, nor could he tell if his sheep would count more than forty thousand, but he knew they were not below that figure. They are sheared twice in the year, averaging eight pounds of wool each, and netting, clear of all expenses, something more than one dollar per head. Were they not thinned out for the market, they would double themselves every two years; and twenty thousand being annually sold at one dollar a head, there is a total income of sixty thousand dollars. Here is a model California farmer—a State Senator, honored by his fellow-citizens with the directorship of various public institutions—who came into Sacramento thirty years ago, with his boots hanging over his shoulder, and who modestly says that he too has grown rich because he could not help it. We have sojourned with nobility in their castles, and have been accustomed to the etiquette of flunky servility which calls for the address of "My lord" and "Your lordship;" but "John Boggs—hullo, John!" is the style our friend receives at Princeton, where he is the lord of manors compared to which an English estate is a potato-patch.

A pleasanter, though longer route to Princeton, would have been to ascend the river by one of the stern-wheel steamers that ply upon it. Our host, Mr. Boggs, gave us a little experience of steamboating when, from the bank near his house, he signalled the captain to haul into the shore and take us all on board for a short trip of a few miles. At this place the stream is scarcely one hundred feet wide, but the romantic beauty of the scenery in frequent turns is wonderful to contemplate. The river is bordered by a forest of oaks for miles, and these great trees are draped with festoons of wild grape-vines, loaded with early clusters that perfume the air. This little excursion was terminated on meeting the carriage that followed us along the road by the shore. Before the advent of the railroad, all passengers and freight were transported on the river; and the wheat produced in the greater part of this district is still sent down to market by steamers as a cheaper conveyance than by rail.

Jacinto, fifteen miles above Princeton, is the capital of the dukedom of Dr. Glenn, for he owns its site and its surroundings. I have gradually introduced you to Dr. Glenn, first describing what might be termed a large farm at Knight's Landing, next a larger one at Princeton, and now coming to the largest estate under cultivation in California, or in the world— fifty-six thousand acres planted in wheat! The doctor's modest cottage is a house indicative of occupation by a farmer of one or two hundred acres. "Father is not at home," said one of the young ladies, "but he is about the place somewhere; if you like, I will go with you on horseback and find him." This arrangement being perfectly satisfactory, we were soon galloping through the wheat fields. After a sharp ride of half an hour, I began to think my little pilot had lost her bearings; but she assured me that her father was only seven miles off, and we should soon find him, and we shortly afterward met him on his return.

The crop of this year was below the average, as the doctor said it would not yield more than twenty bushels to the acre. It is his custom to plant two-thirds of the land annually and allow one-third to recuperate. In this he shows more wisdom and a greater regard for the future than a Californian farmer usually has. He finds that the estate is so large that it is burdensome, and has begun to lease parts of it on shares. It would be well for themselves and for the community if all the great landholders should realize their mistake in extending their territories beyond moderate bounds. Most of them are never satisfied, but are always craving more land. By this means some of the richest are absolutely poor. Every dollar they get being expended in the purchase of other acres they are always borrowers.

In the neighborhood of Los Angeles we were taken by a friend to visit a property of several thousand acres. The proprietor was not the owner of a decent suit of clothes, and as the family had just dined upon all the bacon they had, he could not offer us a morsel of food. The great productiveness of the soil offers irresistible temptations to purchasing more and to borrowing money at high rates of interest. In ordinary seasons a man may be able to pay eighteen per cent. for loans, and at the end of four years to repay the money and to own the land. This state of things encourages the establishment of banks in every small village; but, whatever are their profits, it cannot be healthy practice for a man to keep himself poor in order to grow rich.

The private village of Jacinto is a curiosity. Dr. Glenn owns it, and therefore controls its religion, morals and trade. He will not have any false doctrine, heresy or schism preached in his church, nor any liquor sold in his tavern; and the store, a large two-story brick building, is well supplied with every conceivable necessity, furnishing at just prices all that the people he employs require. An immense warehouse, capable of storing four hundred thousand bushels of wheat, stands on the river bank, where its contents can be slid on board the steamers. There are the stage house, the wagon factory, the blacksmith's shop, the shoemaker, the tailor, the butcher and the baker; here are Sam Lew's store and "intelligence office," the respective laundries of Sue Wan, Clong Sing and Jim Yew, all these establishments being necessary to the support of Dr. Glenn and his family, and of the families of his laborers, or for conducting the business of the ranch. And there sat the lord of the domain, dressed in his home-spun suit, seemingly unconscious that he owned a dollar. As he delights in hospitality, his cottage is always full to overflowing, and it needs no card of invitation to make any lady or gentleman an acceptable inmate. Not content with a welcome to the coming, but with a readiness to speed their parting guests, one of the sons drove us over to Chico in the evening.

Crossing the Sacramento, the road lay for four miles through groves of oaks and wild vines, and, emerging from the river bottom, kept on through nine miles of continuous wheat fields until it reached the town. Chico is a pretty village of three thousand inhabitants, owing its prosperity to farming and to the lumber brought down from the Sierras in a flume for a distance of forty miles, and shipped by the Oregon Railroad running through the place.

General Bidwell has a property of twenty-three thousand acres in the immediate neighborhood, of which one hundred and fifty are planted in vines, and as much in peach, cherry, almond, olive, fig, orange and lemon groves. As from some cause he has not been successful in making wine, he has turned his attention to drying raisins, which industry promises larger returns. His career affords another instance of prosperity founded on energy; for on the very spot where his castellated mansion rears its walls, formerly stood the little adobe hut where he once dispensed liquors and cigars over his bar. He may justly feel a pride in the change of his fortunes.

After a description of Dr. Glenn's farm, that of Mr. Reavis, near Chico, may seem to be scarcely worth a reference, as it contains only twelve thousand acres. Nevertheless, the management of the estate is admirable. After visiting the harvest field, where fifty men busily worked together like so many parts of a clock, we inspected the stables of blood horses, one of which, "Blackbird," had been purchased from Mr. Boggs for ten thousand dollars. The young son of the proprietor said with becoming modesty, "Father hasn't much of a ranch, and doesn't care to have a big one. He sticks to raising wheat, and doesn't care for stock, for we have only two thousand head of cattle and three hundred horses over yonder in the mountains."

The ranches of a few gentlemen have been mentioned, as specimens of the great landholders of California whose enterprise is so creditable to their industry. It may be observed that their present estates have invariably accumulated from small beginnings. Indeed, there is scarcely a single instance of a man's "starting in" with wealth that has not ended in failure, whereas there are thousands of poor men who have become rich by farming.

When these great estates are divided—as they will be before many years elapse—into small farms of one or two hundred acres, capable of being easily worked by single families, and affording them a comfortable livelihood; when seven millions instead of seven hundred thousand people live in California to work, and work to live upon her wheat, corn, barley, oats, cattle, sheep, hogs, fruits and vineyards, all its vast population may boast of a solid wealth derived from its only true source; for it will be the reward of honest labor.

CHAPTER XVI.

REVIEW OF THE MINING AND AGRICULTURAL INTERESTS OF CALIFORNIA—ALONG THE SACRAMENTO—NAPA—CALISTOGA—THE PETRIFIED FOREST—THE GEYSERS—SAN FRANCISCO.

Following the course of the Sacramento River on the Oregon Railroad, we came to Marysville, fifty miles from Chico, still a town of some importance as centre of a large farming population, although the activity it once displayed as a great mining camp of the placer diggings has subsided. To this district the first prospectors were attracted, and for years the gulches and sluices yielded them a golden harvest. Now there are no more nuggets to be found by grubbing or chance, but in their place the fields are covered with golden wheat.

The changes of business and industries give force to a remark made by Governor Stanford. "California," said he, " owes her prosperity to agriculture. If every mine could be sunk out of sight ten thousand fathoms deep it would be for her advantage." Continuing the conversation, he added, as nearly as his words can be remembered, " Mining is comparatively an unproductive industry. All the laborers engaged in it do not earn as much as farm hands upon the average, while they are losers in health, and it gives rise to a species of gambling which robs the whole community. Now, there are three thousand people in San Francisco who live directly or indirectly from the purchase and sale of stocks, averaging in their expenses $3000 per year. There are $9,000,000 which they certainly do not earn, but take from their victims. These men should earn this money for themselves by being producers. Then they would not rob their fellow-citizens ; and if they and the miners were all at work in the wheat fields, our railroads could well spare the profits made from the transportation of ore and bullion." What has been said of Southern California may be quoted as proof that farming is as uncertain as mining when the crops fail, and there is not only a loss of harvest, but of cattle and sheep. It is true that years of drought sometimes occur, but these may always be provided for by selecting lands that can be irrigated, while stock may be preserved by taking proper precautions. The melancholy loss of animal life by starvation, might have been avoided. There was an abundant harvest even upon some uplands, but the farmers, after going through the wheat-fields with "headers," and taking off the tops of the stalks, either brought in their stock from the ranges to feed it down, or they only set it on fire to be rid of it.

If that straw had been cut and stacked, the mute blessings of hundreds of thousands of poor beasts would have come down upon those farmers' heads, and what they would value more, the lives of the animals would have been saved for their profit.

Passing through Sacramento we reached Napa on the 4th of July. The anniversary was there celebrated by a great barbacue, to which all were freely invited. Oxen and sheep were roasted whole in long trenches, and brought upon the grass for a general attack of pocket-knives and fingers, the meat being finely basted by a dust storm that made it a more suitable food for chickens than for the men who had the grit to partake of it. Then was read the inevitable Declaration, that shibboleth of our political faith, which somehow, in spite of its accepted truth, fails to convince the ragged tramp who looks up at the palace windows of the millionaire that all men are free and equal. After that came the oration, an echo of the hundreds of thousands of orations that have resounded through a hundred years, until the want is felt of a new revolution to give birth to an original idea.

From Napa to Calistoga it is twenty-five miles by rail. Here are the Hot Springs, a "resort," as every thing of that kind is called in California. This must be chiefly a resort for people who suffer from a deficiency of animal heat. Enclosed in a deep and really beautiful valley, the sun has a full play upon the soil, sometimes producing a heat of one hundred and ten degrees in the shade, as it did at this time. By a little digging anywhere hot water is reached. The condition of the inhabitants in the summer season may be imagined; it may be agreeable enough in the winter, when fuel is not required on account of the subterranean steam apparatus.

We rode to the "Petrified Forest," six miles from town, on the Santa Rosa road over the mountain separating the Napa from the Sonoma Valley. This wood bears a name likely to mislead one's ideas of the reality. The forest is like all others, the present generation of trees being green and vigorous. The petrifaction is in the trunks of their predecessors, which were discovered buried several feet in the ground, and were exhumed for the gaze of the curious. The proprietor of the land is an ignorant old Dutchman, who told us that the trees were "feefteen t'ousand year old." When asked for the certificate of their birth, he retorted, " Vell, how old you calls them ? " We admitted our ignorance, which gave him the advantage, and he triumphantly exclaimed, "Den vot for you doubts my vord?" The age of the Petrified Forest may therefore be considered as settled. Some of the fallen trunks are in absolute preservation, the bark and broken segments having the exact appearance of wood, although they have turned to heavy stones. They have all the characteristics of the red woods which resemble the sequoias of the Mariposa and Calaveras groves. It may be possible to unearth some which equal or exceed them in size, with a sufficiency of rings to corroborate the Dutchman's theory. The largest one measured thirty-three feet in circumference near its base. What peculiar properties of soil produced the petrifaction must be left to the investigation of naturalists, who may obtain some further information from the intelligent guide.

Calistoga is on the direct road to the Geysers. These hot spouting springs are visited by tourists not only for the sake of the phenomena, but for the drive over the romantic mountain road with the renowned Jehu Foss. It being all up-hill work, there was no opportunity for him to display his skill; so he entertained us with descriptions of the country and the quicksilver mines, formerly so productive to this neighborhood, but at present greatly neglected. Descending somewhat from the highest point, we came at evening to the hotel, twenty-six miles from Calistoga.

As to the Geysers, it is a mistake to suppose that they are high spouts of water. They are simply a group of boiling springs, extending half a mile through a mountain cañon, where we walked amid the hissing and roaring noises of steaming sulphurous gases and over hot lava-beds. There is nothing that is beautiful, but much that is fearful about them. The descent to their valley seemed like the preliminary steps taken by Æneas, when he was piloted by the Sibyl to Hades. It is a fit place for the end of all things to begin; and I seriously opine that on some day these pent-up fires and boiling waters will explode and send the mountain peaks flying in atoms down the abyss. Before this comes to pass, however, a catastrophe is more likely to befall Foss, his passengers and his horses. The great object of this celebrated expert seemed to be to show us how near he could touch upon total destruction and yet avoid it. "Hi! Bummer, mind!" he cried to the nigh leader of his six-in-hand as we were whirled round a point of rocks and descended a grade apparently of forty-five degrees.

Bummer's track was within an inch of the edge, and there was a chasm of hundreds of feet below. If his foot had slipped one inch he would have taken horses, wagon, passengers and driver with him into eternity. In this way we made a run of six miles down the mountain in twenty-four minutes, and I came to the conclusion that in point of comparative comfort, I have experienced more of it in sending down a royal yard in a gale of wind than in driving with Mr. Foss.

A modern Athenian had been "mapping out" for his friend in London the tour of the United States. "You have mentioned," said the Englishman, "many objects worthy of attention in New York, Philadelphia, Washington and other towns, but you have said nothing of your own renowned and beautiful city." "Your appreciative remark," returned the Bostonian, "is sufficient evidence that it was needless for me to refer to a city so universally known."

While the most agreeable routes through the State of California have been described, San Francisco has scarcely been mentioned. She has no history like the Puritan capital, of two hundred and fifty years, no venerable shades of Harvard, no old families who trace their lineage back to a convenient epoch within the range of three centuries; for her aristocracy is not developed, though its bud has the promise of a full-blown flower. But while the queen of the Atlantic has her rivals, who perhaps vainly attempt to surpass her, the empress of the Pacific has none.

Commerce settled upon the noble bay of San Francisco, and laughs at the puny efforts of all the little sea-coast-towns from San Diego to the north to divide the spoils. The history of the city is one of thirty years—scarcely that—for her unkempt infancy of three years should not enter into the account. The "old forty-niners" consider themselves her founders, and when they look back through a vista of little more than a quarter of a century, and turn their gaze upon themselves and their surroundings, they may well wonder if all is reality, and if some part of their eventful lives has not been spent in Rip Van Winkle sleep.

With its three hundred thousand inhabitants, among them scores of men exceeding in wealth the like number in the world, its streets lined with warehouses, banks, churches, shops and princely dwellings, its squares set apart for colleges and institutions of public charity, its hotels unrivalled in extent and magnificence, and, above all, its commanding situation, and climate *sans peur et sans reproche* for at least ten months of the year, San Francisco, though yet in its youth, is the ruler of the Pacific coast, and is fast becoming the commercial monarch to whom the islands of the sea, Japan, China and New Zealand will pay their abundant and willing tribute.

Every observant traveller discovers this at a glance, and it needs not to be told. One learns it all in a day, but it took the weeks that we so pleasantly passed to obtain a correct idea of the natural beauties and the agricultural resources of the State. It would be an ungracious task to criticise certain elements of society differing in many respects from the eastern ideal. Praise might be regarded as fulsome, and dissent as querulous. A regular standard of good breeding is scarcely to be expected of a society recently in a chaotic condition, and now hastily forming out of a mosaic of mankind which first requires cementing before it can receive its polish. This in due time will gloss over all its irregularities.

CHAPTER XVII.

"The Chinese Problem."

The great social question agitating San Francisco, and to a certain extent the State of California, is, "Shall the Chinese go?" Their presence is objected to because they teach immorality and because they "take the bread out of the mouths" of white laborers.

Now the danger of immoral teaching from a class who keep their immorality, which is exaggerated to the last degree, chiefly pent up in their own quarter of the city, is very slight in the way of contagion, and the pretence of their "taking bread from other people's mouths" is very feeble, so long as white hotel-waiters can obtain thirty dollars per month, and chambermaids twenty five dollars per month, including the bread for their mouths and all the dainties offered to the guests.

There is no part of the United States where labor of all kinds commands higher wages than in California, and none where living is less expensive. Food is cheap, and rents not exhorbitant, while people, if they choose, may live out of doors, with advantage to health, the greater part of the year. The Chinese confer a positive benefit upon the State in keeping labor within reasonable bounds, and thus enabling it to raise and export immense crops of grain. It would be well if they should occupy all the servile positions in the cities and drive aristocratic white servants and troublesome "hoodlums" into the country, where they can always find employment.

The worst that can be said of the Mongol is, that he is a labor-saving machine, which is very much needed while labor rules at its present high price. He may be classed with sewing machines, reapers and headers. These are composed of needles, springs and iron teeth, whereas he is a thing of bone and muscle. They are the offspring of art; he is the offspring of nature. *Voilà tout.* The advantages of employing either kind of machinery are equal, and the objections against the one are as forcible as they are against the other.

Our sympathies were certainly with the Chinese when we were told at a large wheat ranche, in reply to the question why none of them were employed: "We dare not do it. If we did, our crops and buildings would be burned, as for the same cause they were burned at Chico."

Last summer I met a sociably-disposed gentleman on the boat running from Vallejo to San Francisco. We drifted on to the Chinese question, upon which he appeared to be thoroughly informed. He was decidedly in favor of importing more Chinese, instead of limiting the immigration. He said that as house servants they were invaluable. He was confident that without their competition the Irish waiters and chambermaids would demand such wages that families in moderate circumstances would be compelled to do all their own work. He thought that instead of interfering with American mechanics they were a positive advantage to the home industry of California.

He gave a forcible illustration of this. A large boot and shoe factory in Sacramento was competing favorably with the eastern market and lessening the demand from that quarter. One hundred and fifty white men and fifty Chinamen were employed in the establishment. About that time Kearney came to Sacramento and said that "those Chinese must go." They went accordingly, and the result was that white men not being able to do the work for which they were appointed, the whole concern was run at a loss and finally broken up, so that the hundred and fifty white men were thrown out of employment by their own act. This was only one of many cases in point.

If I had not been convinced already that the Chinese are profitable to California as railroad builders and fruit-growers this intelligent reasoner would have satisfied me.

On parting at the wharf we exchanged cards, and I found that he was the editor of the—well, I will not "go back" on the profession—but he was the editor of a newspaper having as wide a circulation as any other in the State. "May I use your name in my correspondence?" I asked.

"Good heavens, no!" he exclaimed, "this is only private talk; I don't utter such sentiments in my newspaper!" I found that he did not, for in all California there was not a more violent anti-Chinese newspaper than the ——!

The senseless nature of the excitement against the Chinese should be at once apparent when we reflect that their number is absolutely decreasing in a considerable ratio, while that of the white population is increasing so fast that the next census is relied upon to give California 900,000 inhabitants.

At the close of 1876 there were in the United States alto-

"THE CHINESE PROBLEM." 129

gether 104,963 Chinese. They have since decreased 7,900, leaving 97,063, of whom there are computed to be in California and Oregon 62,500, and in San Francisco and its neighborhood 25,450. What a fearful "invasion of pauper labor" is this!

Now let us tabulate this invading army from data given by the Chinese themselves which correspond with the acknowledged statistics of our own authorities :—

Cigar-makers	2,500
Clothing manufacturers	2,000
Vegetable pedlers	500
Laundrymen	1,500
Shoemakers	1,800
Watch manufacturers	150
Woollen mills	350
Fishermen	800
Jute factories	600
Various small manufactures	1,500
Domestic servants	6,000
Doctors, druggists and teachers	300
Merchants, clerks and porters	2,800
All other occupations	2,150
No legitimate regular calling	1,200
Children of school age (*denied admission to our schools*)	1,309
	25,450

There are twenty-five thousand four hundred and fifty Chinese, most of whom it is admitted are mere sojourners without families, who are expected to capture a city of three hundred thousand people, to reduce its laborers to starvation and to demoralize them utterly! And this list of their occupations is a proof of their "enforced pauper labor!"

We have no statistics of the employment of the other 37,050 Chinese who are about to subjugate a million people in California and Oregon, or of the remaining 34,563 who are scattered like incendiary fire-brands among the 45,000,000 people of the

9

United States. But it is fair to take the same divisions that exist in San Francisco.

This table disposes of the question of pauper labor; and its enforcement may be set at rest by a declaration of six respectable Chinese merchants:—

"We solemnly declare that we, the Six Chinese Companies, are purely benevolent societies. We never, singly or collectively, as individuals or companies, ever brought one of our countrymen to this free country, under or by any contract or agreement, made anywhere, as a servant or laborer. We never have before heard that our people desiring to come here sold their relatives to obtain the means to come. We have never yet let, hired, or contracted one of our people out to labor; neither have we ever exercised the slightest control or restraint over our people after they came here, nor claimed, or demanded, or received one dollar of their earnings. We have never acted, directly or indirectly, as the agent or agents of any one of our people who advanced the means for one of our people to come here.

"LIN CHUCK FONG,
"LEE GE QUNG,
"WING PUEY YUNG,
"WONG SUE FOO,
"LOU KUNG CHAI,
"CHIN KUNG CHEN,
"Presidents of Six Companies.

"San Francisco, February 12, 1879."

Here is a statement compiled from Municipal Reports of City and County of San Francisco :—

HOSPITAL.

City and County of San Francisco for the year ending June 30th, 1878.

Whole number admitted... 3067
Nations of the United States.. 913
" Ireland... 948
" China... 0
" all other countries....................................... 1140

ALMS HOUSE.

City and County of San Francisco for the year ending June 30th, 1878.

Whole number admitted.. 472
Nations of the United States.. 138
" Ireland... 175
" China... 1
" all other nations... 158

CHIEF OF POLICE.

City and County of San Francisco for the year ending June 30th, 1878.

Number of arrests for drunkenness................................. 6127
" Chinese 0

While there can be no question that Kearneyism and newspaper enterprise for political purposes are at the bottom of all the anti-Chinese agitation, there is one element in it that has not been considered. It is a humiliating confession, but there is a dread among business men that the Chinese merchants, by their astuteness and quick-witted comprehension of commerce, will take the profits out of their pockets, as they are accused of taking the bread out of the mouths of laborers.

While figures go far to prove that the Chinese are not burdensome upon the community, as they pay their full quota of taxation, they show, moreover, that they are competing for trans-pacific commerce.

In 1878 the Chinese paid :—

Internal Revenue taxes in San Francisco alone	$550,000
Poll taxes in the State	180,000
Licenses in the State	41,000
Property taxes	220,000
Duties paid on imports	1,768,000
	$2,759,000

In the same year they exported merchandise valued at $3,109,320, of which there were 209,000 barrels of flour.

In short, nine-tenths of all the exports to China were made by Chinese Coolies !

The banking and insurance systems are now thoroughly comprehended by the Chinese. They are establishing their own banks and insurance offices, and they have in serious contemplation the project of a steamship line across the Pacific under their own flag.

This enterprise is perfectly feasible. China, in one respect at least, is more free than the United States. The Chinese may buy their steamships where they please. With ships at a greatly reduced cost, victualled and manned at half the expense, their only necessity at first being that a few European officers should be employed, these hated foreigners may sweep our commerce from the Pacific seas, and the Stars and Stripes, even now rarely seen upon those waters, may totally disappear !

This is another reason why "the Chinese must go." They must go because they are too willing servants, and because they may become too powerful masters.

For the prospective gain of votes, demagogues on both sides, backed up by their partisan adherents, are willing to destroy the tools with which the prosperity of their State was constructed.

Their railroads have been built by Chinese. They have drained swamps that by their labor only could have been reclaimed, and made the most productive land, giving employment to thousands of white men in agriculture.

They supply the markets with fruit and vegetables, which otherwise could not be produced in such abundance. They are the best workers in the vineyards, and they perform menial services that no European would undertake.

It is not true that they invariably work for very low wages. As soon as they work as intelligently as white men, they often obtain equal rates with them. It cannot be otherwise. Employers understand their value, as quiet, orderly, industrious temperate men, and therefore prefer them at the same price.

That they live in crowded dens in San Francisco, not so crowded, however, as the tenement dens of New York, is undeniable, and it is a disgrace to the municipal government which permits it. So far from being personally uncleanly, they are remarkable for the neatness of their dress and the daily ablution of their persons.

Like the Irish, they send money home to their relatives, and are to be commended for it. The gold and silver of California is a product of its soil as much as wheat and wine, and its export is of no greater injury to the country than the export of cereals. When they go home they carry with them for dissemination the knowledge they have acquired, some of which it would be better for them to forget.

We send missionaries back with them in the same ships, to tell their countrymen of American civilization, and of the religion of peace and good will to all mankind, which strangely disagrees with their experience on our inhospitable shores.

Can we remedy all this? Can we convince California democrats and republicans that they have been laboring under a serious mistake in their estimate of Chinese character and of their value to them as immigrants?

Who doubts the ability of Congress to accomplish this desirable end? To its everlasting disgrace, in obedience to the insensate clamor of politicians—but for the President's veto power—it would have humiliated our nation in the eyes of the Christian and the heathen world by the violation of a solemn treaty.

Now let this be partially atoned, by justice to the Chinese.

Because they are yellow, not white—yellow, not black, let our treatment of them no longer give the lie to our Declaration of Independence and to our profession of religion. Let us prove our belief that all men are free and equal, and that God "hath made of one blood all nations of men for to dwell on all the face of the earth."

Let us give the Chinese the boon of suffrage. Then, while they are with us aiding us to develop our industries, they will not be treated as pariahs and beasts of burden. The only danger will be that they may be too much flattered and caressed. And when they return to their home, we may send missionaries with them with better grace, for they can tell the Chinese that the Christian religion is practised by ourselves.

CHAPTER XVIII.

ALONG THE COAST TO OREGON—DISCOVERY OF THE COLUMBIA RIVER—THE BAR—INDUSTRIES OF OREGON—SALMON FISHERY.

The Californian measures every thing by the scale of his own aspirations. A million of dollars for him is not a large fortune. Beets and turnips of eastern immensity are vegetables of a fair size at his agricultural exhibitions, farms of ten thousand acres are modest properties, a tree equal to a New England forest clamped together is not an extraordinary bit of timber, and when he talks of a run among the Sierras or the ascent of Mount Shasta he is merely "going to the hills." As to excursions, he looks upon twenty or thirty miles up and down the bay or a trip along the coast of one or two hundred miles to Santa Cruz and other little outposts as afternoon relaxations from business. A voyage to Japan or China to him is not much in excess of a New Yorker's idea of a visit to Fire Island or Long Branch. As California can be compared to no other country, so a Californian can be compared to no other man, in his estimate of measures, weights, distances and himself. "You ought, by all means," said my friend, " to make a little excursion to Oregon. Everybody goes there now for an outing. The whole 'paseo'"—this is a pleasant little word of the old Spaniards—"can be done in ten or fifteen days. It is only about twenty-five hundred miles altogether, going and returning. There are three lines of steamships. The accommodations are excellent, the fare good, and the price reasonable. Go!" We went.

The *George IV. Elder*, of the regular line, was built by Mr. John Roach, of the Delaware, a gentleman protected by our government in the monopoly of shipbuilding, which means that all Americans are obliged to buy ships upon his terms. This theory of protection does not apply to the lives or purses of the people, but merely to the emolument of Mr. Roach. In this instance, the *George IV. Elder*, of round bottom and needless breadth of beam, not being quite ready to work herself to pieces, pitched all the time that she was not rolling, and rolled all the time that she was not pitching, and finally, though leisurely, landed her passengers in safety. There were one hundred and sixty-five in, on, and around the cabin, and another crowd in the steerage who were much more comfortable in regard to space. We were four days in accomplishing seven hundred and forty miles. One hundred and fifty of them were of river navigation, during which the hitherto sea-sick wretches were able to stand up and make more room for themselves and others.

Coasting along a bold shore for the first two days, the California characteristics were predominant. The grass of the early spring was dry, and the hills, cleared of trees, presented a barren appearance. Yet the dry, yellow grass was good food for cattle and sheep, while here and there, in some shady cañon, their owners lived in comfortable ranches upon the increase of their flocks and herds. Across the Coast Range, and in the interval between it and the distant Sierras, the map tells us of vast plains chosen by an ever-increasing population for pasturage and farms. As we drew to the north and passed the Oregon line, the dull, dry, barren appearance of the coast gave place to verdant grass and thickly studded firs and pines. In Oregon nature does not divide her rain and sunshine in two great halves, as she metes them out in California. Here it rains and shines by turns, as smiles and tears alternate on those happy faces never distorted by immoderate laughter or drawn down by persistent grief. The California farmer is contented in one way, and the farmer of Oregon is contented in another. The first consoles himself for the long winter rains with the fixed assurance that he will have an abundant harvest, reaped at his leisure, stacked and thrashed in the fields without fear of storm and without need of a barn. Then he counts with certainty upon his thirty-five bushels of wheat to the acre. But if the winter be dry, what then? Why he is happy all the same in calculating that two dry winters never come in succession. When short crops and starving cattle stare him in the face, his philosophy is scarcely equal to the emergency.

On the other hand, the farmer of Oregon counts on a smaller crop, but he counts with a greater certainty. There are for him no alternating years of abundance and drought, no perpetually rainy winters and summers of steady sunshine. Providence does not send for him its gifts in large parcels or none, but it sifts them more equally over his path. He must build barns and sheds as he was accustomed to build them in the East, but his store-houses will be filled with plenty. In point of prosperous agriculture and grazing, inasmuch as certainty is preferable to spasmodic luck, the inducements to settle in Oregon are superior to those which California offers. And if taste and beauty enter into a man's calculations, as they always unconsciously touch his soul, the dark green forests, the mossy rocks, the scarcely lighter shade of pastures and meadows, ever present to his eye of sense, educate and refine his inward nature, and give him and his children a wholesome pleasure unknown to those who dwell for half the year in a dust that chokes all poetry out of their existence.

On a beautiful Sunday morning we approached the Heads of the Columbia River. Before us lay basking in the sunshine the smooth expanse of water which Vancouver in 1792 mistook for a bay. It is surprising that, being on a special errand to find the traditionary river or strait which in dreams of early navigators formed the connection between the Pacific and the Atlantic, he should have passed the promising inlet with so little examination. Equally remarkable it is that Captain Gray, of the merchantman Columbia, whose only object was trade and a speedy termination of his voyage, should have turned aside and made the great discovery. The modest skipper did not seek for the fame his name has acquired, but overhauling Vancouver, told him where he might find the river. His information treated with contempt, Gray resolved to prove the truth of his impressions. Turning back from his route, he again sighted the headlands.

The determination of purpose which overcame his scruples may be imagined. His ship was commissioned for no scientific purpose. She was not insured against any such attendant risk. His business was to sell his cargo, to buy another, and to come back to Boston. But the Englishman had ridiculed him, and he would not stand it. The dawn of May 11, eighty-seven years ago, found him again heading for the bar with a fair wind. The water was too rough for a boat to take soundings ahead. The breakers were combing and dashing far out on the shoals from either headland, and in view of the danger before him on this unknown shore, the question arose with startling abruptness, "Shall I haul off before it is too late, or shall I make the attempt?" It was decided in an instant. "Hard a-port your helm ; keep her E. N. E." Slowly the Columbia surged ahead, and gathering way as the wind filled her sails, she dashed onward, rising and falling on the foamy crests. Cool and calm sat the "old man" on the foretopsail yard, with an eye on the darkest and smoothest water ahead, changing the course as these indications were before him. Regularly was "the lead kept going" from the chains. Now she shoals from ten fathoms to nine, and eight, seven, six, five ! She is coming to the bar. Suddenly the measured song, crying, " By—the—he—mark— five !" is followed by the excited leadsman, who has no time to sing, with sharp conciseness, "and a quarter three, sir !"

" Steady as you go ! " calls Captain Gray.

" Steady ! " repeats the mate.

" Steady, sir ! " echoes the man at the wheel. A big sea heaves the Columbia on its crest ; then she settles in its trough ; then rises again, and slides before it.

" By—the—he—deep—four !" is now the song from the chains ; the next cast gives " and a quar-her-ter-five ! " the next " By the—he—mark—ten ! " and the good ship is over the bar.

The long-time fabled great river of the West now found, had come down from its still unknown mountains to meet and welcome the daring sailor. With all this there came to him no feeling of pride or exultation beyond the simple desire to fall in with Vancouver again and to hail him with " I told you so." This he did, and then the Englishman, piloted by the experience of Captain Gray, entered the river and claimed it for his sovereign by the right of discovery! History has told us how the conflicting pretensions of America and England were adjusted, how the title of the former was confirmed, and how the appropriate name of Gray's little ship was given to the river.

The poetry and beauty of the Columbia remain to-day almost as fresh as in 1792. True the Indian wigwams have disappeared. "Vast numbers of canoes come out to meet us" no more as they met Captain Gray. Instead of these, towns and villages are springing up on the river's banks, steamboats are ploughing its waters, and wholesale trade in lumber, wheat, wool and fish has taken the place of a simple exchange of commodities by barter. All these modern improvements mar the great picture of Nature, but they have not yet cut down the boundless forests, they can never level the grand mountains or turn the channel of the mighty stream that rolls through their gorges to the sea.

An early superstition, more inexcusable in our day than that in ancient times hanging over the Cyclades and fearful Scylla and Charybdis, is still attached to the bar of Columbia River. It would not have been surprising if Captain Gray had hesitated to cross it in 1792 when the soundings were totally unknown, or if the navigators who immediately succeeded him had approached the breakers first encountered by the Columbia with nervous apprehension. But nearly a century has elapsed, the river has been surveyed by officers of the British and American navies, accurate charts have been published, experienced pilots cruise in the offing, steam-tugs are always to be found, and yet great fears are entertained by those who approach the coast for the first time, and underwriters actually demand an extra premium on vessels bound to ports in Oregon at any season of the year. In the course of time this unfounded prejudice will be overcome, but while it lasts it certainly is a most needless drawback to the prosperity of Oregon and Washington Territory.

On entering and leaving the river, Captain Bolles kindly gave me the opportunity of examining his charts and observing the courses. This, with what I have been told by pilots and have gained from other authorities, establishes the conclusion that, with equal care and prudence, the bar of the Columbia for the greater part of the year is not more dangerous than that at Sandy Hook. Even in comparatively early experience, from 1861 to 1869, when the north-west coast was by no means so accurately surveyed as at present, there was this authentic record of disaster: " In eight years there were one hundred and ninety-eight accidents, one hundred and ten of which happened to small coasting vessels, and of these only three occurred on the bar of the Columbia. The records of the Pilot Commission show that only nine vessels have been wrecked at or near the bar in the last twenty-five years. Nine disasters in about twelve thousand five hundred crossings give a loss of only seven one-hundredths of one per centum."

Captain Maginn, formerly a New York Pilot Commissioner, who ought to be able to make just comparisons, says :—

"There is deep water on the bar, it having four and one-half fathoms without the addition of the tide, while New York harbor has on the bar but four fathoms, without the addition of the tide, which is six feet. The bar in the Columbia is about half a mile across, while that of New York is three-quarters. The channel of the bar at the mouth of the Columbia is about 6,000 feet, and shoals gradually, while the channel of the bar at Sandy Hook is about 600 feet and shoals rapidly ; the channel across the bar is straight at the Columbia ; that at New York is crooked."

On this authority it is safe to conclude that at high water vessels drawing twenty-two feet may cross the bar, and those drawing nineteen feet may do so at half-tide. At low water and in storms, when the breakers are making the rise and fall of the sea unusually great, it is of course prudent to haul off and await a more favorable opportunity; and it must be allowed that such occasions are not unfrequent in the winter.

This exaggerated dread of a bugbear has greatly retarded the direct trade of Oregon with the outside world, and placed her at the disadvantage of double shipments, making her a mere tributary to California. The Oregon and Washington farmers, upon the average, can produce greater crops of wheat than their neighbor can depend upon in all years, some of which are cursed with drought, but hitherto they have been able to obtain equal prices for their produce. They have had various impediments in the way of success. In the first place, although they are mostly settled in valleys watered by large rivers, these are blocked by natural obstacles, some of which cannot be overcome by canals. Then the railroad system is not far advanced, notwithstanding that it is measurably so for a sparsely inhabited country.

For most of the year, with occasional but very expensive portages, the Columbia River is navigable two hundred and fifty miles from its mouth, and the Snake one hundred and fifty miles from its junction with it in Eastern Oregon. The Willamette, one of the chief affluents of the Columbia, is for nearly all the year navigable for more than one hundred miles. Now, Walla Walla, the best producing county of the State, cannot send its wheat to San Francisco at a cost of less than sixty cents per bushel, a surrender of one-half its value. Near and distant districts will average that ratio. This estimate holds good regarding wool, hides, and all other products. Even without counting the necessary expense of transportation from the fields to the principal shipping ports, the loss to the farmers in ocean freight to San Francisco is from five to seven hundred thousand dollars every year. The great requirements of Oregon and Washington Territory are, therefore, internal facilities of carriage and a direct export trade. The first must await time and capital, the last can be brought about by ordinary intelligence and enterprise. Already the advantages are beginning to be comprehended.

Seventy-five thousand tons of wheat were last year exported, chiefly to Great Britain. This was carried in sixty-nine vessels, and it is incidentally worthy of remark that only nine of these were under the American flag. The whole crop of wheat for the last year was two hundred and fifty thousand tons, only about one-third of which was directly exported. Beside this there was no inconsiderable quantity of barley, oats, fruits, bacon and hides, most of these articles having been sent to San Francisco.

Sheep-farming being a prominent industry, the export and coastwise shipment of wool is annually becoming greater. The quality is of a high grade, and the quantity last year amounted to six million pounds. Not the least important of all is the salmon trade, so enormously enlarged of late that it will soon be destroyed by reckless fishing unless speedy precautions are taken to regulate it. In view of such a result the Legislature of Washington Territory has passed a bill not only exacting heavy licenses, but prohibiting the use of traps, seines and nets of less than eight-and-a-half inch meshes. This will prevent the capture of young fish, and as it is intended to stock the river yearly with spawn the wholesale destruction now going on may be averted. It is expected that Oregon will confirm this action.

In 1877, the thirty-one canneries which we saw distributed on both sides of the river packed three hundred and ninety-five thousand cases of forty-eight pounds each. We had an opportunity to see the operations of several establishments. All is systematic, from landing the fish to shipping the cases. The salmon are first chopped into sections, then into pound-pieces, then put in tin boxes, soldered, subjected to various degrees of heat and to exhaustion of air. The boxes are finally colored, labelled and packed. Chinese are chiefly employed in all this indoor work, as their labor is not only less expensive but more expert than that of white men, who are mostly occupied in catching the fish. They have the use of the boats and nets of their employers and receive thirty-three cents for every fish they bring in. Six thousand men are thus engaged.

It is a curious fact that Columbia River salmon can never be taken with the hook. When the British Commission came out here to investigate matters during the dispute with the United States, it is said that they attached little value to a stream " where the blasted fish would not take a fly ! "

I have touched upon the principal industries of Oregon and Washington Territory bordering upon and divided from it by the Columbia River, which find a profit from abroad. As to the lumber trade having a market at home and in California, indeed all along the west coast of America, it is inexhaustible, for these regions are forest homes. The mineral wealth of the country, yet undeveloped, is incalculable.

CHAPTER XIX.

ASTORIA—PORTLAND—WILLAMETTE VALLEY—SCENERY OF THE
COLUMBIA—THE DALLES—INDIAN TROUBLES—OREGON'S OP-
PORTUNITY—DEPARTURE.

Having crossed the bar of the Columbia, before us on the Oregon side of the river is the little town of Astoria. City it is, like every collection of houses, great or small, in the West. Astoria is the first city in the State—the first that was founded, as it is the first in approach. It came into life with a struggle, was choked in its infancy by the rivalry of the Hudson's Bay Company, and has not yet recovered from the hardships of its youth. Now it lives on its history of the past chronicled in the poetic prose of Irving, on its expectations of the future, and on salmon.

It is supposed to belong to Oregon, but it seems to dread going ashore, so it stays out in the harbor, built on piles. The streets are all bridges, and the cellars of the houses are watery depths. The Astorians say that lumber is cheap, and that plank and water are not dusty. They are satisfied with the land they see in abundance behind them piled up in the coast range of mountains, where they occasionally go ashore to hunt deer and grouse. This aquatic tendency is not peculiar to Astoria. Every town at which we touched on the river pushes itself into the water and has its plank-road streets and drives. Nobody knows why, only it is the fashion.

The steamship discharged a little freight, took on board a little more, and then late in the afternoon steamed away for Portland. We were to lose the anticipated view of the scenery, but the loss was compensated by a brilliant sunset. The refraction of the atmosphere magnified the sun to an unusual size, as in his full blaze he dropped behind the waves and streamed his rays along our path, just lighting us into the channel between the hills that began to encircle us with their shadows. Long after the bright day had left the lower plains its parting rays gilded the snowy summit of St. Helen's, until at last this highest peak was shrouded in darkness.

The morning found us at the wharf in Portland. This commercial capital of Oregon is one hundred miles from Astoria, near the mouth of the Willamette, which pours into the Columbia and is its largest affluent. The city can be reached by vessels drawing sixteen feet, and having been established early, has maintained a business pre-eminence scarcely warranted by a situation much less favorable than that of Astoria. It has its banks, great shops, and not a few semi-millionaires, who live in costly if not elegant houses, for wood, the universal building material, is not susceptible of architectural beauty. This sentiment may be treasonable to the shingle palaces not only of Portland but of San Francisco, where such structures cost a million of dollars, and yet are ugly in proportion to their pretentious magnificence. Portland is wood above and wood below, wood where'er we go; and now perhaps we have discovered why it is built over the water, on which it has so frequent occasion to call for extinguishing its fires. Its population is fifteen thousand.

The California and Oregon Railroad is a projected thoroughfare, finished at each end, but exceedingly open in the middle. It extends from Sacramento north to Redding, and from Portland south to Roseberg, with a stage coach interval of two hundred and eighty miles. It is seldom used by travellers to California, who prefer the more comfortable steamship route, unless, as does not often happen, a day or two are worth gaining at the cost of no inconsiderable fatigue and expense. When the inducements become greater the whole line may be opened, but the day is far distant when it can derive a profit from through passengers and freight. We made an excursion upon it as far as Albany, eighty-one miles from Portland. Its course is along the banks of the Willamette River through the valley of the same name. Every rule of pronunciation is set at defiance by calling this word Will-Hammet, but, as the river belongs to the Oregonians, they are not to be held to account for naming their own pets as they please.

Scarcely do we leave Portland when we dive into a primeval forest of fir and pine, giving out balsamic odors and yielding a most grateful shade. Flickering rays of sunlight dart through the deep shadows, and the sunbeams have full play on the river flowing by our side, sparkling between its green borders. Fifteen miles and we reach the falls of the Willamette—great rapids that come tumbling down with a roar to the site of the " old city of Oregon."

Old? Yes; it was a trading post fifty years ago, ere Oregon was a State, or even a territory. It is now a thriving manufacturing village, its flour mills having a merited celebrity. The falls are overcome by a short canal, allowing steamboats of a light draught to pass upward.

We now come into a rich farming district, wheat being the chief product. Land is worth all prices, according to its improvements and nearness to the railroad or river, most of the government sections being taken up. The railroad has many acres still for sale at low rates. Thirty bushels of wheat is an average crop, and thus far the harvests have never been interfered with by drought or insects. Winding along through a well-cultivated region, amidst wheatfields and orchards, with pretty farm-houses ensconced in pine groves which an unusual eye for taste and comfort among new settlers has left undisturbed, we come to Salem.

Salem is neatly laid out with wide and shady streets, has three thousand inhabitants, and, as the capital, yearly contains the representative wisdom of one hundred and fifty thousand people. The State House was pointed out to us. It was within its walls that the Cronin certificate was signed, and, therefore, although the political scheme was unsuccessful, the State House of Oregon will be as memorable in history as those of Louisiana and Florida, where the machinery of President-making was better oiled and made to run more smoothly.

For thirty miles we traversed a country similar to that already passed, and were assured that it continued along the whole line of the road to Roseberg. Then we reached Albany, a town not much inferior to Salem. This was the limit of our excursion. By no means did we see the whole of the Willamette Valley, extending with its connections over a fine agricultural country one hundred miles long and fifty miles wide. It is one of the most productive tracts of what is called Western Oregon, a term comprising that part of the State lying between the seacoast and the Cascade Mountains, running from north to south one hundred miles in the interior, from the forty-second to the forty-sixth parallel of latitude; and this is but a small part of the State. Eastern Oregon has more than twice its extent, and its soil has equal capabilities. The whole of the State embraces sixty millions of acres, very few of which are not susceptible of cultivation. Vast tracts of the mountains are timber lands, and still larger districts are ready for cattle, sheep-raising and farming purposes. In fact, there is no State of the Union where there is less waste land in proportion to the total area.

With all these advantages added to a convenient geographical position and a salubrious climate, the present and future population of Oregon ought to be prosperous and happy.

Beyond its commercial value, its trade and fisheries, its sites for cities, and its valleys producing wheat and fruit, the Columbia is beautiful. As Niagara is never considered with calculations of its mill-driving water-power, and the Rhine is not estimated according to its importance as a highway for transportation, so the great river of the West will ere long be visited by tourists, painters and poets for the gratification of a higher taste than the lumberman, the fisherman or the farmer connects with his practical vocation. Unconsciously our people are being educated to this standard.

As the memory of the rich morsels gathered in the universal reading of the present age sweetens the daily toil of the laborer, so the pictures of nature presented to his eye are ever hanging, though unseen, in his workshop, his cabin and his tenement. He joins an excursion party for the pleasure he anticipates from the "refreshments" and a dance. He takes his children to "give them a little fresh air," but he gets more than he bargained for in gaining for himself elevation of thought, and for them lessons from a teaching higher than that of their school-books.

As we leave Portland to visit the Dalles we find among our fellow-passengers all sorts and conditions of men, women, and children too; some from the town and many who have come from San Francisco to enjoy the wonderful scenery of the Columbia River. They have taken it home with them as we have done, and it will last us all forever.

The "Wide West" is, as all the river steamboats are, a stern-wheel boat adapted to the navigation of shoal water. She appeared to be about fifteen hundred tons measurement, an immense raft carrying all her cargo on deck, and all her passengers above it in an elegant saloon, where there is luxurious furniture and well-spread tables, and in roomy staterooms, where every appliance for comfort is at hand. Do you remember the little steamboats on the Rhine with their narrow limits? You may compare them with the "Wide West," as you may compare the Rhine with the Columbia in size and scenery. You may do this without detracting one iota from the Rhine of its beauty or its history.

Here we see nothing as yet of vine-clad hills, although our descendants may, nor are there any remnants of feudal castles. But there are hills that would be called mountains there, and mountains so-called even in this land where ordinary mountains are spoken of as hills. They are on each side and around, even above, as they seem ready to topple over from their summits thousands of feet high, all covered with grand forests of pine and firs from their base to their tops, where the tallest of them seem like bushes and shrubs. The castles of the Columbia are the masonry of Nature's hand, deftly chiselled by floods and glaciers, piled up in regular, irregular and fanciful blocks—battlements designed by an Almighty architect, and existing from an age approaching the eternity of the world's beginning. I do not propose to describe the indescribable. You may import it in miniature by photographic piecemeal, but to know any thing of its beauty and sublimity it must be seen.

Turning the point of the Willamette, by which we entered the river twelve miles below Portland, we again ascend the Columbia. Six miles above the junction, on the Washington Territory side, lies the military station of Vancouver. The hardships of a soldier's frontier life are lightly estimated as we look upon the green lawn charmingly sloping from the base of the mountains, and dotted with the neat quarters of the officers and barracks of the troops; but when we consider their perilous duty in Indian warfare, we think them entitled to all the enjoyment they can get in so lovely a home. This was an old post of the Hudson's Bay Company, and in early days was the scene of such dangerous and romantic adventures as are now pushed far beyond its limits.

As we wind through the tortuous channel, occasionally catching glimpses of Mount Hood, eighty miles away, crowned with perpetual snow, eleven thousand feet in the air, we come to the "Gorge of the Columbia." For more than fifty miles we pass through and among the mountains of the "Cascade range." The river at its mouth, six miles wide, pinches into a deep and narrow channel as it cuts through perpendicular cliffs with smooth, straight sides, three thousand feet high, where sometimes the cataracts, beginning with a pouring stream at the top, reach the base in a scattering spray.

Passing up forty-five miles from Vancouver we come to the Lower Cascades, where the rapids are so impetuous that navigation is interrupted. Here the steamboat discharges her passengers, to be transferred to a railroad six miles long, cut through the rocky banks of the river. Reaching the end of the portage we take passage in another steamboat of equal size and similar construction, called the "Mountain Queen," and are carried by her to the portage of the Dalles, sixty miles beyond. There is again a railroad transportation of fifteen miles, and navigation is resumed by another steamboat, which goes one hundred and twenty miles further to Wallula, and if the state of the water allows, many miles above, far into the territory of Idaho, across the limits of Oregon.

We reached the Dalles in the afternoon, when, by the courtesy of General Sprague, the superintendent of the line, who accompanied us, a special train was provided, by which we had an opportunity to see the rapids and to return to the Mountain Queen at night. "Dalles" is an Indian word, signifying a deep narrow, racing, roaring, boiling, swirling, seething, leaping rush of waters. It must be a more expressive word than is afforded by our language, and it is wisely retained.

We followed the torrent up the fifteen miles of its course. Sometimes it became smooth and wide for an instant, then, darted down in its mad career through the lava-beds, impatient of restraint. In one spot the great Columbia is narrowed to a channel only ninety-five feet wide, and of a depth which the rapidity of the current has never permitted to be sounded. This was the limit of our voyage. Beyond, the scenery is not so interesting, the mountains being less densely wooded above the Cascades, and the river coming quietly down to the rapids and gorges where it begins its wild activity.

A few days more, had they been at our disposal, might have been profitably passed in visiting Walla-Walla and the other farming regions on the upper Columbia and Snake rivers. It would not have been prudent, however, just then to penetrate the country so far that a return might be uncertain. The Indian depredations had driven many of the frontiersmen to seek safety in the settlements, and some of them were so thoroughly scared that they came on board our steamboat at the Dalles and went with us to Portland.

In many cases they had left their crops already ripened, to be destroyed by the Indians, or to perish for want of gathering. The distress and loss to these poor settlers cannot be estimated by people in the East or by the paternal Government at Washington. It might be, if every member of Congress owned a tract of land in the neighborhood of the Indian reservations. In that case we should hear less of the reduction of the army, and some means would assuredly be devised to prevent the recurrence of these unending border troubles.

This is by no means my first acquaintance with the frontier or with its dangers. Here, as elsewhere, we see the effect of cause—the cause, mismanagement, and the effect, inevitable disaster. Mismanagement is notorious in a system that encourages it, and to this the uprisings of the savages are to be attributed rather than to their inherent disposition. The Government and the settlers are equally to be blamed for what has happened: the former, for its small appropriations, made smaller still by Indian agencies; and the latter, for encroaching upon the reservations.

Our little army is employed in punishing the Indians for the crimes these provocations have led them to commit. This condition of things will never cease unless with their extermination, till Indian agencies are abolished, and the army, now used to chastise the savages, driven by their injuries to raiding, shall have the jurisdiction which will render its present occupation needless. This authority should be still further extended. It should reach white men as well as Indians, and should punish with equal severity violence on either side. The true policy is to place every reservation, and a large area of territory around it, under absolute military control. With a sufficient force, probably no greater than we have at present, order would be preserved. These are the convictions of the most intelligent persons in the border settlements.

The principal Indian tribes in Oregon, Idaho, and Washington Territory are the Spokanes, including the Pend d'Oreilles and Cœurs D'Alènes, this tribe, under the leadership of Chief Moses, being the most formidable in numbers of any in the North-west, having a fighting force estimated at two thousand warriors ; the Nez-Percés, on the Nez-Percés reservation at Fort Lapwai, Idaho Territory, the tribe, which under Chief Joseph, created the Indian disturbance of 1877, and the Umatillas, on the Umatilla reservation, in Umatilla County, Oregon, forty miles inland from Umatilla, on the Columbia River, who number about one hundred and fifty warriors. Umapine and Black Hawk, of this tribe, led the party who attacked and killed Egan, the Piute chief, during the recent fight in the Blue Mountains near their reservation. In this part of the country, also, may be included those on the Columbia River, who are non-treaty Indians, gaining their subsistence by hunting and fishing. Their numbers are variously estimated at from two hundred to three hundred. The Piutes belong on the Malheur reservation in south-eastern Oregon. The Bannocks are placed on the Fort Hall reservation, in south-eastern Idaho.

The fighting force of the Bannocks and Piutes, who combined in the raid of the last year, is estimated at four hundred. The Bannocks and Piutes, also the Utes and Snakes, are all branches of the old Shoshone tribe. The total fighting force of the combined Indian tribes of the north-western States and Territories, by a late estimate, is placed at sixteen thousand. On the Umatilla reservation are three hundred thousand acres of the finest wheat lands in eastern Oregon, less than one per cent of it now being cultivated by the Indians, while the remainder is used by them as a range for their horses, which they raise in great numbers, one of the old Umatilla chiefs, Homily, alone owning several thousand. This land will produce an average of forty bushels of wheat to the acre the first season, and from forty to sixty bushels annually thereafter.

One great cause of Indian insurrection is very evident. As in the Black Hills, the gold in the reservation was too great a temptation for white men to withstand, so on these rich lands all treaties are set at defiance. It is the old, old story of the wolf and the lamb. It was this accursed hunger for land, equalling the hunger for gold, that instigated the Nez-Percés war of 1877.

This tribe was particularly inoffensive, more intelligent than others, and rapidly adopting the habits of civilized life. They were noted for their strict adherence to the treaty made with them many years ago. The war began by no fault of theirs; simply by the encroachment of the settlers. It became necessary to punish them for asserting the rights in which Government failed to protect them. They were conquered, scattered, and removed, and now their enemies have taken up their cultivated lands under pre-emption laws. This is the punishment for good behavior and the reward for robbery!

The Bannocks, in Idaho, driven to despair, have now joined the hostile Indians. Our troubles, instead of being ended, are but begun. The Indians are in arms, or ready to take up arms, all over the sparsely-settled districts of the western territories. Innocent or guilty, they must be subdued. Soldiers must fight in a bad cause. Those agents and traders who have stirred up the insurrection will pocket their profits and keep out of harm's way. The farmers who have stolen land will suffer justly, but others who were guiltless must suffer with them. Harvests will perish, and houses will be burned, immigration will be checked, and no little money must be expended.

The worst feature in the Indian's warfare is his vengeance upon the innocent for the deeds of the guilty. Now the Governor of Oregon proposes to adopt the same policy. In his special letter to the sheriff of Umatilla County, dated July 18, 1878, he says: "It is not necessary, in my judgment, that any of the Indians taken should have been personally present at any particular murder, in order to make them amenable to the law. Their depredations in Umatilla County may be regarded as parts of a general combination or conspiracy for the commission of a crime, and all who are in any way connected with it may be regarded as principals." In other words, "Shoot an Indian because he is an Indian wherever you may find him."

Oregon wants peace, but she might get it in a different way. She should appeal to the general Government to be just, rather than to her people to be vindictive. When peace is finally restored, a great future of prosperity will open before her. The district where the Indian war has raged is one of the richest within her borders. She has already begun to connect it by railroad with Puget Sound, where the security of the harbors of Seattle, Tacomah, Port Townsend, Olympia, Stillicom, and Bellingham Bay, and their plentiful depth of water, will give her a thriving commerce, and enable her to reign with California as joint queen of the Pacific.

Steaming down the Columbia, on our way to San Francisco, as strangers who, having passed through the long galleries of the Louvre, are charmed with new pictures on their return, so we see upon either side of the river picturesque rocks, mountains, valleys and lawns on which the changing sunlight has thrown reversed shadows, and made them new objects of delight.

Again we cross the bar, and imagine the old Columbia steadily pursuing her way out of the channel she had surveyed, and the proud satisfaction of Captain Gray in having discovered the noble river that has made the name of his ship immortal.

CHAPTER XX.

FROM CALIFORNIA EASTWARDS—THE MINES AND GARDENS OF GRASS VALLEY—LAKE TAHOE, CARSON AND VIRGINIA CITY —THE SINKS OF THE HUMBOLDT—THE GREAT AMERICAN DESERT—ARRIVAL AT SALT LAKE CITY.

The westward-bound traveller too often sees but one point for which he goes as fast as steam can propel him—San Francisco. He might with advantage read the beautiful poem of Whittier where he describes the search for the waterfall, unsuccessful in its end, but along such a path of beauty that the waterfall itself is forgotten. When the old familiar lions, the city and its suburbs, the Geysers and the Yo-Semite have been seen, he turns his steps homeward with equal alacrity, traversing the backbone of the continent unmindful of its vertebræ. These spreading branches are almost as important as the great trunk of railroad itself. Without them it could not exist as a profitable investment. The trans-continental tour cannot be made with the fullest pleasure in the limited time usually allotted to it. Neither time nor money should be an object when both knowledge and pleasure are to be attained.

There is a little way station, called Colfax, about two hundred miles west of San Francisco. Like all the rest, it has its station-house and "saloons." As we arrive at many of them, we see the dust-covered Concord coaches drawn up ready to carry passengers right and left to the mines, and long trains of wagons awaiting their freight. Away they go, without much difference in speed, for hundreds of miles, leaving us to wonder concerning their unknown destinations. Here and there the business of the adjoining country has so much developed that side railroads have been constructed, making the increase from ten to a hundred fold. Such are the roads to Denver, to Salt Lake City, the narrow gauge to Montana, that leading to Eureka and the broad track to Virginia City, Nevada, the home of the bonanzas. We had traversed all these, and as for the fourth time we are going toward home we are still so little in a hurry that we cannot resist the invitation of Mr. Coleman, who was fortunately our fellow-passenger, to make an excursion on his narrow-gauge road, and visit Grass Valley and Nevada City, and to descend into the Idaho Mine.

Coming from the west everybody crowds upon the platform or about the windows to get a view from "Cape Horn" of the valley below, where one may step without difficulty twenty-five hundred feet and be picked up in fragments. The idea of this fate for a train-load of passengers would be something appalling but for our faith in the engineering science that constructed the road, and confidence in the brakemen who hold our lives in their hands. Across the terrible chasm, and piled up around, the monarchs of the Sierra, in regal robes of snow and forest-green, with crests of rock, look down, we may fancy, with more of admiration than contempt, upon the little insects who have defied their power and march in tortuous lines over their summits, and bridge their depths with spiderwebs. Approaching the high cape from the east, the view is still more startling of mountains piled on mountains till the distant peaks commingle with the skies. This is magnified as we plunge down the narrow gauge to the valley of the American River under the very base of Cape Horn, where the train we have left is seen slowly creeping around its verge.

On a serpentine track we glide for fifteen miles, diving into abysses, spanning rivers, and making steep grades of a hundred and twenty feet to the mile, always through a forest of enormous pines and firs. Mr. Kidder, the superintendent, tells us of the difficulties overcome and the final success of the enterprise. It is no stock-jobbing speculation; but was built by the brothers Coleman and a few other gentlemen for their own and the public good. They demand no higher rates of transportation than are sufficient to ensure the interest on their investment, with which they are content. If all railroad corporations were actuated by such motives, gamblers would be poorer and the people would be richer.

The town—I beg its pardon, the city of Grass Valley, where we first arrive—has seven thousand inhabitants, and Nevada City, three miles beyond, is about one-half its size. They differ from ordinary "mining camps," generally devoid of any pretensions to beauty or taste, where instead prevails a perverse desire to set these qualities at defiance. To save a hundred yards of travel every tree is cut down for timber or fuel, not a spear of grass is allowed to grow, and the rudest architecture abounds. It is the fixed purpose to make every thing as ugly and uncomfortable as possible, and to proclaim by all the surroundings that the supreme, the only object of life is to grub for gold. Here, at variance with all the habits of miners, there is refinement, education, society, pretty homes lost in shrubbery of orchards and vines, and the air is perfumed with flowers.

These lovely little places should eschew their vulgar titles of cities, content to be as we shall always remember them, villages of this enchanting valley. We had no claim upon the hospitality of the people, but their houses were open, their tables spread and their carriages freely offered. After driving through the shaded streets we were taken to see the workings of some of the mines.

These are of two kinds—gravel and quartz. A gravel mine is a magnified exhibition of the first rude process of washing out gold in tin pans, by which the early miners gained their wealth from the abundant placers, the surface deposits of ore swept down by water-courses from the hills. These were soon exhausted. Now, gunpowder and the artificial apparatus of hydraulic hose are brought to bear upon the gravel hills. They are first undermined, and then blasts, frequently of eight or ten tons at a time, are exploded, pulverizing solid hills to be played upon by streams of water with a force attained by descending pressure. The dust washed by processes far in advance of the original hand-pans, results in vastly greater abundance of gold. In this way the "Milton Company" alone obtained the value of $308,000 this last year. About one-half the mines of the Grass Valley and Nevada districts, as well as at Bloomfield and other places on stage routes from the railroad, are of this description. The quartz mines are of more uncertain value, but many of them are even more productive. We had the opportunity to examine only one, the "Idaho," the richest of all. It belongs chiefly to the Messrs. Coleman, who own the majority of its thirty-one thousand shares, which have paid already one hundred and eight dividends of seven dollars and fifty cents each per month, and promise good results for a long time to come. Into its depths we descended eleven hundred feet, and then far below the busy world on the earth's surface, wandered about in tunnels and drifts, lighted by tallow candles, meeting troops of begrimed miners and hearing the explosions of giant powder echoing through the vast catacombs, astonished at the ingenuity and perseverance of men who seem willing to penetrate to the very centre of the globe, and to explode this great terrestrial ball itself for the sake of the glittering dust it contains. In gravel and quartz mining alike, gunpowder is the prime agent of development, and we sometimes wonder how the gold and silver of antiquity was produced in such quantities without its use. Now, it is indispensable except in simple placer workings. The gravel loosened by its force, as described, is washed by hydraulic pressure, or the hard quartz is pulverized by steam operating on powerful stamps. The result of both processes is the fine dust from which the pure gold is extracted by the amalgamation of quicksilver. We were pleased and instructed by what was seen in the mines, but our more cheerful remembrance of Grass Valley is of its romantic approach, its groves, gardens, and its hospitable people.

Returning to the Central Pacific road at Colfax, we ascend eight thousand feet through rocky defiles and around the hanging precipice of the famous Cape Horn, whence we take a last view of the beautiful, exchanging it for the grand and the picturesque. Hour by hour the grass exchanges its verdure for faded russet, until the sage-brush usurps its place. The garden trees are succeeded by the live-oaks, and these in turn by the scrubby cedars. The cedars, too, after a while give up the battle for existence, and all is bleak and barren rock excepting where on either hand the peaks are crowned with perpetual snow.

Reaching at length the highest point, we rapidly descend two thousand feet, coming in sixteen hours to Truckee, the first town of any importance. Its business is derived from its lumber trade. The continual cutting of timber, and the carelessness of woodmen causing extensive fires among the pine forests, are rapidly exhausting a great source of wealth. Already tens of thousands of acres are laid bare, and water flumes bring the timber many miles from the heights above.

We leave the train at Truckee with the intention of visiting Lake Tahoe and Virginia City. The traveller from the East should land at Reno, and reverse the trip by taking the railroad to Virginia, thence crossing to Tahoe, and meeting the Central Pacific again at Truckee. An open wagon is the conveyance, much more suitable than a covered coach, as it affords such commanding views of scenery that people are not disposed to complain of hard seats and a lack of springs. If one has time, a previous day may be passed profitably in a drive around Donner Lake, a pretty basin, but not comparable to Tahoe in extent.

From Truckee to Tahoe the drive ascends for fifteen miles along the banks of a noisy torrent, and for most of the way through a dense forest of giant pines. Descending from the last divide, a scene of wonderful beauty and grandeur spreads itself before and around—the clear, placid lake lying at our feet, circled with a vast amphitheatre of mountains, some of them even at this season capped with hoary crowns of snow, and all sloping from their rocky belts, beyond which no vegetation thrives, through one thousand feet of forests of unfading green. The great mirror, sixty miles in circumference, reverses its variegated frame as the morning sun throws the shadow of the rocky peaks far out upon its expanded plane.

The water is so clear that the bottom may be seen at a depth of twenty fathoms, and so light that its touch is almost like that of air. It is nearly impossible for the best swimmers to float upon it, and a body that sinks never rises again. Far down, the water is cold as ice, and marvellous stories are told of unfortunates who have fallen overboard in some of its greater depths. There, it is said, they can be seen occasionally, when the lake is especially calm and clear, lying as they have fallen, and resting forever in their watery shrouds.

There are old legends of Indian love and hate, offering an excuse for future poets to invent Hiawathas and Minnehahas, and to clothe squalid savages in garbs of imaginary tenderness and nobility.

But more practical notions induced us to seek the comfortable inn, which we assuredly found at "Campbell's Warm Springs," on the eastern shore. From this point the best view of scenery is to be obtained; the fishing is excellent, and the pleasure of hauling out salmon trout weighing twenty-five pounds is equalled only by that of greeting their appearance afterward on the table.

A little steamer called the "Governor Stanford" daily circumnavigates the lake, stopping at all ports on the California and Nevada shores, for the State lines run through its deep waters. A day may be pleasantly passed on her deck. By all means take this excursion.

From Glenbrook, on the Nevada side, a stage runs to Carson, on the railroad to Virginia City, distant fifteen miles. There is nothing to recommend the dusty mountain road, excepting that the stage is driven by a celebrated break-neck coachman named Hank Monk, whose delight is to frighten women and children. It is his boast that he "scared Horace Greeley into fits."

We did not avail ourselves of this route, as our landlord

offered us saddle-horses to cross the divide that separates the Warm Springs from Carson. The trail is twenty-five miles long, and we hoped to accomplish the distance in a few hours. Our guide lost his reckoning; and we wandered for a whole day through pathless solitudes, until, late in the afternoon, we fell in with a strolling Indian. Instead of taking our scalps, this gentle savage piloted us in the right direction, so that we reached Carson in the evening. During a ride so tedious and difficult, the romantic scenery in abundance, did not so much engage attention as the prospect of food and rest.

The busy little town of Carson derives its chief trade from the great mines of Nevada. On the route over the railroad to Virginia City on every side were to be seen sluices, crushing-mills and smelters. Everybody in this district seemed to be living on a diet of mineral ore. That would be their actual subsistence if they depended upon raising food from the ground. There are scarcely fifteen blades of grass in the whole district. The railroad, in curves, tunnels and spans, and creeping along precipices, claims precedence of all other roads for reckless locomotion. A story is told of the death of an engineer who leaped down a chasm of a thousand feet at the sight of an advancing light, which proved to be the lantern suspended from the rear car of his own train.

After the few hours' twist on this gigantic corkscrew we reached Virginia City, whose foundations are over fabulous millions of tons of silver and gold. Upon the profits of digging these metals and gambling with them its people live. The town has been burned since our last visit, and has risen from its ashes in somewhat better form, though it still hangs its streets and houses loosely on shelving rocks and over deep excavations.

Nearly all the mines are unproductive, that is to say, they pay no dividends. "But what's the odds?" said a Virginian; "the stocks go up and down, and they are just as good for speculation as if they paid like bonanzas. In fact, they are better, for they fluctuate more, and there is a greater margin for profit." He did not say anything about the margin for loss.

We visited two famous bonanzas—the Consolidated Virginia and the California, first going through the laboratories and works above ground. Some of them were intensely interesting and curious—none more so than the weighing office, where the scale turned at an infinitesimal part of a grain. The appearance of the reeking miners who came up from the depths decided us not to accept the invitation to descend to their infernal regions, as curiosity in such respects had been already gratified.

We came away, rattling down the railroad, flying past the mills and crushers we had seen in the morning, and leaving behind the mountains of gold and silver without a pang of envy towards Mr. Fair, who, though worth $20,000,000, passed a part of every day far down in the hot and darksome dens of the mines, so that he might daily report the indications to his partners, in San Francisco. One thing we discovered, and it is this, that in speculation all outsiders are fools, and only the men who have the "inside track" are wise; for knowledge is power, and ignorance is the victim of chance. On some day, sooner or later, the near approach of exhaustion is discovered. The partners are duly notified. Perhaps on the same day there are "well authenticated" reports of immense deposits "in sight," and the stock is parted with for the accommodation of new investors, whose property will be found to consist of a big hole in the ground.

This is precisely what has since occurred.

It is fifty-one miles by rail from Virginia City to Reno on the Central Pacific. There we resumed the direct route to Ogden.

The road passes through a country often described by the guide books, which has many points of good scenery and is here and there diversified by large tracts of pasturage. Naturalists have studied its peculiarities with an intense curiosity to discover the meaning and intention of its phenomenal "sinks," where streams and lakes disappear, as they imagine to rise again on the Western side of the Sierras and finally to enter the Pacific. This theory is supported by the fact that on the Western slope of the range, water suddenly gushes out from the ground in such quantities that rivers of considerable size start at once in their course, but it has not been satisfactorily demonstrated.

The solution would be of as much practical value as the discovery of the North Pole, and the investigation would involve less hardship and expense. A scientific corps might be detailed whose business it should be to throw chips into the Humboldt river and watch for their appearance in the Santa Ana. This modest suggestion is made with a view of "appropriating" a little more money from the Treasury in addition to the amount annually expended for purposes of similar utility.

The stations along the route, mark the locations of small towns of apparent insignificance, but many of them are the depots of valuable mining districts in the interior with which a large trade is carried on, and whence an abundance of ore is brought for transportation to San Francisco and the East. Some of the most noteworthy of them are Wadsworth, Humboldt, Winnemucca, Battle Mountain and Elko. At Terrace, we come to the Western limit of what is called "The Great American Desert," once undoubtedly an inland sea, now settled down to the comparatively small surface of the Great Salt Lake. We get an extended view of its waters at early morning when Monument Point is reached. After a few hours the train arrives at Ogden, the terminus of the road at its junction with the Union Pacific.

There we take passage for Salt Lake City over the Utah Central Railroad for a distance of thirty-eight miles. This road, now owned in part by the Union Pacific, to which it is a most profitable auxiliary, was built under the direction of the late Brigham Young. That politic leader of the Mormons, finding his hopes of isolation destined to be thwarted, turned his mind to making his defeat successful in a pecuniary way. He resolved to balance his loss of religious influence by worldly gain, and entered heartily into the railroad enterprise, detailing his people to build, not only this road, but also many miles of the main trunk Line. His success is apparent, for at his death he held, at a cost of little or nothing to himself, a large amount of the bonds of the Utah Central road which annually pays to its stockholders a dividend of twelve per cent, on a capital stock of a million and a half of dollars.

CHAPTER XXI.

SUNSET AT SALT LAKE—THE MORMON JERUSALEM—THE ASSEMBLY OF THE SAINTS—THE LATE BRIGHAM YOUNG—THE CLOSE OF THE CONFERENCE—SOCIETY IN UTAH.

Bierstadt should paint for us this dissolving view of Salt Lake City. He should sit at this upper window as the sun is going down beyond the Oquirrh Mountains, and, looking eastward upon the Wasatch range, under which this beautiful city is nestled among gardens of fruitful trees and shrubbery, he should watch the changing colors, catch the passing shades, and follow with his artistic eye the long shadows as they creep up the inclined plane that leads to the foot of the mountains, see the sombre tints climb higher and higher among the rugged crags, until they reach the snow-clad summits and suddenly change into sunlight, which rests for an instant, a narrow gilded strip of light, and then vanishes, leaving the dark outline against the clear sky. He should seize some best moment of this serene death of the day, and transfer to his canvas a scene that cannot be expressed by words.

I do not wonder at the poetic faith of these Latter-Day Saints; that they should so often exclaim, " Beautiful is Mount Zion, the joy of the whole earth," and that they should quote the inspired prophecies of Isaiah as foretelling the glories of their kingdom.

The time of our arrival was the season of the semi-annual conference of the church. Salt Lake City is the Mormon Jerusalem. Here is their holy of holies, the site on which their great temple is slowly creeping up from its foundations, to be the wonder of the world; here is their enormous Tabernacle; here their beautiful streets, ere long to be paved with silver and gold; here dwells their great high priest, and his chief Levites make it their home; here, the Sanhedrim being assembled to preside over the semi-annual conference, the tribes of Israel have been gathered together. From north and south, from east and west, down from the mountains and up from the valleys, they have poured into the city, nominally to confer with one another about the interests of Zion, but in reality to receive counsel and dictation.

Since the railroads have been constructed, the means of access to the town have been increased, and the throng of people is greater than ever. But the picturesque effect is diminished. The streets and market places are no longer crowded with wagons and saddle-beasts. These may still be seen in great numbers, and every night in the outskirts of the town the light of camp-fires falls upon them. Altogether the scene and occasion are such that a stranger would not willingly be absent.

The Tabernacle is the chief attraction. There sat the Prophet on his pulpit throne. Around him were his councillors; ranged below him were the Twelve Apostles, and all about him were gathered the Council of Seventy, while presidents, elders, and bishops of high and low degree were the numerous satellites of his train.

St. Peter's Cathedral is more splendid than this Mormon

Tabernacle, and the cardinals flaunt in scarlet robes; but Brigham Young, in his plain clothes, with his white handkerchief always tied about his neck, surrounded by his body-guard of ill-dressed, illiterate men, possessed a power and influence over his people such as the Pope would not venture to exercise on those who call him the Vicegerent of Christ.

For one, I have never been disposed to reverence, esteem, hate, or slander him, but to regard his character from a strictly impartial point of view.

When we looked around upon that great assembly of twelve thousand persons, representing ten times as many more, whose condition in this world his sagacious administration had so greatly advanced, and in whom he had inspired such joyful anticipations of the life to come, I did not wonder at their enthusiastic admiration of him; and when outside, I saw the small Gentile minority, some of whom were scandalized by the revolting practice sanctioned by him, while many of them opposed him because he was an obstacle to their political influence, I was not surprised that he was honestly detested and maliciously abused. It must be admitted on all hands that no religious fanatic ever succeeded more peacefully in obtaining such an ascendancy, and no one of them has, upon the whole, used it more wisely and beneficently.

Not touching upon the objectionable doctrine, he urged the people to the completion of the temple, advising every one who could afford it to devote half a dollar monthly to the object; and then, taking some of the rules of the "united order" as a text, proceeded to enforce their observance on all present. I quote a few of these rules:

"First—We will not take the name of the Deity in vain, nor speak lightly of His character, or of sacred things.

"Second—We will pray with our families, morning and evening, and also attend to secret prayer.

"Third—We will observe and keep the word of wisdom according to the meaning and spirit thereof.

"Fourth—We will treat our families with due kindness and affection, and set before them an example worthy of imitation; in our families and intercourse with all persons, we will refrain from being contentious or quarrelsome, and we will cease to speak evil of each other, and will cultivate a spirit of charity towards all. We consider it our duty to seek the interest of each other, and the salvation of all mankind.

"Fifth—We will observe personal cleanliness, and preserve ourselves in all chastity. We will also discountenance and refrain from all vulgar and obscene language or conduct.

"Sixth—We will observe the Sabbath day, to keep it holy in accordance with the 'revelations.'"

All the other rules are equally commendable, and some of them, relating to "foolish and extravagant fashions," might well be preached in cities where they are less likely to be practised.

In the assembly of the saints the proportion of old men is very noticeable. The seats were dotted with white heads, like blossoming trees amidst the green foliage of spring, and, like the sturdy weather-stained oaks of the forest, these venerable men still hold their own among the young saplings springing into life beside them. They were the old pilgrims who traversed the desert a quarter of a century ago, and yet bravely hold on to life, and enjoy, in the evening of their days, the well-merited reward of their toil in the ease and comfort they have earned for themselves and their descendants. Many of their aged wives are remaining with them, "mothers in Israel," worthily entitled to our respectful admiration; haggard, worn out with hard labor, and too many of them carrying heavier burdens on their hearts than they have borne upon their backs, yet unswerving in that faith in God which overcomes the faithlessness of man, they are among the truest heroines on this earth. Hundreds of young men were present, dressed in the home-spun clothing made by their mothers and sisters, strong and athletic lads, and hundreds, perhaps thousands, of girls, whose simplicity of costume, although still to be admired, is fast giving way to the omnipotence of fashion. Last and least, but not least to their mothers, was the little infantry of babies, brought here because they cannot be left at home, and because to exhibit them is the greatest pride of a Mormon mother. A few Gentiles, who came from motives of curiosity, were added to the immense crowd on Sunday, the closing day of the conference.

The benediction was spoken by one of the apostles. The great organ pealed forth the first notes of that magnificent, and, to these people, appropriate anthem:

> "Daughter of Zion, awake from thy sadness:
> Awake, for thy foes shall oppress thee no more."

The well-trained choir threw their hearts as well as their voices into the music, and when its last notes had died away, twelve thousand men, women and children poured out in the streets and scattered to their homes.

It might be supposed that such an influx of people from the country at the time of the conference would have brought no little money to hotels and the shop-keepers. But this would be a mistake. Scarcely a Mormon name was registered at the hotels, for the countrymen were quartered upon the faithful in the city, or camped in and under their wagons in the streets and outskirts of the town. As to money, although there is an abundance of food, clothing, and home comforts, it is an exceedingly scarce article in Utah. When at Lehi, the bishop told us, not many years ago a book was wanted wherein to keep the accounts of the settlement. A suitable one was in the hands of an Englishman. The price demanded for it was fifty cents, and that cash. Eggs, potatoes, chickens, and such common currency were obstinately declined, and as ten cents was all the ready money that could be collected, Lehi was obliged to wait a considerable time for its account-book. Within twelve or fifteen years, impecunious applicants for tickets at the theatre have procured them at the office in exchange for potatoes, onions and cabbages.

At every meeting of this conference there was a crowded audience, who listened as attentively as circumstances would permit. These circumstances were babies, of whom there must have been always at least a thousand present. There was an all-pervading continual infantile wail, and at times, when this came in chorus, the speaker was obliged to wait for a lull in the storm. Many of the discourses were moderate in character, and some of them dwelt with sincere earnestness on the necessity of a religious and virtuous life. Frugality, temperance, chastity and industry were urged upon the people, and while the open attacks of the "enemies of Zion" were deprecated, moderation and forbearance were counselled even by that violent declaimer John Taylor. When this old apostle did break out with occasional bitterness, we were willing to excuse him. He was one of the earliest converts, and suffered all manner of persecution for his devotion to Joseph Smith. He was imprisoned with him at Carthage, and when Joseph and his brother Hyrum were dragged from the jail by a mob and killed in the street, Taylor at the same time was repeatedly shot. He still carries three bullets in his body, and it is when these give him an extra twinge of pain that he scowls fiercely upon us Gentiles, and reproaches us as if we had actually participated in that murderous affray.

But most frequently the saints were reminded how the Lord in all times of their past tribulations had delivered them from the hands of their enemies, and how the same God would do it again, however much the heathen might rage, and whatever vain things the people might imagine against them. The oft-repeated story of their miraculous deliverance from the army of crickets was again and again rehearsed. They were told how, in answer to their prayers, a great army of gulls overshadowed the land, and, swooping down on their tormentors, gorged themselves with their prey, and vomiting them when full, returned again to the abundant feast, until, when these angels of deliverance took their leave, not a cricket was left in the fields. This apparent miracle is a matter of history, and as prayer undoubtedly preceded it, the prayer and the gulls are naturally connected. So now the Gentile ravagers of the land are to be disposed of in some such providential manner. It may be safely assumed, that whatever course the Government or the people of the United States may take in regard to these "Latter-Day Saints," there will be no armed resistance by them or withdrawal from the territory. If "the Lord God of Israel" does not deliver them from us as he did from the crickets, they will patiently submit, like the Jews in their Babylonish captivity, and like that ancient people, who awaited their return to Jerusalem and the rebuilding of the temple, the Mormons will expect in the fulness of time to be gathered together, that they may reign as kings and priests, all nations being subdued unto them.

George A. Smith, an apostle of a milder type than Taylor, delivered the last address.

We have often seen children running into the country stores on errands like this: "Ma wants a pound of sugar, a quart of molasses, a frying-pan." The articles were furnished and paid for at the established rate in eggs, butter, or some other domestic production. In this way trade was carried on at conference time more extensively. Wagons came in loaded with all descriptions of farm produce, and when they departed they carried to the country those articles of necessity that could not be produced or manufactured at home. Thus trade was brisk without money.

You might imagine that one-half of Brigham Young was born in Pennsylvania and the other half in Massachusetts, so strongly was he impressed with the idea of "protecting home industry." Indeed, there are many Gentile shop-keepers to whom this doctrine, so constantly enforced by him, is more repugnant than his practice of polygamy. As home industry is carried out, however, it is not a misnomer for taxation in favor of monopolists. It is a wise plan, by which simplicity of living and frugality are encouraged for the benefit of the people themselves. For this purpose, undoubtedly, no small part of the tithing is applied, in the construction of mills and factories, the digging of irrigating ditches, and other works of public improvement.

The Mormons are drawn mainly from the most ignorant and debased populations of Northern Europe. At home they were fortunate if, as serfs of the soil, one-tenth of their earnings remained their own. Here their tithing is nominally ten per centum, although upon an average not more than one-half of it is paid in. It results, therefore, that, as they become property-holders instead of ill-paid laboring peasants, and are enabled to hold on to more than nine-tenths of their earnings instead of paying it in toil to their masters, they can well afford to pay tithing to the church as an equivalent for their opportunities and instruction.

The condition of society in Utah may be briefly summed up. There are two classes of Mormons—the bigoted and the liberal. The first would perpetuate polygamy and drive the Gentiles out of the territory, were it in their power. Their influence is decreasing, while that of the liberals is on the increase. Superstition and lust are the allies of the former. Railroads, newspapers and fashions are filling the ranks of the latter. These are more efficient missionaries than ministers or tracts, and more powerful forces than legal enactments.

There are two classes of Gentiles—the meddlesome, and those who attend to their own affairs, exerting a peaceful influence upon their neighbors. The first, many of them office-holders or office-seekers under the Federal Government, and desirous of high positions in the territory, are constantly stirring up absurd rumors of Mormon insurrection and outrage, frightening away immigration of other sects, and thus playing directly into the hands of the Mormon priesthood. The last, the most estimable and useful class of all, are business men, who are developing the resources of the country, by opening the mines, building railroads, bringing in capital and men to aid them in their enterprises. They are the civilizers of Utah.

CHAPTER XXII.

OUT INTO THE COUNTRY—THE GREAT SALT LAKE—MORMON
AND GENTILE TOWNS—ELECTIONS—OPHIR CAMP—SUCCESS-
FUL BUSINESS MEN.

Scarcely a traveller on the pleasure trip to California omits to spend a day or two at Salt Lake. In a short stay tourists are unable to form correct opinions of every thing they see and hear, although they often persuade themselves that they have acquired the fullest information. Yet they do succeed in furnishing the press with such abundant descriptions of the town and its imme-diate surroundings that I should not be thanked for again trav-elling over their narrow but well-beaten paths.

I prefer to take my readers at once on excursions over those less frequented. These journeys of several hundred miles have been chiefly accomplished on horseback, by which pleasant and exhilarating method of travelling we were enabled to see more of the country, and to form more correct ideas of its peculiar people, than by observation in any other way.

My wife and myself were every where hospitably entertained in a region which fortunately for our purpose was generally with-out hotels. It is almost superfluous to remark, that as ladies are more communicative with each other than with a sex less accustomed to questions and answers, there were unsurpassed opportunities for obtaining information of domestic affairs.

It would certainly have been impolitic and ungracious on our part to have undertaken missionary work. When the subject of polygamy was introduced by our hosts, we did not fail to accept the challenge to dispassionate argument, but our object being to investigate, rather than to instruct, we looked upon society as we found it, extracting all the amusement it afforded.

Without more preface, we will leave the city on a pleasant day about the close of September, and as we travel west and south will see the Great Salt Lake, the mountains, the valleys, the mines, and the people.

The distance from Salt Lake City to Ophir cañon is fifty-five miles. When the Utah Western Railroad is completed as far as contemplated, this will be one of the most agreeable excursions from the city. It was a tedious, dusty drive in the stage-coach. Still, there are many pleasant views to be had from the road, passing across long desert wastes and over spurs of the mountain range. We reached the shores of the Great Salt Lake after a drive of three hours. Such is the optical illusion caused by this rarified atmosphere, that the city, left eighteen miles behind us, seemed to be only four or five miles distant, the houses being distinctly visible. The formation of the land contributes to this deception, ridges of mountains running north and south, and enclosing valleys of a width of about twenty-five miles, with no intervening elevations. We drove for an hour along the southern bank of Salt Lake, fanned by the breath of its sea air, and looking over its waste of waters dotted with mountain islands. It required but little imagination to transport ourselves to the shores of the Atlantic, for extending, as it does, ninety miles to the north, no land could be seen beyond the line of the clearly defined horizon. Some years ago a steamboat of three hundred tons was built for freight and passenger traffic, in connection with the Union and Central Pacific roads; but her fair prospects were ruined by the construction of the Utah Central, and she now lies at the wharf, her only value consisting in her occasional use for pleasure excursions.

How this great basin of salt water came to be deposited in the interior of the continent, has been a study for geographers and naturalists. The changes taking place in its character at the present day are observed with much interest. It was first discovered by a party of trappers, long before the religious discovery of Joseph Smith. When they had tasted of its waters they supposed that it was an arm of the sea coming in from the Gulf of California; but, on their attempt to sail into the Pacific by that route, they experienced the same disappointment which befell the Dutchmen in their exploration of the North River, although they might have been led to just conclusions from different tests.

The trappers should have realized that the water was too salt, and the Dutchmen should have found that the water was too fresh to communicate with the Pacific Ocean.

Salt-making has been a business of great importance on the banks of the lake since the occupation of this territory by the Mormons. The water is so densely saline that it is impossible for a body to find the bottom. It is a capital place to acquire the art of swimming, with perfect safety. In former times three barrels of water left to evaporate, would produce one barrel of salt; but it has so weakened in the last twenty years that four barrels of it are now required to obtain that quantity. It has become fresh, therefore, in a proportion of somewhat more than one per cent. yearly. Hence it follows that in less than one hundred years the name of Great Salt Lake should be changed, for, by that time, it will, like Mormonism, be cleared of all its impurities.

We notice the regular water lines, called benches, distinctly defined on all the mountain ranges surrounding these valleys, affording unmistakable evidence that in former days they enclosed vast inland seas. The deep alkaline soil of the bottoms has led to the supposition that these seas were of salt water, and that they have been completely evaporated, Salt Lake being the sole survivor, and that destined to dwindle to a puddle and then to dry up forever. But the last part of this theory is negatived by the evident intention of the lake to assume something of its original proportions; while it is becoming fresher, it is growing larger. Within the twenty-nine years that the country around it has been settled, it has encroached along its low banks nearly a mile upon the land, and deepened five feet. Several fine farms are now permanently under water, and the road on which we travelled has been moved far inward to accommodate its aggressiveness. At the same time that this change is going on, atmospheric causes for a part of it are apparent. The climate is becoming more mild, although it is still excessively dry. But each succeeding season brings a greater rainfall. This has doubled within twelve years.

The lake is fed by the Bear and Weber rivers on the north, and the Jordan on the south, besides some small rivulets that find their way into it. Every year their volumes increase, and contribute to the filling up of the great basin into which they pour. Notwithstanding, the increase of the lake cannot be thus accounted for, as they are still but insignificant streams. It must be true that new fresh-water fountains have burst from the bottom. A like phenomenon has produced the lake near which we afterward passed at Stockton, where, on the ground encamped upon by Connor's army, there is now a body of water two miles square, and of considerable depth. If these changes go on as they have commenced, the Zion of Brigham Young will ere long become completely submerged. His enemies will say that a second flood has been commissioned to overflow the desert that he reclaimed, because of the sins of the people, and that, like Sodom and Gomorrah, these modern cities of the plain have been overwhelmed as a punishment for their unnatural crimes. But those judgments are yet afar off. Brigham taught that when Utah is destroyed all the earth will perish likewise, excepting that favored spot, Jackson county, Missouri. There it was, a divine revelation commanded him to build a temple which is destined to rise again from the ashes of the one destroyed by the Nauvoo mob. All the lowlands around it will rise at the same time, and the chosen remnant of mankind will flock to this elevated plateau, from whence, like Noah looking over the bulwarks of the ark, they will behold the drowning Gentiles struggling in the deep waters, while Mormons, in dry white robes, with harps in their hands, shall, like Nero, touch the strings, in mockery at the ruin of the universe. Then Jackson county itself is to be caught up, and its glorified saints be distributed among the stars of the firmament. Thus the gradual rise of Salt Lake is not an indication of their destruction, but a harbinger of their glory.

Leaving Salt Lake far behind, our way led over the spur of the Oquirrh ridge, which there terminates and forms the eastern boundary of Tooele valley. Soon after dining at a wretched "half-way" house, we came in sight of the pretty little town of Tooele, that springs into life by the side of a mountain stream which enriches it by its irrigation, and presents it in beautiful contrast with the surrounding desert. It is not like a town laid out in blocks and squares, but is literally an accumulation of garden spots. The trees and vines were loaded with apples, pears, peaches, melons, and grapes, which are dried and preserved for use and exportation. Entering one of the gardens, we were offered an abundance of the delicious produce. The peaches were large and luscious—quite equal in flavor to those gathered on the Delaware.

This little village, now so peaceful and quiet, was lately the scene of intense political excitement. The election quarrels at Tooele have not related to Republicanism or Democracy. Such trifling issues did not affect votes in any degree. The great question was, shall Judge Rowberry, the Mormon bishop, who for years had presided at the Probate Court, retain his office, or shall the Gentile Brown occupy his place? In short, it was a religious fight. Bunyan's " Holy War " and Milton's " Paradise Lost" can only convey an idea of the fury of the battle. Mormon hosts were marshalled against the Gentile cohorts, the one considering themselves the armies of the Lord, and the others willing to be called the soldiers of Lucifer, so that they might gain the victory. Mormonism pressed every man and woman into its service, and the Gentile element ransacked all the mining camps of the country for its supplies. It was Lowlander against Highlander—the saints dwelling on the plains against the irreverent "cusses " of the mountains, who had invaded the soil heretofore sacred to the religion of the prophet. It was the first organized attempt to gain a Gentile foothold in any part of the territory. The means used for the assault were as unscrupulous as those wielded for the defence. A federal official descended from his dignity to mingle in the broil, threatening, when he was interrupted in his speech, to " punch the head " of his assailant, and to "boot out" the county clerk if he did not "dry up." Parson Smith, of the Methodist persuasion, is such a muscular Christian that when he was damned by some devout Mormons, he replied that he was not allowed to swear, but, throwing off his coat, said he "would lick the whole crowd, three at a time." Per contra, in a rather more quiet style of warfare, when they found the election was going against them, the Mormon judge and his clerk carried off the records of the court, which were not recovered without much difficulty.

There was doubtless a great deal of illegal voting on both sides, from Mormon women who paid no taxes, and from Gentile miners who constituted themselves residents of two or three different camps at the same time. The end attained was a Gentile victory.

Like travellers on Sahara, we had espied the green oasis of Tooele from afar. We had entered beneath its shady trees and luxuriated in its fruitful gardens, and now, leaving it regretfully behind, we were whirled through clouds of dust, over the desert again. All was a barren waste of stunted sage brush and alkali, till after three hours' drive we came to the Gentile settlement of Stockton, presenting itself in strong contrast to the charming little village of the saints. There the people, having planted their own vines and fig trees, were content to sit down beneath them and enjoy their fruits, with no ambitious desire of aggrandizement; satisfied with the sure returns of husbandry, from which, after paying their tithing to the church, there is an abundance left to supply all the absolute wants of life. Tooele is a picture of happiness, if not the realization of what can never be fully attained; Stockton seemed a representation of misery sought for and found.

Pitched on one of the bleakest spots that could be selected, where no trees can take root, and scarcely a sage brush can show its head, built of rambling piles of logs, the only exception an abortive frame-house called a hotel, where bad dinners are eaten and worse liquors are quaffed, it is the home of a few workmen, who are employed in the neighboring furnaces of ore. What wages these men earn to repay them for passing any part of their existence in this execrable hole I do not know, but I am sure that a Tooele Mormon would not exchange his home for this, unless some special "exaltation" be promised in the world to come.

Passing the lake of recent formation, we drove on toward Ophir. From the level of Salt Lake our ascent had been gradual. Over what appeared to be vast plains, the grade was scarcely discernible, but now it was quite apparent as we drew on toward the foot hills of the range looming up gradually before us.

The sun had been pouring hotly down all day, and it was an inexpressible relief and pleasure when we entered the mouth of the cañon, and the first tall cliff on the left threw its shadow over our path, permitting us to trace its dark outlines on the opposite mountain, whose summit was still in a blaze of brightness. In this delightful coolness of evening below, under the light of sunshine from above, we followed up the cañon for three miles, and arrived at the city of Ophir.

Like all the mining "cities" of these mountains, Ophir is a mere camp, containing a few stores, bar-rooms, and shanties for the supplies and accommodation of the miners, who are mostly distributed in the hills, only visiting the cities for their necessities, or for the enjoyment of Sunday after their own fashion.

One of the buildings serves the purpose of city hall, lyceum, dance-house and church, as occasion demands. The day after our arrival the pulpit scaffolding was occupied in the morning by an Episcopal clergyman, and in the evening by a Catholic priest, both of whom came in the same coach from Salt Lake. When the latter preached, his Protestant brother aided with us in making up the congregation, numbering a little more than a dozen. On the previous evening the hall had been crowded with dancers, who kept up a hideous noise till morning. Nevertheless, it is fair to say that Sunday was very quietly observed, and there were few cases of drunkenness which caused much disturbance.

Ophir citizens are not church-goers as a class, but they are as tolerant as they are ignorant in religious matters. The other Sunday a Methodist clergyman officiated, opening the services by requesting them to sing the hymn commencing,

"O for a closer walk with God."

After the meeting one of the congregation thanked him for his preaching, adding: "But, parson, you was more comp'mentry than we deserves. I dunno's Ophir camp's any better'n the rest of 'em ; we all walks a good deal closter the other way."

Whenever a stranger comes into these camps he is immediately encompassed by a crowd of kindly disposed gentlemen, who are willing to divide their interests in the most promising mines, which only require a little of his money for their development. They have prospects of wonderful "indications," "true fissure veins," "limestone and quartzite formations," "hanging and foot walls," "carbonate," "chloride," and other certainties of producing unlimited quantities of rich ore, thousands of tons of which are frequently "in sight." They want you to invest in the "running of tunnels" and the "sinking of shafts," and then to "put the mine in the market," in New York or London. As to "prospects," the mountains are as full of them as sandbanks are ever bored by swallows for their nests.

The laboring miners are universally poor. They keep themselves industriously in that condition, toiling away at their "prospects" until their flour and bacon give out, and then working by the day in the large mines until they get money enough to buy powder and provisions to work on another prospect, when they find a "trace" or "cropping out" that affords them any hope. They have known or have heard of a few men who, having "struck a good thing," have risen from a condition like their own to the rank of millionaires, and why should not the same good fortune at last be theirs? Instead of gambling with dice and cards, they gamble with the spade and pick, working harder and gaining as little.

Among the thousand blanks there is occasionally a prize. The Walker brothers have drawn their full share. They came to Utah as members of the Mormon Church, toiled in the cañons, cutting and drawing wood, gained a little property in this way, invested in land and merchandise, paying their tithing with regularity, until they accumulated a property on the income of which they did not care to pay ten per cent. One day they were reminded of their duty by Brigham Young, and sent him a check for ten thousand dollars. Brigham returned it with a notice that it was insufficient, whereupon they tore it up, paid tithing no longer, and left the church.

They say the Lord has prospered them ever since. Brigham said the devil was their friend. No matter who has assisted them, the Walkers have done something for themselves. Their great warehouses are potent rivals of "Zion's Co-operative Mercantile Institution," and every hole of ground into which they dig becomes a mine of wealth. They own them in every cañon, and here in Ophir they reign supreme. What wonder is it that poor men, who but a few years ago worked side by side with these Walker brothers, should ask themselves, " As we have been equals once, why should we not be equals again ? "

CHAPTER XXIII.

CAMP FLOYD RULED BY A BISHOP AND THE BISHOP RULED BY HIS WIFE—WILLIAM HICKMAN—LEHI AND THE BISHOP WHO RULED HIS WIVES AND HIS DIOCESE—THE GARDEN OF ISAAC GOODWIN.

The pursuits of Utah people may be classed like medicines, "vegetable" and "mineral." The Mormons are almost strictly agricultural, and the Gentiles devote themselves almost universally to mining labor and speculation. Brigham encouraged his saints to cultivate the soil, and preached farming to them as a religious duty. The wisdom of his advice is apparent in the prosperity attending its practice. They abandon the precarious chances of the mines to others, who too often, after years of unavailing toil and broken down with disease, are forced to admit the worldly wisdom of the prophet. The entire attention of the dwellers in the mountains is given to silver mining, smelting and milling.

Where there is an abundance of lead present in the ore—and it frequently runs from forty to sixty per cent.—the silver is extracted by the process of smelting. The furnaces generally purchase the rough mineral as it comes from the mines, on a basis of forty to fifty per cent. lead ; that is, if the ore yield that amount, the smelter takes it for his work and delivers the miner one dollar per ounce for all the silver that it contains. If the basis agreed upon falls short, the miners pay the smelter the difference per ton. If it overruns, the payment is reversed. Good smelting ore is that which being clear of pyrites comes up to the basis required, and then yields to the miner—pays him for the cost of his labor and transportation—thirty ounces of silver to the ton.

Besides the mines of smelting ore, there are many of milling; that is, they produce a greater amount of silver than some of the others, but so little lead that the silver cannot be extracted by the smelting process. It is therefore crushed in stamp mills. This is milling ore. It is likewise mostly purchased by those who convert it into bullion. The rate given is nicely graded according to the assay. The lowest ore which will pay for crushing is that yielding $40 per ton ; on this is returned twenty-five per cent.; on that yielding $100, fifty per cent. ; $200, sixty-five per cent.; $500, seventy-nine per cent.; $1,000, eighty-three per cent. These are mentioned to give an idea of the scale of intermediate assays. But expenses are very heavy; charcoal and coke are the only fuels that can be used for smelting, the former becoming every day more scarce in this thinly wooded country, and coke has been supplied from Pittsburgh, Pa., at a cost of $30 per ton. As to the mills, there is not a sufficiency of the ore they require to keep them in operation more than four months in the year. Nevertheless, when well managed, smelting and milling both give large profits. The great requirement for Utah mining, is the proper fuel for smelting purposes. When this is obtained more abundantly, the low-grade ores, which will not pay for working, will give steady employment to all the furnaces at present partially operated, and will cause many more to be profitably run. The railroads now being rapidly constructed in the south and south-west will bring coal cheaply to market. Some of this, especially that from San Pete, two hundred and fifty miles from Salt Lake, it is claimed, can be coked, but owing to the quantity of sulphur it contains, the experiments thus far have not been entirely satisfactory. We spent a day in climbing the mountains on horseback and on foot, with the purpose of looking at some of the mines on the summit of Zion mountain. At an almost perpendicular height of twenty-five hundred feet above the village, and consequently eleven thousand feet above the level of the sea, is a mine owned by the Walker Brothers, which they work to supply the demands of their mill, getting out yearly, without any special development, the interest on the sum of $1,500,000, the price at which they offer to sell this property. As we wound up the mountain on the opposite side of the valley to a still higher point, we looked down upon their extensive works and tramways, on which the ore slides to the mills.

Our trail led first to Dry Cañon, to arrive at which we passed through Jacob City. This city, not "set upon a hill," but hanging like a collection of crows' nests on the side of a mountain, cannot be approached on wheels. Sure-footed horses and mules are rather doubtful of their foothold in its streets paved with boulders and drained by the gully of a torrent. If heavy rains should swell the stream, as they are liable to do, or an avalanche of snow, which every winter threatens, should descend, the flimsy structures of Jacob City would fly into the abyss below, like a pile of shingles before the storm. Precarious indeed is the existence of the capital of Dry Cañon. As we ascend, we see on the left the celebrated "Mono" mine, one half of which has been sold for $400,000. We met Mr. Gisborne, who owns the other half. The net income of the mine is said to average $60,000 per month. When we looked at Mr. Gisborne, living in Jacob City, clothed in a shabby suit that at most could not have cost twenty dollars, smoking a cigar made far away from Cuba, and all his surroundings betokening a man in debt for his last meal, we asked ourselves, what is the use to him of an income of $360,000 per year? A little boy once wished he was a king, for "then he would swing on a gate all day and lick 'lasses." We perhaps would do something similar if we had the income of Mr. Gisborne. We would buy a house on the Fifth avenue, loaf about the streets of New York, visit the clubs, and do nothing. We would have the dyspepsia and die of *ennui*. I apprehend that Mr. Gisborne values his immense fortune only as a proof of his success as a business man, and is far happier in his mountain life, in exuberant health, than he would find himself if he followed any bad advice that we might give him.

On the other side of the valley is the scarcely less noted Chicago mine. There we dismounted and descended a shaft hundreds of feet, through tunnels and drifts, dropping down on ladders, crawling on all fours through damp caverns, as we carried lighted candles in our hands. Here we saw the ore, deep buried for ages, now to be excavated, smelted, refined, coined and made into wealth for the luxury of those who will never see and pity, as we have done, the hard toil by which it is obtained. A very productive property in the mountains is a beautiful spring of water, running in a small stream over a great cliff of a thousand feet, descending in thin spray to an unapproachable chasm. The proprietor located this claim, and there he has established himself for the sale of all the water on the mountain; for it is only after the melting of the snows that, for a short time, the watercourses are known in this "Dry

Cañon." There is no drilling or blasting needed to produce wealth for this fortunate man. He sells the water for two and a half cents per gallon, realizing thousands of dollars annually without the outlay of a penny. The "Mono" and the "Chicago" may give out, but the spring is not likely to dry up.

Leaving our horses at a place where their further progress was impracticable, we proceeded on foot, often swinging by our arms from one craggy rock to another, over the topmost ridge, to survey some prospects in which the gentlemen who accompanied us were interested. The location of a "prospect" is determined by various indications, the chief of which is the presence of a yellow ochre-colored dust. This leads to "croppings," the ore on the surface containing mineral. These "croppings" afford encouragement for the miner to sink a shaft, upon which he works nine times out of ten without success. We return to the place where our horses had been left, and mounting them again, rode over the divide above the Chicago mine to the side of the mountain sloping down toward Ophir.

If we could have taken passage in a balloon, or held on to the tail of a kite, we might have mounted to the top of the perpendicular cliff above the village of Ophir, and dropped down on the other side to the settlement of Camp Floyd in Salt Lake valley; but, until ærial navigation is more advanced, a stage wagon performs the mail and passenger service between these towns along the road over the foot hills, making a circuit of eighteen miles.

It was a delightful drive, for, as we were hurried away at an early hour, the sun, rising out of sight on the opposite side of the mountains, had barely reached their summits before we had completed this first stage of our journey, so the road lay under the shadows, while far away in the west was the view of gilded peaks gradually brightening to their base, and the sunlight came step by step over the plains to meet us, till the dazzling sun himself mounted to the crest on our left, and poured around us the full blaze of day. By this time we had nearly approached Camp Floyd, once the location of a military post, but now a little Mormon village, where all vestiges of its former occupation have given place to cultivated fields and orchards.

Bishop Carter presides over the spiritual interests of the people, his office also giving him the right to counsel them in temporal matters, in accordance with the recognized authority of the priesthood. It is a grave cause of complaint against the Mormons that they do not encourage the presence of any of the three learned professions. Unless the town is unusually large, the bishop is able not only to do the preaching, but to settle all disputes and to cure all ordinary diseases, by "the laying on of hands," quite as effectively as they are treated by the administration of drugs. It is only in cases that require the prompt services of a surgeon that he is forced to admit the inadequacy of his spiritual power.

Bishop Carter, who rules supreme over all other households in Camp Floyd, we were told had lately found that laying on of hands has not acted well in his own case. He was originally, as he is now, a monogamist. But not long ago he saw fit to have a revelation commanding him to take another wife. Mrs. Carter did not see the angel who brought the message, for that angel was careful to avoid her. The bishop, however, trusting in divine protection, went up to Salt Lake " on business," and returned in the evening with another woman. It was then that he experienced an effectual laying on of hands, and Mrs. Carter No. 2 felt the laying on of a broomstick. Feminine muscular

Christianity prevailed over spiritual enforcement, and the bishop was made to realize that the power of a determined woman is one that cannot be withstood by a Mormon any more successfully than by a Gentile. The difficulty was settled by the bishop's marrying No. 2 after all—to another man. Mrs. Carter keeps a very excellent hotel, the breakfast provided for our company evincing that, as far as the travelling public are concerned, the lady at the head of the house is able to meet all their requirements, as well as those of her husband, alone.

The distance from Camp Floyd to Lehi is eighteen miles. As we drove out of the town the driver pointed to a seedy-looking vagabond, apparently sixty years of age, who was walking slowly along, smoking his morning pipe. The expression of his countenance was truly diabolical, and betokened a scoundrel whose society one would instinctively avoid. This was the notorious Bill Hickman, whose residence is in the neighborhood.

Why the fiend is permitted to live is a mystery. His confessions of bloody deeds, if true, should expose him to the vengeance of Gentiles whose friends he has slain; if false, the wonder is that he is not riddled by Mormon bullets. It is a mark of the astonishing forbearance of this people that, believing him to be a malignant liar, they allow him to go about the country unmolested; and the only accountable reason for his safety from the wrath of the Gentiles is, that they hope at some future day to use him as a witness to prove the murders committed by him at the bidding of the church. But the troubled conscience of the desperado is never at ease. He must have revelations, and terrible ones too; he must have angel visits at night, for the angels of darkness must hover around his unquiet bed, and hell must yawn at its side. He walks the streets by day armed with two revolvers and a belt of cartridges, looking furtively about him to see if some avenger is not nigh. He steeps his damning memory in rum, yet dares not drink himself totally insensible, lest, if found dead drunk away from home, he should never wake again. So fearful is he of a surprise that he never enters a bar-room where other men are present without standing with his back to the bar when the liquor is poured out for him. And thus he lives in a continual hell.

Happily he soon passed out of our minds, as after a short drive across the plains we came to a slight elevation, from which, in the distance, we could see the pretty town of Lehi, not far from the northern bank of Utah Lake. The lake extends in a southerly direction twenty miles, and is five or six miles wide, its western limit washing the foot of the Wasatch mountain.

It is of fresh water, and contains an abundance of trout and other fish. Its outlet is the Jordan river, a narrow but deep and sluggish stream, connecting it with Great Salt Lake, forty miles north. Far away to the south stretched the glassy lake, reflecting the noonday sun; the rugged mountains its background, and the town, sheltered in the foliage of fruitful orchards, fringing its northern edge. Lehi is a much larger settlement than Camp Floyd, and contains 1,500 inhabitants under the paternal care of Bishop Evans, to whom we had been commended as willing to provide us with better accommodations than those at the little hotel.

The Bishop is a jolly old Pennsylvanian, who came to this territory many years ago, and has contributed his share to increase its population, not being under such salutary restraint as his brother Carter. His No. 1 being dead, No. 2 has been advanced to the rank of chief mate, six more of his female crew living in cabins of their own. He was very communicative on family matters. He evidently regarded No. 2 as the most valuable wife, on account of her producing qualities. "I ought to have more children than I have," he said. "Why, I should have quite a family if all the rest of them kept up with her. She has had fifteen, and all the others together have not had but twenty-four."

Discoursing upon matrimony in general, he observed that he considered all Gentile forms null and void. "But," he added, "I wouldn't take a woman that belonged to a Gentile, because I consider it mean. I don't justify Parley Pratt in having done it—no—I want to avoid even the appearance of evil." The self-complacency of this prelate was something of the sublime, as he continued, "No, I would not take such a woman even if she asked me to, as these others did."

"Do you mean to say, bishop," asked my astonished wife, surveying the unctuous pluralist, "that these women ask for the privilege of marrying you?" "Yes, ma'am," he replied, with some hesitation; "three of 'em went for me straight, and the rest of 'em hung round gitten me to ask 'em."

In this way did the garrulous old fellow go on until we were glad to be shown to our room. We had no reason to complain of our bed and board, nor of the attentions of No. 2, who manifested her interest in our welfare by shouting, as we left in the wagon, to be driven by our host to the station after breakfast, "Look out now for the bishop; after all what he said last night, remember the more men have the more they want. When a man has one wife he's tolerably well satisfied; but when he gets another he keeps going on, and there's no knowing where he'll stop."

Lehi is upon the Utah Southern Railroad, thirty-one miles south of Salt Lake City. Here we had arranged to meet a party of friends, who were to leave the town in the morning train, and accompany us on a visit to the American Fork Cañon. To while away the time before they should arrive, we sauntered about the neighborhood of the station, under the shade trees of the wide streets, and looked with longing eyes upon the fruitful orchards surrounding almost every house.

Entering a gate, and asking if the owner of the premises would sell a few peaches, we were met by a plump refusal. "No," replied an elderly man, "but you can take as many as you please. Come in and let me show you my garden." A second invitation was not needed, although it was extended with equal cordiality by his wife. The garden was what is called a double lot. It comprised two and one-half acres of ground, every foot of which, except the walks, was under complete cultivation. Nothing can exceed the richness of this soil, irrigated at pleasure from the mountain streams. Although subject to grasshopper visitations and the like casualties, a drought is never apprehended, for that is impossible.

Mr. Isaac Goodwin, who so kindly entertained us, was a Connecticut farmer, but has lived here for twenty-eight years. He was an earlier Mormon than any of the first settlers of Utah, for he was a California pioneer. The little band of 321 pilgrims, of which he was one, that sailed in the ship Brooklyn from New York for San Francisco, landed there in July, 1846. This was two years before the discovery of the gold that brought such a different class of pilgrims to worship at its shrine. The Mormon settlers formed the colony of San Bernardino already described, then, like Utah, a part of the Mexican territory.

Mr. Goodwin gave us many interesting reminiscences of

their early sufferings and privations, and of their final success in acquiring, by peaceful overtures, the friendship of the Indians whom the Mormons have always had a peculiar tact in conciliating. If gold had not been discovered, if the Mexican war had not supervened, if Brigham's revelations had not induced him to order the colony to break up and remove to Utah, we should have seen at this day what an empire these indomitable enthusiasts would have obtained in a country where nature did not oppose such obstacles as they have here overcome. No railroad would have approached them or ridden over them rough-shod, but they would have been allowed to work out the problem of their distinct civilization unmolested in their freedom of action.

But Providence determined that they could be put to a better use here in paving the way for a higher civilization than their own. Goodwin was the man who, with only one companion, travelled across the continent, successfully braving natural obstacles and hostile Indians, until they met Brigham Young on the eastern slope of the Rocky Mountains, and told him of the fertility of the soil of California. It was by his report Brigham was induced to act in accordance with his revelation, as the Mormons believe, but, as we are inclined to think, from the conviction that he would not be allowed to remain there. Their first settlement here proved of the greatest advantage in aiding emigrants to cross the plains in the earlier days of the occupation of California, and subsequently in the construction of the Union and Central Pacific Railroads, which have bound them in the embrace of our common country.

We are fond of listening to the tales of these gray fathers of the land, especially when, as coming from such a one, they bear the impress of unquestionable truth. He was a man of great sagacity and general information—a New Englander imbued with those Puritan principles that make martyrdom an absolute pleasure. Yet, like all who come here from that section, his faith in Mormonism is not exceeded by that of the most ignorant and superstitious Dane or Norwegian.

As Mr. Goodwin talked, we supplied ourselves abundantly with peaches, plums and grapes. Still waiting, not impatiently, for the train, we entered the tidy little cottage, where the proprietor and his only wife devoted themselves still further to our entertainment. "I have a kingdom of my own," said he, "without going into polygamy: this old lady, seven children, and thirty-three grandchildren. I believe in the doctrine for those who like it, but God never required it of me. Matrimony is a 'straight and narrow path.' I like to go it alone. Now you hang a plummet down from the wall and let it drop between two women. Each of them will say it swings nearer the other one than toward her. I might be straight up and down like that plummet, and though the women mightn't say any thing, both of them would think I was leaning the wrong way from her. So much for *two* women. Now hang yourself like a plummet in a circle of half a dozen, and then you can make some calculation what kind of a time you would have through life."

Thus within the last two days we have seen three different representations of matrimony. Bishop Carter is a monogamist because he dare not open the door to another woman ; Bishop Evans is a pluralist because he likes polygamy, although he says the seven women will cleave unto him whether he wants them or not ; and good, honest, straight and narrow-walking Isaac Goodwin gets along through the world in peace and contentment with only one wife, because he loves her too well to take another. Let those of troubled conscience at home, who think that "no good thing can come out of Nazareth," be consoled with the knowledge that there are many more like Goodwin in the Mormon church, and that such leaven as this will yet leaven the whole lump, if meddlesome fingers will but leave it alone.

The shrill whistle of the engine was heard in the distance, and we hastened to meet our friends in the train, parting reluctantly with those, who now bade us farewell, loading us with fruits and benedictions.

CHAPTER XXIV.

SORGHUM—LUZERNE—THE AMERICAN FORK CAÑON.

We entered the train at Lehi and were landed at American Fork station in a few minutes, the distance being only three miles south, along the shores of Utah Lake. While waiting for the cars in which we were to be taken over the narrow-gauge railroad to the cañon, we had an opportunity to inspect a sorghum plantation. The surroundings reminded us of Louisiana and Cuba, excepting that the whole arrangement was on a minute scale, and that a few white men and boys were doing the work there performed by an ebony crowd.

An inexperienced cockney would readily mistake a plantation of sorghum for a field of broom corn, which it so much resembles. It is thickly planted, like sugar cane, and similarly harvested and ground. The stock has the same saccharine property, though in a lesser degree. The grinding apparatus is not unlike a cider mill, and was worked by a patient mule, busily engaged in making his distances on the small circle. The juice is boiled down from one kettle to another, until at last it acquires the consistency and flavor of good southern molasses. But its sweetness refuses to consolidate itself into anything better than what Jack of the forecastle calls " long sugar." The cultivation of this cane is rapidly increasing in Southern Utah, where the climate is exceedingly favorable. One hundred gallons of molasses are produced to the acre, and this, clear of all the expenses attending it, nets to the planter one hundred dollars. If a farmer in New York State or New England could make $10,000 per annum from his farm of 100 acres, he would not have his present complaints to make.

Another very productive industry of this district is the cultivation of what is called luzerne, and in California styled alfalfa. Four crops are here cut in a year, while further south seven harvests of it are obtained. The old Scripture simile of the " desert blossoming as the rose," beautifully and poetically expresses the change that has taken place in these valleys in twenty-seven years, but it is inadequate to give an idea of a land whose very paths drop with the fatness of rich abundance. Leaving these fertile plains behind us, we were shown to an open observation car, which the superintendent of the American Fork Railroad had added to the train for the comfort and pleasure of our party.

Messrs. Howland & Aspinwall of New York are the chief owners of the Miller mine, the principal property in this cañon. It is located at the highest point, twenty-three miles distant from this, the nearest station on the Utah Southern Railroad. Although the mine was at one time very productive of valuable ore, it was almost inaccessible, on account of the roughness and steepness of the trail. To overcome these obstacles, this narrow-gauge road was constructed for fifteen miles. Its cost, comprising the equipments, has amounted to nearly four hundred thousand dollars. So great has been the expense and so much disappointment has been experienced in the productiveness of the mine, that although the road has been graded for a great part of the distance, the eight miles at the upper end of the cañon is still only a rough wagon road. But an unselfish happiness should be theirs. Among the many tourists who avail themselves of the pleasant means they have afforded the public of visiting some of the most magnificent scenery in the world, we tender them our hearty thanks.

The excursion must now be made for the whole distance on a wagon road, the railroad having been discontinued.

We began a gradual ascent over the foot hills for three miles, drawing nearer and nearer to the grand massive range of seemingly impenetrable mountains, till they loomed up like impassable barriers to our progress. Suddenly a chasm was opened between two enormous perpendicular cliffs, and through this narrow valley a way was afforded hardly of sufficient breadth to allow of the passage of the train. Creeping up a grade of 316 feet to the mile, we wound round one point after the other, sometimes under the dull shadow of dripping rocks, and then coming out into the warm sunlight that fell upon hill slopes carpeted with the loveliest velvet green, and figured with clumps of pine trees and autumnal tints of wild shrubbery.

It was a glorious day of this most glorious season of the year, when Nature in her harvest robes is joyful on the plains, and in her mountain plaids surpassingly attractive. The mountains, as they gathered round us, in our ever-changing progress, seemed to leap for joy, and the sparkling brook danced to its own melody. The sublimity and beauty of the scene spread over our little company such a feeling of awe, that at times we were lost in silent admiration, and again were carried to such ecstasy of delight, that words could not be found for its expression. Scenery like this always forces from the observer the conviction that all he has seen before is tame and insignificant in comparison.

So the White mountains, the towering Appenines, Mont Blanc, the Bernese Oberland, and even the Yo Semite faded away into dim pictures of the past, in the transcendent light of this almost unknown cañon of the Wasatch Mountains.

A bountiful lunch was provided for us at Deer Creek, the terminus of the railroad, and then, some in a wagon, some on horseback, and one on foot who arrived first of all, we ascended the cañon for four miles to " Forest City," a municipality comprising some smelting works and charcoal furnaces for its public buildings, and four shanties for the inhabitants of its various wards. The Miller mine is four miles still higher up. Two of us ascended to it by a bridle path, varying our route to examine another newly developed mine.

Finally, by a zigzag trail we reached the Miller at a short distance from the summit of the mountain, a few moments before the sun went down. His last rays lingered long enough to light the high peaks, while the deep valleys were almost shrouded in night. There we stood, 11,000 feet above the level of the sea, and surveyed the great panorama of alternate day and night, extending to mountains around, and over chasms below.

It was the very night of the full moon, when she rises at the moment of the setting of the sun. Strangely then the picture changed; the splendor and the grandeur faded and vanished away, but a softness and a beauty succeeded, even more pleasing than the magnificence of the day. The sharp outlines of the mountains were toned down to the smoothness of grassy mounds, all colors were blended into a grayish blue, the hills were drawn together, and the hazy bottoms of the valleys rose to the appearance of elevated plains. So contracted did all things now appear, that but an hour before were spread abroad in immensity.

Daylight and darkness are alike in mines. Mr. Epley showed

us a part of the works which had been commenced four years ago. He lives at the mine during the winter as well as summer months. For weeks at a time he is often alone, so far as congenial society is concerned, but in his little cabin there is a choice library well stocked with standard works. There, when the snow flies and the tempest howls, he sits with Shakespeare, Addison, Pope, Macaulay, Scott, Cooper, and Dickens, besides a number of scientific gentlemen, whose companionship we should not so much covet, and communing with these, is at peace, though all without is elemental war. " Is it not cold ? " we asked. " Not very ; the glass seldom falls to 10 deg. below zero." " A great deal of snow, is there not?" " Why, yes ; about forty feet deep." " Hard place to live in the winter?" " No ; not with my books." Happy Mr. Epley !

By moonlight we descended to Forest City, and, after our long and romantic ride, were right glad to enjoy the supper, at which we were anxiously awaited by our companions. In the morning we were rattled down to the railroad station at Deer Creek, where we again took the observation car, descending without the company of an engine. A brakeman sat at each end of the carriage and moderated its speed, and thus we glided smoothly down.

CHAPTER XXV.

PROVO—FACTORY AND CO-OPERATIVE STORE—THE TWO MOR-
MON SECTS—THE CHILDLESS BISHOP AND HIS MORE FOR-
TUNATE BROTHER.

We came again to what was then the terminus of the Utah Southern Railroad, a pretty little city of 4,000 inhabitants, fifty miles from Salt Lake, where the mountains overshadow it from the east, and the waters of Utah Lake ripple on the shores at its feet. This is Provo.

We came on a lovely summer afternoon, for it was the Indian summer of October. The mountains were still hiding in their rocky clefts clumps of shrubbery, variegated with every hue. Quantities of apples, peaches and plums were yet remaining upon the garden trees, and winter seemed to be far away.

But as evening drew on, dark clouds gathered over the Wasatch peaks, and dropped in misty curtains over the valley, the trees swayed in the fitful gusts that filled the air with dust, and the placid lake scowled darkly, and broke into a miniature sea of white-capped waves.

In the wild night the rains descended and the winds blew, and when the morning dawned the streets and gardens were overflowed by water, floating away the fallen fruit and leaves, and the mountains, from their summits down to an even, dark line, where the snow changed to rain, were covered with a white mantle, concealing beneath its folds alike the bare rocks and the autumn-tinted shrubbery. Winter had come.

Within doors we were comfortably lodged, fed and warmed by Bishop Miller, and there we proposed to remain until summer should return, not for months, but for a few days.

Utah seasons are not like those described by Thomson as changing with great regularity. They come and go. The autumn here is not a season by itself. It is made up of alternate summer and winter. "Wait a day or two," said the bishop, "and summer will come again; then you can go on your way. In the mean time I will look up a couple of good saddle beasts, and you can go out between the drops and see the city."

We readily acquiesced in the title given to Provo. It is one of the earliest Mormon settlements, and its prosperity always was a pet delight of Brigham Young. To describe the laying out of one Mormon town is to describe them all. There are the same methods of rectangular streets, bordered on each side by running water, and shaded by cottonwoods and locusts, all the house lots and orchards enclosing cottages, and every thing about the localities betokening quiet contentment.

As we go further from the metropolis we see less of what in the East is styled comfort, and as we become accustomed to its absence we are apt to think that our idea of comfort is after all one of luxury not absolutely necessary to the enjoyment of life. Good taste is invariably displayed in the selection of town sites. This is involuntary, but the effect is none the less charming. Each settlement, large or small, nestles under some mountain range and at the mouth of a cañon. The streams that run down these narrow defiles are caught in ditches before they waste themselves on the plains, and are made useful in irrigating the village gardens and the fields surrounding them.

At the mouth of Provo Cañon this little city is not only well watered and pleasant to the eye, but, owing to the volume and rapid fall of the river, is happily situated for manufacturing enterprise. We were shown through the largest cloth factory in the Territory, a capacious stone building which, with its machinery, cost over $200,000. It has been in operation six years, and besides giving employment to one hundred operatives, is a very profitable concern to its stockholders. The blankets, flannels, shawls and cloths turned out by this establishment are finished goods that would not disgrace the counters of the fashionable dealers in our great cities. It is certainly creditable to Brigham Young that he introduced the best breeds of sheep into Utah, and in such a short period followed the experiment from the beginning to the end, and through all the processes produced these proud results.

The manager of the co-operative store explained the working of the institution. Like the woollen factory, it is a stock concern, and as far as possible is made subservient to the profit as well as the wants of the community. The shares are issued at twenty-five dollars each, in order to induce all classes of people to participate in the copartnership.

In no community are wealth and poverty more evenly distributed. It may be said of Provo, a city of 4,000 inhabitants, that there is not a rich man or a poor man in its limits. It would be difficult to find anywhere an assemblage of an equal number of inhabitants so contented with the answer to Agur's prayer, " Give me neither poverty nor riches."

Our host, the bishop, was one of the "early pioneers." I have previously noticed the unusually large percentage of old people we everywhere meet. It would seem that the pilgrimage over the desert in 1847 gave to everyone who undertook and finished it, a new lease of life. These old folks never die, for they have earned a claim to immortality. The bishop was an intimate friend of Joseph Smith the prophet, sharing with him many of his adventures and persecutions.

His conversation elicited the truth of a very important but much disputed matter of church history. The question has often been discussed, was Joseph Smith, the originator of the Mormon sect, a polygamist? The Josephites, or as they are sometimes called, the members of the "Reformed Church of the Latter-Day Saints," deny it emphatically, claiming that his own life was one of purity, and that he did not countenance impurity in others. They accordingly discarded this pernicious doctrine which they say is a device of Brigham Young.

In almost every other dogma of their religion they are in accord with the dominant sect. We have listened to their preaching and never discovered any other material difference. They use the same religious books in their worship, and argue from them the prohibition of polygamy with as much earnestness as Orson Pratt displays in its advocacy. They all accept the Bible as a literally inspired book from beginning to end.

The outside Christian world, desirous of establishing a purer form of worship in Utah, would best attain its object by encouraging this sect of Josephites. The prevalence of their teachings would reform Mormonism, and that certain result would be better than all that can be accomplished by uncertain missionary effort. It may be said of this, in general terms, that it is a waste of time and money, and that all that the Presbyterians, Methodists, and Episcopalians have done in the Territory has been among themselves, few converts having been made from Mormonism.

When a Mormon apostatizes he almost always becomes an

infidel or a spiritualist. It will be admitted by most people that Christianity of any kind is better than infidelity, and no unprejudiced person can study the Mormon religion and its effects upon those who embrace it without coming to the conclusion that if it could be shorn of its one objectionable excrescence, it would confer as much happiness upon this condition of society as any other form or creed could bestow. I should like to see the Mormons complying with the law of the land, which has made polygamy a crime, but apart from this I have not the least desire for their conversion.

Unfortunately for the Josephites and for the reformation they propose to bring about, they will be unable to establish the fact that Joseph Smith was a monogamist. His earlier writings and practice, and all the teachings of his "Book of Mormon," were clearly in favor of monogamy; but, however willing to be virtuous was his spirit, his flesh became weak, and for several years before his death he was living in violation of his own precepts. There are old men in Utah who say that he had at least nine wives.

Our friend Bishop Miller produced this conclusive testimony. He and another member of the church told us that the revelation of polygamy was read openly three years before the death of the prophet, and that they had heard it. Moreover, Bishop Miller was married to his wife No. 2, at Nauvoo, by Hyrum Smith, the brother of the prophet Joseph, two years before those two men were killed by the mob at Carthage.

Such proofs, easily brought forward, will lessen the influence of "Josephism." But despite of them, the name itself of the sect, and the purer morality of its teachings, will be powerful arguments in its favor. Combining with other causes, they will surely produce the needed reformation in the church.

The surroundings of our host evinced that he was a prosperous man. Yet there was sometimes a shade of melancholy passing over his genial face. This was always apparent when children were referred to in conversation. At first we thought that he had lost some of his little ones, but we afterward discovered that he had had no little ones to lose. *Hinc illae lachrymæ.*

Two comely and agreeable matrons in his household took excellent care of him. Besides, he had been owned by four more, now deceased; and yet the poor bishop was childless. Each woman thought it the greatest curse that could fall upon her, and their general head considered that he was six times accursed.

True, they had been exemplary Christians to the best of their knowledge and ability, conscientiously fulfilling all the duties of this life, but they had done absolutely nothing toward peopling the "celestial kingdom." Those crowns of glory to be fitted on to the heads of their productive neighbors were not for theirs, and their "exaltations around the throne" would be of a low degree.

How much happier both in this life and in the life to come is and is to be the condition of one of their venerable townsmen! He is ninety-two years of age and the father of sixty children. The eldest is seventy years old and the youngest is sixty-seven years his brother's junior. We were sorry that this patriarch was not at home. How delightful it would have been to see him trotting these two children of seventy and of three on his knees, and to hear him repeat from "Mother Goose"—

<blockquote>
"Tom Brown's two little darling boys!
One wouldn't stay, and t'other ran away—
Tom Brown's two little darling boys!"
</blockquote>

CHAPTER XXVI.

THE JOURNEY TO THE SOUTH—THE HOTEL AT PAYSON—OUR LANDLADY'S CHOICE—MORMON AND GENTILE AMENITIES —HOSPITALITIES OF THE BISHOPS— MOUNT NEBO—ENERGETIC CONDUCT OF A BISHOP'S WIFE—SAN PETE VALLEY—WAR, THE CONSEQUENCE OF MISS WARD'S OBSTINACY —A MONOGAMOUS MORMON TOWN—REFLECTIONS OF MRS. PRICE—THE COAL MINES.

After two days the storm abated, and on the third morning the sun rose brightly over the mountains, now covered nearly to their base with snow. Winter seemed to have fixed his permanent abode among them, while summer was permitted to return for a short visit to the valleys. It was summer, with all its agreeable warmth, but not too hot for travel; summer, lacking somewhat of the pleasant views of green meadows, ripening harvests, and fruitful trees, but compensating these losses by enhanced beauty of mountain scenery.

The bishop had secured two ponies of promising character, but with peculiarities subsequently developed. As we were provided with our own outfit of saddle and side-saddle, we had nothing more to ask for, but cheerfully agreeing to pay half a dollar a day for each of the animals, for the time they might be required, we packed our luggage, and, mounting them, bade the bishop and his family good-by for the present. Then, over a ground made soft by the late rains, we took our course to the south, along the eastern shores of Utah Lake.

On the first afternoon we passed through Springville and Spanish Fork, and arrived at Payson, eighteen miles from Provo, in the evening. The road lay along the "bench" below the Wasatch mountains. By turning our faces to the left we could enjoy a continual view of winter magnificence, and then looking down upon the bottoms, find enough of summer still there to make a pleasing picture, while beyond the dark blue waters of the lake contrasted beautifully with the snowy Oquirrh range in the west.

As we rode up to the door of the neat little inn, we were agreeably surprised to meet Judge Emerson, who, with a party, was on his return from the Tintec mines to Provo. This gentleman, although a Federal officer, is highly respected and esteemed alike by Mormons and Gentiles.

The Mormons accept his decisions as made in accordance with the spirit of the law he is placed here to enforce. No one of them, excepting the most bigoted, can complain of him for being the agent of the Government, and no Gentiles, excepting the mischief-makers of the "ring," assert that he is too lenient to the Saints.

His present journey was an instance of his ability to hold their mutual confidence. There had been a dispute concerning a mine between a Gentile and a Mormon. Each of them, desirous of avoiding legal expenses, had agreed that the judge should go with them to the spot, and there decide the question. This had been done, and all parties were returning amicably together. The arrangement was especially agreeable to us, as it afforded an evening of pleasant entertainment.

In the course of conversation a Mormon of the party observed that, although he was a "pluralist," and was very happy in his domestic relations, he recognized the right of Government to enforce its law against polygamy, provided it was constitutional. He and many other reflecting men were perfectly willing that some test case should be brought into the courts, in order that the vexed question might speedily reach the highest tribunal and be forever set at rest. This desire has since been gratified.

The little hotel at Payson was a model of comfort. It had lately been established by a young couple, the husband a Gentile and the wife a Mormon. The linen and the table service were faultless. There was no abominable stove to burn out the oxygen and poison the atmosphere, but a soft coal fire was flaming cheerfully in the grate, and every thing reminded us of the easy luxury of an English country inn.

We asked our pretty landlady how she came to marry a Gentile. "Why, isn't he handsome?" she replied ; "and then he is good, and then—and then—I wanted every bit of him to myself! Father didn't like it, mother didn't like it, but I did."

We had known of similar vagaries among other young women, and as fathers and mothers become reconciled to them after a while, we sincerely hope that the obdurate hearts of these Mormon parents will relent. Payson, containing about 2,000 inhabitants, is a thriving farming town.

In the morning we went on our way south, leaving the shores of the lake, which here has its south-western limit. We had passed out of Salt Lake valley before coming to Provo, and now on reaching Santaquin, came to the southern end of Utah valley, following the new grade of the Utah Southern Railroad. Every mile this thoroughfare progresses is a gain to the mining and agricultural interests of the South. These Utah railroads are dependent upon no land grants, concessions, or subsidies of any kind. In the exact proportion of the demand and necessity for them, they are constructed by the people and for the people who need them. Bonds are issued for two-thirds of the cost, and they are not dependent upon Government charity or the chances of Congressional action. There is no watering of stock. In short, they are built by honest men for honest purposes. To meet the wants of the newly developed mines at Frisco, this road is now under contract to be extended one hundred and fifty miles in a south-westerly direction, and by other connections will doubtless in due time reach the Pacific. At Santaquin we reached, by a somewhat sharper grade, the more elevated valley of Juab, three or four miles wide and thirty miles long, Nephi, sixteen miles south of Santaquin, being its shire town.

Progressing ten miles in that direction, we came to the small settlement of Willow Creek. We were provided with an encyclical letter from a church dignitary in Salt Lake, addressed "to all the bishops south." It was intimated therein that we were in search of information, and we were accordingly commended to the courtesy of these country ecclesiastics, who were requested to furnish refreshments when the lack of hotels obliged us to claim their hospitalities. We found them assiduous in contributing to our comfort, and ready to impart all the knowledge they possessed. Many of them are in very moderate circumstances, but all have enough and to spare. A Mormon brother is always welcome to board and lodging gratis, and even a Gentile often finds it difficult to make them accept any remuneration.

At Willow Creek we accordingly called upon Bishop Kay for the requirements of ourselves and our animals. Again we found an early pioneer, and listened to the oft-repeated story of crossing the desert.

Salt Lake City is 4,300 feet above the level of the sea. We had mounted 700 feet in a distance of ninety miles. Here, directly against and almost above the village, is Mt. Nebo, the highest peak in the Territory. It was incomparably magnificent, clothed in its spotless robe shaded into a delicate pink at its summit, 7,000 feet above us.

The wonderful rarefaction of the atmosphere plays curious freaks with our estimation of distance. I said to the bishop that I should like to spend a day, if time allowed, in going up to the peak. " Well, " he replied, " you might start this afternoon and if you did not freeze in the night you might possibly get there by sunset day after to-morrow. You remind me of an Englishman travelling through this back country a few years ago. He thought everything looked so near that he hadn't far to go, and he never could understand why he could not get along faster. At last he got on a little ahead of the party. They came up to him on the bank of a small brook two feet wide. He was taking off his boots to wade over. ' Why don't you jump across? ' somebody asked him. ' Aw, you see,' replied the Englishman, ' I've been deceived so often that I fancied this brook might be half a mile wide, and I might be obliged to swim ! ' "

After dinner we rode to Nephi, over a level bench of sage brush for most of the way.

I have described Nephi in the mention of Payson and Provo. There is a sameness of beauty in them all. It contains about 2,000 inhabitants, and two hotels, one of which we know to be well kept by Mr. Seeley, an old Californian. " Are you a Mormon or a Gentile ? " I asked. " Nary one, " replied Seeley, " I'm a neutral." He had been to California in search of gold, he said, and had not found it. So he had come here in search of peace and quiet. Surely he has attained it.

California and Utah solve the problem of longevity. The gold hunters went to California in 1849. Ten years earlier the religious enthusiasts came to Utah. At San Francisco the veterans of '49 have the annual meetings of their society. Very few of them are now left ; of these too many are broken down old men. *Auri sacra fames* produces an equal appetite for whiskey, and together they craze the brain. In no country is suicide so common, or old age so rarely attained, notwithstanding its unrivalled climate, as in California. In Utah, where winter howls among the mountains for half the year, and the toil of the farmers in the valleys is incessant, the robust exercise of the woodman and the quiet existence of the agriculturist, their temperate habits and the training of their minds in continual regard to the practice of religion in this world with reference to its hopes for the future—these conditions bring but little wear and tear on the human frame. Men live out their three score years and ten, and if by reason of strength they be fourscore years, the Psalmist would admit that their strength is not always labor and sorrow.

The extensive Tintec silver mines can be reached from Nephi by an easy grade for a narrow gauge road of twenty miles in a westerly direction, while it is also the nearest and most convenient junction for the narrow gauge road contemplated and surely to be built for the San Pete valley, that will contribute its coal and its grain. This is reached by the Salt Creek cañon, through which we took our road.

The ascent is very gradual, little of it being on its steepest grade of 200 feet to the mile. The cañon is so wide that the height of the mountains at its sides is not fully realized, and there are always perplexing ideas of distances. By a circuitous track we wound along, keeping mainly a southeast course, but often steering due north. In this way we circled Mt. Nebo, until we had a full view of its eastern slope, as beautiful in the morning light as its western side appeared in the sunshine of the previous afternoon.

With the exception of a saw-mill and one cattle ranch, there was no sign of habitation or life upon the road until we came to Fountain Green, the first village in San Pete valley, into which we descended from the divide, after making fifteen miles from Nephi. Bishop Johnson not being at home, Mrs. Johnson gave us a kindly welcome, and spread before us an abundant and cleanly meal.

Polygamy is not much countenanced in San Pete, as would appear by the energetic conduct of our hostess not long ago. I have related the experience of the bishop of Camp Floyd, when he pursued matrimony under difficulties. His brother of Fountain Green fared even worse. He also conjugated surreptitiously. When Mrs. Johnson discovered that he had another house, she dressed herself in male apparel, and armed with an axe, destroyed the honeymoon. Fortunately mistaking the bedpost for one of their heads, she hacked it into a broken shaft over the grave, as it were, of love nipped in its early bud.

The valley was originally called by the Indian name of San Pitch, a chief of this region. San Pitch headed the war which devastated these settlements ten years ago. As in the difficulty that occurred at Eden, Troy, and thousands of other places, a woman was the cause of this trouble. Barney Ward, an old settler before the time of the Mormon occupation of the valley, was on such terms of friendship with San Pitch, that he promised him his daughter in marriage when she should become of a suitable age. But when that time arrived, the young woman was found to have a will of her own. She rejected the advances of the swarthy Ute, and he took vengeance on the whites for the jilting he had received. The innocent people who had begun to settle in the valley were murdered or driven out, their habitations laid waste, their crops burned, and their cattle stolen. All this happened because of the obstinacy of Miss Ward.

At the close of the war the Mormons returned, and again built their homes, fortifying their villages with rude forts for defence in case of other outbreaks. The wisdom of their precautions has been obvious, for two raids have since been made upon them, the last of which occurred five years since when several individuals were killed, and a large number of cattle driven off. Already nine towns, including Fountain Green, containing altogether ten thousand people, have been rebuilt, and are in a flourishing condition.

The valley is forty miles in length by four or five in breadth, and is very productive of wheat, barley, and oats. Potatoes are raised in great abundance, and celebrated for their excellent flavor. The average grain yield of San Pete is 450,000 bushels, a great part of which is exported to the mines of Pioche, Tintec, and other districts. The chief future product of San Pete will be its coal, already attracting much attention, and promising great results.

After dinner we rode from Fountain Green, on the west side of the valley, south to the small collier hamlet called Wales. This is an absolutely monogamous Mormon town. There had been a feeble attempt on the part of the male members to introduce polygamy, but the women so rudely handled the intruders on their domestic peace, that the men surrendered unconditionally, and now the single broomstick reigns supreme. No woman has presumed to dispute the sway of a rightful wife since the last audacious hussy was mounted on a rail, and carried by these

Amazons down to the meadows, where she was dumped and left to find her own way out of the neighborhood.

A kind old Welsh couple took us into their little log hut of two rooms, giving us the best. There were holes in the roof, the sides and the floor, thus affording plenty of ventilation without windows. Mrs. Price told us heart-rending tales of the poverty they had endured before they were now so comfortably situated. Her husband had been superintendent of a colliery in Wales, with a good salary which he had abandoned for the sake of his religion.

"I've often wondered," remarked the thoughtful old woman "why we couldn't have been Mormons in Wales as well as here, and had some comfort in life besides what we get in religion. They talk about coming to these holy mountains—well, and aren't there mountains there too, and don't they belong to the Lord just as much?"

She did not see the advantages of martyrdom. She had experienced it enough not to yearn after more, and she was the first emigrant we had found in all Utah who was willing candidly to confess that she was sorry she had come, and would now prefer to be living in her old home.

In the morning we rode up to the principal coal mine in the cañon, three miles behind the village. The president of the company, the secretary, the treasurer and the superintendent, were all living together in a comfortable log cabin, serving them for sleeping, cooking meals, store-room, offices of their various departments, and other general purposes.

They received us very politely and escorted us further up the cañon to the place where the works are in active progress, explaining all matters of interest by the way.

The veins are distinctly traced for seven and three-quarters miles. It is a solid stratum of five feet and eight inches, enclosed in flat limestone walls, and running into the mountain at a pitch of twenty degrees. Along this incline they have run a shaft two hundred and fifty feet, and from various points have drifted tunnels of from four hundred and fifty to six hundred feet. Sixty men are now employed at the works. The actual cost of mining is $2.50 per ton, and it is sold at $4 on the dump. The coke is made at the mouth of the cañon, and the full cost of it there turned out is $4 per ton. It cannot probably be made for less in Pennsylvania.

CHAPTER XXVII.

TOWNS AND VILLAGES IN THE SAN PETE VALLEY—GERMAN PREACHING—PROVIDING TABERNACLES FOR DISEMBODIED SPIRITS — BRIGHAM YOUNG'S JOURNEY—THE MOUNTAIN MEADOW MASSACRE—LIFE AND CHARACTER OF THE APOSTLE GEORGE A. SMITH.

We left the hospitable mud thatch of Mr. Price at Wales on a lovely Sunday afternoon. Sabbath, it might more appropriately be termed, for all animate and inanimate nature seemed to be at rest. The slow pace of our lazy ponies was so near to a standstill that so far as using them is considered, we could not be accused of breaking the commandment, for they certainly did no work.

As for ourselves, we did not "sit under" any preacher, but on our saddles we sat under the smiles of the great Creator, who made such days as this for the enjoyment of his creatures.

Descending the bench sloping from the western mountains, the little villages of Mount Pleasant, Spring City, Maroni, and Ephraim were in full view on the eastern side of the valley, their green orchards variegating the sage-brush deserts. The towns were all abandoned and destroyed when the Indians ravaged the valleys of San Pete, Sevier, and the surrounding country. Their present condition evinces the energy the settlers have displayed in rebuilding their homes.

The forts they have constructed are not unlike many old European fortresses of the middle ages, being provided with loopholes for rifle shooting, as those were for the use of bows and arrows. This is quite sufficient, as the Indians are unprovided with artillery, though some of them have been furnished by greedy and unscrupulous traders with the best Henry rifles. We occasionally met bands of them armed in this way and belted with metal cartridges.

These fellows, although now peaceable perforce, carry in their devilish faces the inclination to pull the triggers of their fancy weapons whenever they can do so with impunity. Most of them, however, are but rudely armed, some still carrying old flint-locks, and not a few relying upon their original bows and arrows. But the same disposition is left in them all to use whatever will serve the purpose of getting a white man's scalp.

It was but twelve miles' travel from Wales to Ephraim, the most southern town of importance in the valley. As we came down from the western bench we passed over three miles of river bottom watered by the San Pete, a narrow, sluggish stream tapped by irrigating ditches several miles above. The villages on the benches are watered, and their gardens made productive, by the torrents from the cañons, while the farming lands are spread over the rich bottoms of the meadows.

The cattle either find pasturage on the benches and in the cañons or are herded on the low lands. Ephraim contains about 1,700 inhabitants. As we entered it on this quiet Sunday evening, it would have seemed like a city of the dead had it not been too beautiful for such a melancholy idea.

The Mormons believe in spirits of the air. These might

have been dwelling here unseen. They could not have had a more heavenly home on earth. Lovely as were the many villages we had seen, this last one, with its neat cottages, and streets shaded by long lines of trees, with not a sound to break the stillness, but that of the running roadside streams, and the setting sun gilding the snowy mountains in its background, leaves in our memory one of the fairest pictures of the journey.

At last the herd boys came driving in their cows, and the blowing of their horns, the tinkling of the bells, and the lowing of the cattle awakened the little town from its dreamy repose. A few people came out from their cottages and leaned listlessly over the fences. From one of them we obtained a direction to the inn.

Ephraim is almost entirely settled by Danes and Germans. In the evening we attended the "meeting" in a large, tastefully built church. It stands in the centre of the stone fort, presenting a formidable appearance, surrounded by walls and bastions. The preaching might have been in Danish so far as it conveyed any instruction to us. Few of the speakers had pure English at command, but they all seemed to comprehend each other with the same accustomed facility with which we understand "Pigeon English" in China. The church does not encourage the continuance of old national habits or language in Utah. Therefore the new comers are required to speak in English as best they can.

Now and then we could make out a little of the discourse. In descanting upon the "United Order" which Brigham Young was laboring to introduce, one of the brethren observed, "Ven de Presdent tell vat he tinks am recht, I vas alvays know das ist recht: who vas ever know him tell lie? If angel vas coom down from himmel and vas say something diffrent, I moost believe der angel vas lie. Cause vy? Vasn't ter duyvil fix himself up like angel mit shnake's face and coom to ter garten mit Adam and Eve and tell 'em lies? Brigham Young is ter great prophet. I don't believe vat all de priests in de voorld say agin him. He is yoost like Lijah ven he shtand oop agin der vier hoonderd und fumfsig prophets von Baal, and beat dem all."

The next day I had a pleasant talk with Bishop Peterson. He is the "husband of one wife" and several more. He looked upon polygamy as a hardship but a duty, expressing not only a perfect willingness but a wish that the question might be fairly tried by the supreme court. If the law of 1862 and the Poland bill are declared to be constitutional he will cheerfully refrain from being married again. In fact he would be glad of an excuse for not complying any longer with revealed orders, when the orders of the Government legally enforced, oppose them. The mind of the bishop must now be relieved.

One of the Mormon theories being that the air is full of disembodied spirits in want of earthly habitations in which to do penance for their sins, in order to obtain salvation, our good friend has hitherto considered it his duty to "provide tabernacles" for them to enter. He who provides the greatest number of tabernacles is instrumental in saving the greatest number of distressed spirits, and is accordingly a benefactor to the spirit world, deserving of the highest exaltation.

This is a man's excuse for polygamy. The woman gains for herself also exaltations in proportion to the tabernacles produced. This glorious hope of the future reconciles her to the humiliation of her condition, to the mere participation of her husband's affection, to a small share in his property, to jealousy, heart-burnings, domestic quarrels, and all the unmentionable miseries of this damnable system. It is true that Brigham Young urged it only upon those men who think that they are able to support more than one family, and upon those women only who think that they will be happy in the relation. But I have not yet seen one man who has become richer by polygamy while I have met hundreds who were impoverished by it, nor in all the families we visited in our extended tour, where the subject is always broached by the Mormon women themselves, have there been found but three individuals among them who claimed to be happy.

Bishop Peterson gave us an interesting narrative of the Indian raids and the consequent sufferings of the settlers who, unable to defend themselves, sought shelter in the rocky fastnesses of the mountains.

The United States Government afforded them not the slightest aid. The bishop observed, with no more bitterness than was warranted by the fact, that the only troops sent to Utah came as enemies, not as friends to the Mormons. He thought it unreasonable in the Government to exercise control over their social relations, while it treated them as a separate and distinct people by leaving them to fight their own battles.

We were taken into the large co-operative store, and told with pride of the great dividend of sixty per cent. declared last year. This seems enormous, but it is really nothing more than the taking out of one pocket and putting into the other. Almost every purchaser is a stockholder. If he gets sixty per cent. dividends—always, by the bye, payable in goods—it is only because he pays sixty per cent. too much for all that he buys. The system varies from a high tariff policy, inasmuch as the people who pay the high duties that make high prices do not receive again the profits. These go into the pockets of monopolists. The Utah farmer pays himself back. The people of the United States pay manufacturing corporations. That is the difference.

In a succeeding chapter will be found a relation of the experience of travel from the little town of Ephraim to the southern point of our journey. Among the places worthy of remembrance on the route, Richfield, the county town of Sevier valley, is most prominent. The valley, fifty miles long, watered by the river of the same name, is easily irrigated, and although it has not been under cultivation until recently, has abundant promise for the future.

We happened to be in Richfield, as in Gunnison, at the same time with Brigham Young and his party of about twenty persons, on their way to " Dixie," as the extreme south of Utah is termed.

The imperial crowd being entitled to the best hospitalities of the people, unbelieving Gentiles could expect but poor accommodations unless they chose to attach themselves to the suite. Brigham himself was very ill, making no public appearances on the route, and although we were acquainted with several of the elders who accompanied him, we kept aloof from their society, as their journey was a sort of religious procession of praying and preaching in which we were not especially interested.

When notice was given that he was expected in a settlement on his line of march, a cavalcade went out to meet him, and when he departed he was escorted in the same way until met by other horsemen. The poor old gentleman could only look from a window of his carriage and thank them with a silent blessing. It was perhaps his last journey. Thirty years ago, in his full vigor of mind and body, he made his entrance through the wild Emigration cañon into what is now the fruitful United States Territory of Utah.

Then it was a Mexican desert, uninhabited, save by roving savages, unproductive of a blade of wheat. He had now left the city whose foundations he then laid. More than a hundred miles north of it the country is already thickly peopled, and as he travelled through these valleys three hundred miles to the south, he beheld thousands of acres that had just yielded a bountiful harvest, thousands of cattle and sheep grazing upon them, and in the hills, orchards, and gardens, lovely villages, and above all tens of thousands of happy, industrious people settled in these towns and on their farms, every one of whom was indebted to his energy and foresight.

I cannot yet comprehend his character. I cannot believe that a man of his astuteness could have been totally led away by the delusions of Joseph Smith, nor can I think that one of his unswerving fidelity to the religion he embraced, maintained and successfully propagated was a consummate hypocrite. At all events I am persuaded that he became at last convinced of his own sincerity. He looked upon the end of his labors as justifying the means taken to achieve the grand result.

There have been committed in the early years of the settlement by the Mormons, single murders rivalling in atrocity those now perpetrated in the mining camps with horrible frequency by Gentiles ; but to reproach the Mormons as a people with wholesale atrocities as premeditated, or to accuse Brigham Young of instigating them, are slanders worthy only of those who invent them and sustain them for base political ends.

The Mountain Meadow massacre, a crime unparalleled in barbarity by either Mormon or Gentile, furnishes the chief ground of these accusations. I have made inquiries in every direction regarding this celebrated, most wretched affair, and am thoroughly convinced that the emigrants themselves excited the animosity of the Indians, who were joined by white men of notoriously bad character. The emigrants were butchered from motives of revenge and plunder. Brigham Young and the

Mormon Church had no more concern in its perpetration than the Pope of Rome or the Catholic Church has in any murder committed by men who acknowledge their authority.

The preaching of "blood atonement" as a doctrine of religion in former years will forever stand against Brigham Young, although he long ago discontinued its advocacy. His maintenance of the polygamous practice was a disgrace to his name, but it is contemptibly mean and unmanly to vilify him for crimes of which he was not guilty and to refuse him the credit due for the good that he accomplished.

His conscience, unless it was perverted by fanaticism, must have marred the satisfaction with which he viewed the accomplishment of his work. Still, it would not be wonderful if he drew the balance greatly in his own favor. Like the patriarchs whom he sought to imitate, whose good deeds were many and whose misdeeds were few, he was ready to depart in peace and to be gathered to his fathers.

President George A. Smith, next in council to Brigham Young, accompanied him on this journey. Mr. Smith was my favorite apostle. We had often heard him preach at the Tabernacle in Salt Lake. His views were more liberal than those advocated by many of his co-religionists, and his plain, practical teachings were instructive to Gentiles as well as to Mormons. He was fifty-seven years of age, of tall, portly figure, with a face of infinite jollity and expressive humor. This cropped out so frequently that the audience always expected to be entertained when "Brother George A." held forth.

His private character was without reproach, excepting on the score of polygamy. I do not believe all we hear of the grasping propensities of the heads of the Church, for on visiting Mr. Smith at his residence in the city, we found him living in the simplest manner consistent with ordinary comfort, and I scarcely know one of the apostles, elders, or bishops not engaged in some lucrative business of his own, who maintains a style above that of a laboring mechanic.

Mr. Smith was the historian of Utah. He came out originally with Brigham Young, and his personal experiences, united with the material he had diligently collected from other sources, would make volumes of exceeding interest and entertainment. On the occasion of his visit to Richfield we attended the crowded meetings and listened to the discourses of Mr. Smith and several others.

Mr. Smith told of his adventures thirty years ago, when he explored the south of Utah, before the idea of a settlement in the region was seriously entertained; of his camping out when the mercury stood 19 deg. below zero: how an Indian and a lonely trapper stole his mule; of the lesson he then got "never to trust a mule, an Indian, or an old bachelor;" how after the settlement was made at Salt Lake he preceded Fremont three years in the exploration of this valley of San Pete; how his party was snowed up for a whole winter in the neighboring mountains, and how under difficulties and dangers he had travelled the whole territory from north to south, three or four times a year, for several years, to get an accurate knowledge of its topography.

Then he gave the people some very good advice: "Make the most of materials at hand, without procuring luxuries from abroad. Skin every dog or cat that dies or is killed. If that don't give you leather enough for shoes besides what you get from cattle, make the soles of wood; wooden soles are preventitives of rheumatism. They are better than the sponge soles you import from the East. Raise your own sheep. Manufacture your own wool. Make your women useful as well as ornamental.

Work outside, and they will be encouraged to work inside. You have got everything you want right here at home—the best of land, the best of cattle, the best of religions, the best of everything. Thank God for his continual mercies. Pray to Him morning and evening, and at every meal. When the railroad is completed you can have some luxuries you cannot now procure, and you can pay for them in the abundant excess of your own productions. Pay up your tithing like good Latter-Day Saints; not a particle of it shall be misappropriated. We want more temples for the Lord, and whatever excess there is shall go to bringing people from all parts of the earth to participate with you in your blessings. Never get into debt. When you take up land pay for it as soon as you can, whether obliged to do so or not; for I have always noticed that people get into debt when they are flush and have to pay up when money is scarce. To those of you who were so unfortunate as to have come to this country with your clothes on, I would say, get clothed at once with all the rights of an American citizen. You have a judge in this district who is a just and honorable man, and who does not consider himself a missionary sent here expressly to convert you. If you are drawn on a jury don't shirk your duty. Don't lie before God or man. If a man is indicted for polygamy entered into since the law of 1862, and it is proved, convict him accordingly. We know that law is unconstitutional, and we can beat them in their own courts. Don't be nervous about it. Take a little valerian tea and put your trust in God. Everything will come out all right. Show to the world that you are a quiet, law-abiding people. We have stood a good deal, and we can stand it to the end. May every blessing attend you. I ask it of the Eternal Father in the name of Jesus Christ. Amen."

We have listened to worse sermons than that.

Soon afterwards, the whole community of Utah was saddened by the death of this excellent man. His history is almost as remarkable as that of Brigham Young. Indeed, he was the right hand of the head of the Church. He most sincerely believed in the inspiration of his cousin Joseph Smith, and from the date of his baptism into the Church of the Latter-Day Saints in 1832, he devoted unselfishly every day of his life to its interests.

He seemed to entertain the same ideas of polygamy which, in a letter to me, he attributed to the founder of the sect. He says: "He was a rigidly moral, virtuous, and pure man, and nothing but a sense of the awful responsibility of disobeying the Almighty caused him to teach or practice a principle which increased manifold the responsibilities and burdens of men." A Gentile finds it hard to believe that duty is the motive to influence a man in that direction. Nevertheless, knowing the honesty of the writer, I can credit it in his case at least.

I am indebted to him for many anecdotes of the early settlement of Utah. The following extract from one of his letters is characteristic of frontier life.

The school-room and school library of the pioneer schoolmaster teach us how education may be obtained under difficulties.

" St. George, Washington Co., Utah,

Nov. 14.

Dear Sir : Your letter from Cove Fort of November 7 has been received. I should take much pleasure in giving you the desired information concerning the settlements in the southern country, with the history of which I have been familiar from the beginning, were it not that my time is so much occupied with other duties as to render it impossible.

I camped with my party in Cove on the 4th of January,

1851. We ploughed the first ground and sowed the first wheat; built the first saw and grist mill—two hundred and twenty miles from any other. I taught the first school opened in the settlement ; and some of my scholars are now the principal men in the county. My first grammar class of eighteen had only one book—a copy of Kirkham's grammar—the instruction being given by lectures and repetition. Our school-room was out of doors by an immense fire of dry cedar and pinion pine, around which we spent the evenings of the entire winter.

Walker, the Ute Indian chief, who had for half the generation been the terror of the entire California frontier, came to our camp with his warriors, and we were very much pleased to find he was disposed to be friendly. He was mourning over the bad luck he had had on his last raid for stealing horses, which he said San Pitch, his brother, had made a failure of ; although he was lucky in stealing one thousand head of horses at one haul, he got sleepy, and the Spaniards overtook him and got back eight hundred of them. I persuaded Walker to quit that business, as the Americans had got possession of California, and they would surely scalp him if he continued it. Walker and his Indians never made a raid on California since, though they had made one annually for twenty-five years previous."

Every right-minded man entertains a respect for sincerity of belief even in those from whom he differs in many questions of doctrine and practice. No one can fail to appreciate the practical character of this pioneer of religion for his sect, of civilization for his countrymen at large. The good that he has done will live after him in the grateful memories of many others besides those for whose interest his life was especially devoted.

CHAPTER XXVIII.

IMPRESSIONS OF TRAVEL IN UTAH UPON THE FEMALE MIND—THE STORM IN CLEAR CREEK CAÑON—COVE FORT—THE UTE INDIANS—ANGUTSEEDS AND KANOSH—ON THE WAY TO THE NORTH—FILLMORE—SCIPIO—LOST ON THE DESERT—THE TINTEC MINES—RETURN TO SALT LAKE CITY.

As it is my desire to introduce some of the readers of these notes to follow upon our tracks, ladies will appreciate my candor if I enable them to form an idea how travelling in these regions strikes the female mind. With this purpose I introduce a familiar letter from my wife to her daughter which has the merit and the interest of not being intended for publication. It is fair to say that the inconveniences experienced were unusual, and that they were endured with patience and fortitude, and that their recollection has afforded an enjoyment corresponding to the difficulty of surmounting them.

"COVE FORT, November 9.

MY DEAR———: We made a delightful journey on horseback of about a hundred miles from Provo. As I am not able to ride comfortably more than twenty-five miles a day, in order to gain time and to obtain the least uncomfortable lodgings on the road, whenever there is an opportunity I shall avail myself of the mail carrier's conveyance. Your father meantime will lead my horse or fasten him to the wagon.

In this way we started from Ephraim on Monday afternoon, for Gunnison, the most southern town in San Pete valley, on the Indian reservation, and distant twenty-five miles. The stage proved to be a rickety open wagon with two seats.

The country was very barren and uninteresting—sage-brush plains, with low hills. We passed a settlement called Manti about half-past six o'clock. Here we changed horses, and I had a cup of tea, made in a miserable adobe cabin, which warmed and made me more comfortable for the next two hours. Your father rode his horse, and mine was led by the side of the horses of the wagon.

I had for a companion from Manti to Gunnison an Irishman named Reed, an educated man, who was converted and came to this country some twelve years ago. He told me that I was the first "outsider" that he had seen during that time. From the bitterness with which he spoke of England's course towards Ireland, I fancy that his discontentment drove him out West. Here he embraced this religion and provided himself with an extra wife.

We reached Gunnison about half-past eight o'clock. It was very dark, but it appeared to us a very small collection of houses, and we found to our dismay that Brigham Young, with some of his family and friends, on their way south to St. George, had arrived and occupied every house. At last we found a Danish cobbler who consented with some reluctance to take us in his little adobe cabin of two rooms.

While your father attended to the horses and to the arrangements for the next day, Mr. Ludwigsohn made a great fire in the "living room," and his wife being out, I surveyed the premises, while my heart sank within me. A very small room, with one bed and filled with chests and hanging clothes evidently of Danish manufacture, and with that indescribable odor acquired by age, sea voyage, and travel—this apartment was intended to accomodate Mr. and Mrs. Ludwigsohn, two children, a young brother and sister, and ourselves, while the "living room" had a double settee for the use of three Mormon brothers who had come from the next settlement to meet President Young. I felt quite desperate, and suggested to Mr. Ludwigsohn that we might occupy the settee in the "living room," and not disturb the rest of the family, as the stage would leave at four o'clock in the morning, and we should not sleep much at any rate. His wife soon came in, and with four children and the four men, their little room was very full. She gave us some bread and milk, made up the settee with clean sheets and blankets, and then went away to nurse a sick woman.

After discussing as usual their religious tenets, the father, four children, and three men went into the bedroom. Where or how they slept I cannot say. We kept up the wood fire all night, for it was very cold, and of course I could not undress; but I rolled myself up in my plaid, and actually slept well.

At four in the morning we arose, and your father arranged the horses, one to saddle and the other to lead. Pretty Mrs. Ludwigsohn returned from her sick friend and gave us some bread and milk. The stage, a light spring cart for mail carriage, arriving, I mounted by the side of the driver, a young Dane, and we started in the darkness of the early morning.

The country was barren and desolate, a valley with abrupt hills on each side. We were three hours driving to Salinas, a most forlorn, wretched looking collection of huts. Here we stopped to breakfast, having driven fifteen miles. "Dirty" would not express the condition of the hut in which we breakfasted, or of the woman who ruled there and her six children. To do it justice I must reserve it for oral description. Suffice it to say, I did breakfast on tea, eggs, and bread and butter, while trying to be oblivious of the surroundings.

The unfortunate people of this settlement had been driven away many times by the Indians, who seven years ago made a raid upon them and stole everything, cattle, horses, grain, etc., leaving them absolutely destitute. So much excuse can be made for their poverty, but not much for their filth.

On leaving Salinas we found ourselves in Sevier valley, and after driving some three miles came to a gully in the road, about ten feet deep, called Lost Creek. Here the driver advised me to jump out, as, he remarked, "Wagons generally upset in this mean hollow." I did not require a second suggestion, but jumped out over the wheel. Down went the horses, down went the wagon over the holes and rocks at the bottom, not wrecked, but stranded. Your father and the driver were obliged to unharness the horses, pull up the wagon, and finally succeeded in righting the whole concern upon the opposite bank without other damage than breaking the bit of the led pony. Meanwhile I was in high spirits, as I had been saved from the agony of going down with the horses and wagon.

We continued our road on the east side of the valley, following the foot hills for seven miles, when we entered a mountain pass called the "Twist," which exceeded all the roads I had ever heard of for misery. It was originally an Indian trail winding round and about the foot of little hills, and had been much washed away by the late storm. Sometimes the right wheel would be on a high bank and the left wheel in a deep rut; then these conditions would be reversed. The descents were not long, but nearly perpendicular, and the wagon jumped up and down and swayed about like a ship in a heavy sea.

This state of things continued for five or six miles, during which time I said many prayers. We reached Glenwood, a small settlement, about twelve o'clock, and I entered the postmaster's house to warm myself. His wife opened the mail-bag, and I had much quiet amusement at the distribution of the letters. Four or five children assisted ; the baby played with the postal cards, and the odd letters were put away in a stocking box. We dined with these people, and then drove across to the west side of the valley, to a settlement called Richfield, making our day's journey thirty-seven miles.

We found this small town in great excitement, awaiting the arrival of President Young. I had risen at four o'clock that morning, and now sat in the wagon waiting for shelter until six o'clock in the evening, when Judge Morrison, the postmaster, coming into the village with the President, kindly offered his hospitality. His wife was down south on a visit, but her four small children, fourteen, ten, eight, and five years of age, were keeping house. The Judge lived on the next block with another Mrs. Morrison.

This lady came round and arranged a bed for us, while we took entire possession of the sitting-room, lighting a great wood fire. Although I found a Miss Morrison aged eight doing the family washing in a tub much larger than herself, and with a washboard of about her own size, I doubted her capacity for cooking, and we gladly accepted the proposal of Mrs. Morrison No. 2, to take our meals at her house. We remained one day in Richfield to recruit.

Our next journey being forty miles through the mountain

pass of the Sevier, and through the famous Clear Creek cañon, I did not venture to attempt it on horseback, and your father engaged Judge Morrison to carry me through in a light spring wagon, and to lead my horse.

We accordingly left Richfield on Friday morning at nine o'clock. The wind commenced to blow on the previous afternoon, and howled and whistled all night, filling me with many forebodings for our journey. Although it still continued very strong in the morning, the clouds seemed to follow the ranges of mountains on each side of the valley, and we hoped for a clear day. We should have started at seven o'clock for a forty miles mountain journey in these short days, but the Judge is one of those unfortunate men who leave their properties and belongings out of repair, trusting that the Providence of the shiftless will carry them through every necessity and danger. His horses he represented as fine animals, but they proved to be unfitted for travelling, having been used entirely for ploughing and teaming.

We drove down the valley, twelve miles over a level plain of sage-brush, to a wretched-looking hamlet of adobe huts, called Joseph City, situated at the extremity of the Sevier valley. The wind, although very strong, was from the south, and not as piercing as it might have been from another direction, but it was in our faces and very uncomfortable. After leaving Joseph City we turned to the west, making our way over and through the foot hills at the edge of the mountains, following the windings of the Sevier river.

At one o'clock we arrived after four hours' driving, at the entrance of the mountain pass called Clear Creek cañon. Here we found a camp of teamsters and a fire, and we stopped to rest and feed the horses and to lunch. While thus occupied the sun disappeared behind a gray bank of clouds that loomed over the mountains. Very soon came some premonitory drops, and before we could get on the wagon cover and attach the horses, we were overtaken by a heavy rain. There was no shelter and no course before us but to proceed and face the storm, which now descended the sides of the opposite mountain in driving sheets of sleet.

The mountains were very high and the passage narrow, allowing room for only the creek and the road ; and as we slowly ascended, winding about, the wind fiercely facing us at every turn, the rain changed to snow, and we soon found ourselves in a whirling tempest of rain, sleet, snow, hail, and wind, while the howling, near and distinct, of some wolves on the mountain gave us an intimation of our probable fate, should any disaster befall the horses or vehicle.

Still we plodded on, urging our horses to their best ; the scenery, at all times grand, magnificent, sublime, under such circumstances became really terrible. Sometimes we were covered with snow, then the sleet would come, and it would change to ice, and my wraps were frozen stiff about me ; the rain and the snow dripped over me, and I was wet through. Your father galloped on to keep himself from freezing, as he had no shelter, even of a wagon cover. Unfortunately the Judge had omitted to bring strings for the cover, and it could not be secured at the sides ; the wind, coming in great gusts, would raise it, frozen and stiff as it was, and shake it until it seemed sometimes as if we should be carried off in the whirlwind.

Each turn made the scene more grand and more fearful. The famous gap in the mountains, where they rise in great palisades of rock on each side, is a perfect wonder of nature, and the entire pass, twenty miles in length, in sunshiny weather must be of surpassing beauty ; but as we were exposed to the tempest, the moments seemed hours, and the hours were long.

At every turn we made, new mountains seemed to block our path, and when we vainly hoped the summit had been reached, the little brook would come gurgling down as if to mock our anxious hearts.

It was twenty minutes to five o'clock when we really reached the summit. The storm had then abated a little, but the daylight was almost gone, and we had long and steep descents of nearly six miles before we could reach the valley and the shelter of Cove Fort. Judge Morrison did not know the road, and it soon became so dark that we were obliged to trust to the horses. Your father took the lead, and we followed in the wagon. It was ten hours since we started from Richfield, and for five of the ten I had been exposed to the driving storm ; and now again there gathered and broke over us a tempest of wind, hail, and rain, and I was quite broken down and in despair. I thought we must surely perish in the darkness, when a shout from your father and a stream of light from an open door proved to us that we had at last found a refuge in Cove Fort."

I doubt not that the writer for the occasion, in depicting the adventure happily ending at Cove Fort, has convinced those of her sex who may propose to follow her through Utah, that there are some inconveniences and possible dangers in the way.

There are truly many annoyances and some perils quite unavoidable on a journey like this, but these as well as the enjoyable incidents work up admirably into winter drawing-room tales. In this case, leaving out of the account the feminine trials, which must draw sympathy from feminine hearts, there was not a little in the passage through the cañon in the wild storm and the darkness of the night that made the danger far from imaginary.

With an inexperienced guide, a pair of broken-down horses, a treacherous road covered with snow, alternate gusts of snow hail, and rain, the freezing of garments until they became stiff as boards, no habitation within many miles—these were circumstances in which no lady would care to be placed for the purpose of enjoying scenery.

For my own part, as I ranged along ahead on horseback, hoping to discover some place where we might find shelter, the pelting hail blinding my eyes, I had little leisure, inclination, or opportunity to gaze about at the wonders of this grand defile. In one instance only, and that lasting but a moment, as I rode upon the narrow track by the side of the torrent, where the chasm at most was fifty feet wide, did the storm relent, so that I could look aloft two thousand feet, where the overhanging cliffs came so closely together that the leaden sky made but a thin strip overhead.

Fort Cove was built by the Mormons twelve years ago, for a place of refuge, when the Indians were committing their depredations. Now it was a welcome refuge for us. A family is maintained here for the purpose of affording entertainment to travellers, many of whom pass this way on their road to the south and to Nevada. We paid little attention to its massive walls and battlements when we arrived, but the blaze sent out by the cheerful fire upon our dark surroundings, as the door was thrown open, warmed our hearts with gratitude to those who had provided this asylum.

The idea of building the fort and afterward devoting it to its present purpose originated with Brigham Young. As we took possession of the room he had vacated in the morning, we prayed the good Lord to forgive him his sins and to put this good work to his credit in account.

In the morning we took a survey of the fortress. It stands at the outlet of the Sevier pass, through which we travelled the previous night. There is a lofty background of mountains in the east, an extinct volcano on the south; on the north and the west are spread out the extensive plains of Dog valley, the Beaver range looming up twenty-five miles beyond. The walls of the fort are of solid limestone, eighteen feet high and one hundred feet each side of its square. It is not intended for a defence against artillery, but opposed to a moderate cannonading, it would stand for a long time.

The Indian outbreaks which have three times within the last twelve years partially desolated the neighboring settlements, may possibly recur, and Fort Cove revert to its original use. The ferocity of the untamable Indian nature is liable to crop out at any moment. Should one of them be killed in a quarrel, or even accidentally, a general raid on the peaceful farmers will be likely to ensue, and murder, rape, and arson will follow in its train. It is well that this place of refuge remains, to which men, women, and children may flee from the wrath to come.

Here the Mormons have tried to domesticate a few of the Utes. Last year they began the experiment mildly by breaking up the land and planting wheat for them, only requiring the lazy aborigines to take off their own crops. Unfortunately an early frost killed the wheat. The Indians attributed this to the Divine displeasure at their abandonment of their primitive habits, and consequently very few of the half-tamed creatures will be induced to try it again.

Angutseeds—Red Ant—is the chief of this tribe of Utes. He is a friend of the whites, and possesses considerable influence not only over his immediate dependents, but with the other tribes in southern Utah.

This instance will show how a great war may arise from a trifling provocation. Fourteen or fifteen years ago a chief, the notorious Black Hawk, went to a person at St. Peter's, with whom some flour had been left for him by the Indian agent. The man was drunk, and whipped Black Hawk. The chief took revenge by murdering a herdsman. The herdsman's friends killed another Indian, and these murders originated a war which lasted three years and cost $1,500,000 and numerous lives.

Red Ant did all in his power to restrain the others, but was in this case unsuccessful. In several instances he has prevented quarrels which might have had equally fatal results. Tamaritz—White Horse chief, who sometimes calls himself Chenowicket—"saved by Almighty power"—is another celebrity among the Utes, with whom the settlers are now on friendly terms.

"Ah," said the bishop, who gave us many Indian incidents, "we have had a hard time in keeping peace as well as in fighting these Lamanites, but our greatest enemies have been the white men, for they have always been the aggressors. We ask no aid from the Government, only this—let it keep its agents away."

Formerly the Moquis tribe was powerful in these regions. They had a civilization of their own, living partly in towns. At Richfield some ruins of their dwellings were pointed out, and we picked up some specimens of their crockery which proved that they were advanced in manufacturing skill far beyond the Indians of the present day. Two or three hundred years ago, after many bloody battles, they were finally driven beyond the Colorado, by the victorious Utes.

The Navajos still remaining in Utah, like all the other tribes nomadic in their habits, are wonderfully proficient in weaving cloth. We purchased some of their blankets, beautifully woven in variegated colors, and perfectly impervious to water. The mills of Manchester or Lowell have never produced anything of the kind that can equal them.

Beaver lies twenty-five miles south of Cove Fort. We intended to continue our tour to that town, having travelled already two hundred and forty miles in a southerly direction from Salt Lake, but the shocking condition of the roads, and the prospects of more inclement weather, were considerations inducing us to return from this point.

The homeward route led us over an entirely different ground. We now returned by way of the valleys on the west of the ranges, which had been upon our right.

Twenty-five miles from Cove Fort are the two adjoining nominally Indian settlements of Corn Creek and Kanosh. In the former we made a short stay for dinner. Kanosh is supposed to be the dwelling place of the chief of that name. Here he owns an adobe hut where he keeps a squaw, while he ranges the mountains and valleys in an independent way, on his own account.

Kanosh is a devout Mormon. He preaches to his tribe "to love God, and not to drink whiskey, or tea and coffee; to love God because he is good, to hate whiskey because it is bad, and to abstain from tea and coffee because they are dear." Not a bad Indian that, General Sheridan, after all!

Fillmore, once the seat of the territorial government is a pretty village of two thousand inhabitants. The town and the county of Millard, of which it is the capital, were both named in honor of the President, who was in office at the time of their settlement. Fillmore is about forty miles north of Cove Fort. The road approaching it from the south is dreary, and possesses no attractions beyond those of the sublime mountains that ever wall the sides of our way. An old volcano looms up in the west, which has been an active operator in its day. Immense blocks of lava are strewn for many miles over the plain, and from the mountain side there runs far to the north a black wall once a stream of fire.

There is a good hotel at Fillmore, its chief attraction. Refreshed by its excellent larder, we pursued our way the next morning, making a short day's journey of twenty-eight miles, to Scipio. This is a wretched little hamlet, looking more wretched still after passing through Holden, an American settlement, where the houses are all of frame or brick, and the appearance of the people emphatically what is called " well-to-do."

Scipio, if he is an uneasy spirit, wandering about in the hope that some polygamist will provide him with a "tabernacle," must wonder why his name was disgraced by attaching it to this little collection of Danish hovels. It is better to be a spirit of the air than to live in any tabernacle here.

The situation is as charming as can be imagined. In the centre of a green meadow, aptly called Round valley, it is closely circled by a range of high mountains, a tiara of snow now crowning their summits. We were almost inclined to camp in the streets of the village, but the uncertainty of the weather obliged us to seek lodgings under some roof.

The bishop was not at home, and the bishopess (if we may coin a new name) No. 1 was not able to accommodate us, as she had a large family of children requiring all her room. She said that she knew of no other place where we could find shelter. Here was an illustration of polygamous jealousy, for we afterward discovered that bishopess No. 2 had one of the best houses in the village, small, it is true, but tolerably comfortable.

This more amiable young woman gave us a room, and with her sister joined us in a game of cards. Occasionally the poor little bishopess would start at any noise from the outside, with evident fear that the virago was coming in upon us. It is not unlikely that when their joint head came home she was made to suffer for hospitality to unbelieving Gentiles.

On the following day we went on through Juab valley, stopping at a small village called Chicken Creek. Here a young gentleman, who was tending sheep, informed us that he came from "Ioway" two years ago. "Father," he said, "told us all along the road that we was coming to Zion. Well, this is the cussedest old Zion I ever want to see. I'd rather have a foot of ground in Ioway, than all these here mountings of the Lord, and I guess the Lord would too if he had ever seen Ioway!" After riding forty miles from Scipio, we reached Nephi in the evening.

In the morning we turned from the main road with the purpose of visiting the Tintec valley and mining camps. There is scarcely a mountain in Utah where silver may not be found. There are mines of low grade ore in the immediate vicinity of Nephi on Mt. Nebo. These will not yield any profit until fuel becomes cheaper, but at some future day their value will be assured. The Tintec mines being of a higher grade, and mostly producing milling ore, are not so dependent upon the cost of coal and coke.

We had been rather unfortunate in being misguided on more than one occasion. This time a young man was also going on horseback to Tintec. He knew the trail perfectly. He had driven cattle across frequently. It was eighteen miles to the Miller and Shoebridge mills. He knew it. No, he did not.

We started under favorable circumstances, for it was a glorious day. Crossing the divide, we looked back through the narrow vista formed by the precipitous cliffs, upon the lofty summit of Mt. Nebo, and then descended into a valley, between which and Tintec there is an intermediate range. Had the intelligence of our guide equalled his professions, we might have crossed the narrow plain of separation and entered a romantic cañon that would have speedily led us through into the valley beyond. But he chose to follow a wagon track, the course leading far to the south in order to cross the spur of the mountains. We travelled on over a broad expanse for hours, until this point was reached. Then rounding it, we made our way again to the north.

"I guess we'll get out of this now and take a short cut across the sage-brush," said Mr. Daniels. Short cut! We wandered on till the sun, having long ago passed his meridian, descended over the western peaks and left us in approaching darkness on a desert waste, where there was no water for ourselves or for our animals, no sign of a habitation, and no hope of any other covering at night than could be found under the threatening clouds.

Our intelligent leader had lost his way. He was evidently uncertain if Tintec was in this valley or the valley beyond. We shot a jack rabbit, and proposed soon to camp and to make our supper of this providential supply. Just as we were about to resort to that necessity we fortunately struck the wagon road again. Encouraged with new hope, we pushed our thirsty animals along, and were soon overjoyed at beholding the smoke from the chimneys of the Miller and the Shoebridge mills. Arriving there after this tedious journey of thirty-five miles, we were welcomed, without letters of introduction, by Superintendent Lusk and Secretary Berkley of the latter establishment.

Captain Lusk is an old sailor, and I felt immediately at home with one of my own profession, from which no one has ever withheld the credit of generous hospitality. We shall always cherish with gratitude the kindness with which he attended to our necessities, providing us with a substantial supper, feeding our horses, and then, as his accommodations were limited, though freely at our disposal, in consideration of my wife's fatigue from her long ride of thirty-five miles, sending her in his buggy six miles further, to Diamond City.

Diamond City, a *lucus a non lucendo*, as it appeared to us when coming out from the hotel of Mrs. Jones in the morning, is the chief mining camp of Tintec. There are others, Silver City and Eureka, rivalling Diamond City in splendor and architectural magnificence. They are alike in the style of their bar-rooms and in the quality of their "tanglefoot." They all do a good business, and yet they are the most quiet mining camps we have seen.

Perhaps the hard journey of the previous day gave us sounder sleep than we usually enjoyed, but certainly we were not disturbed by conventional noises in the streets, nor by the shrill music and the loud stamping of the dance-houses. It was several days since a murder had been committed.

It is asserted that the ore of these mines averages in value $75 per ton at the dump. If ten dollars be assumed as the cost of getting it out and hauling it to mill, where it is converted into bullion at twenty-five more, there is a profit of forty dollars on every ton.

But let not the reader be so sanguine as to come immediately to Tintec for the purpose of making his fortune. There are heavy expenses in continual development, great cost of shafts, tunnels, and timbering. Sometimes there is a "pinch," and the vein for many days, perhaps weeks, is nearly lost; and then there are many other contingencies, expected and unexpected, that should enter into the calculations. The forty dollars suffer many subtractions.

Division is the safest mode of arithmetic in mining calculation. You are shown a mine that will, beyond all doubt, allowing for every thing, give you forty per cent. annually on your investment. Divide this by two. Result, twenty per cent. To be a little more sure, divide it again. Result, ten per cent. Keep on with your division for still greater security—for there is nothing like being perfectly safe—until you get down to zero. Then, for fear of any possibility that you may be brought into debt by assessments, inform the gentleman who is urging you to purchase, that you have concluded not to accept his offer. That is the only perfectly safe way of dealing in mines.

At Diamond City we met a gentleman from New York, advanced in years. His whole soul appeared to be centred in mines. Here he stays through the heats of summer and the frosts of winter, daily superintending his workmen, careless of the comforts of life that he might enjoy at home, finding more pleasure in roughing it in this little mining camp, than he could realize surrounded by luxury and educated friends.

With him I visited the Mayflower and Gold Hill mines, which certainly were rich in the quality and abundance of their ore. The ride to them for three miles over a bridle path cut into the almost perpendicular mountain cliffs, affords an extensive view of the Tintec ranges and valleys, embracing the whole of this rich district. The air, keen and invigorating, was as delicious to me as the contemplation of prospective wealth to my companion. I left him burrowing in his mining den, and descending to the village we resumed our journey.

Mounting our horses at noon, we kept on the ascent for four miles until reaching the divide, about seven thousand feet above the sea level, constantly looking back upon the great picture of heights and depths in the south and west. But when the highest ridge was reached, beyond which we had as yet only seen the blue ocean of sky, there was presented to our admiring gaze one of the greatest paintings ever touched by the incomparable hand of nature. A long slope of two thousand feet terminated at the western shores of Utah Lake, on which the coloring from the heavens had descended. The plains beyond it were not perceptible, for the snowy Wasatch mountains seemed to have drawn themselves down to its eastern edge. They were fifty miles away, but the atmosphere had so closed the far and near together that if some great artist had stood beside us, he would have found the splendid immensity, as it were by transposing the lens of a camera, brought down to a size that he could readily transfer to his canvas.

We had progressed but a mile or two on our descent, when ominous clouds began to gather on the mountain tops. Slowly they crept down upon the plain, circling round to our side of the valley, and drawing their dark curtains over the bright scene that we had but just contemplated with such infinite delight. Then came rain and hail on the wings of the howling wind.

"The sky was changed, and such a change!"—a change we might well compare with that witnessed by the great poet when he saw the placid Leman made angry by the tempest that swept from Jura to the joyous Alps, as they talked aloud in their shroud of mist. But he saw all that from the windows of his hotel. Our experience was from the saddles on our horses.

We galloped rapidly on until the plain was reached. Thence, passing through the wretched little town of Goshen, we waded for a few miles through mud and darkness, the storm still raging, till we arrived at the inn where we had once before been so agreeably entertained. Welcome again a good coal fire, and welcome the smiling face of little Mrs. Macbeth!

On the following day we arrived at Provo, having been absent three weeks. Here we returned our horses, and proceeded by rail to Salt Lake. We had leisurely traversed a distance of four hundred miles, having passed over but eighteen miles of the road for the second time.

CHAPTER XXIX.

IDAHO—SODA SPRINGS—NATURAL CURIOSITIES—THE UTAH
AND NORTHERN RAILROAD—A JUMPING TOWN—THE BAN-
NOCK INDIANS—POLICY OF THE GOVERNMENT.

After visiting the renowned watering-places of Germany, France and America, we are contented of late to come year after year to this remote corner of Idaho, satisfied that at last we have discovered the true fountains of health in an atmosphere of purity beyond comparison.

This is Soda Springs—not Saratoga with its magnificent hotels, balls, regattas, and races, not Carlsbad, Baden-Baden, Kissingen or Vichy, with their *dolce far niente* under shady trees and in cur-gartens, where soft strains of music usher in the day and lull one to sleep at night, the only variations, the casinos and booths where curiosities and coffee are sold by pretty *madchens;* where all that is desired and dispensed is the luxury of pleasurable laziness. Soda Springs is the reverse of all this : a little hamlet of a dozen log huts far away from the world of society and business, ensconced in a lovely valley seven thousand feet above the level of the sea, with ranges of mountains two thousand feet higher on every side; the rapid Bear River, rushing through its green meadows, where herds of cattle, the only property of its people, find choice pasturage; where the warm sun comes down by day, and the cool breezes sweep over at night—this is our summering place.

True, we have none of the allurements of the great spas, but we have what is far better, nature in her wild majesty, an elastic, stimulating air, curiosities of volcanic formation, and what is the chief attraction to invalids, an endless abundance and variety of mineral springs.

They gush out of the ground, warm and cold, in all directions, and need no tubing to increase their volume, but boil and sparkle in their great pools like reservoirs. The favorite springs are chiefly magnesia, soda and iron, highly charged with carbonic acid gas, so agreeably refreshing that it is fortunate there are no doctors to limit indulgence in their use. At the continental spas we did not object to short allowances of the nauseating water. Here we should rebel if not allowed to drink our fill of the reviving springs.

I would fain tell those suffering from maladies not absolutely incurable what certain relief may be found in these wonderful waters, and that long and tedious as the journey to reach them may be, it will amply repay their toil and expense by its lasting benefit.

The place itself is nothing as a town. It is merely a sort of Mormon outpost beyond the confines of Utah, with scarcely fifty inhabitants. At one time it was of some importance as a military station, and afterward derived a little business in supplying the mining camp of Cariboo, forty miles north of it. The removal of the post to Fort Hall, and the failure of the water at the mines, have nearly depopulated this once thriving village, and unless means are found to renew the working of the mines, this settlement must rest its future on its attractions as a health resort.

The springs are resorted to from the surrounding country. Men, women and children come in great Bain wagons, with sail-cloth awnings, turn their horses out to feed on the wide prairies, make their beds in, under and around their vehicles, gather cedar and sagebrush for their camp-fires, and are at home without further trouble. In this way they pass days and weeks, and are happier during their stay and more robust on their return than if they had indulged in the luxuries and dissipations of hotels, instead of gaining their own food by their guns and rods, and cooking it themselves. The free air of these mountains is sustenance beyond meat and drink, a consideration which few invalids regard. Most of them are rigidly exact in diet, while entirely indifferent how much poison they take in by their lungs.

There is not much to be said for hotel accommodation at the springs. Our little party took possession of a vacant log cabin, and extemporized chairs, table and bedsteads, the latter rather unusual luxuries insisted upon by the ladies. Our beds were made from fresh hay, and with the addition of a cooking stove, obtained from a neighbor, we were "fixed." Perfectly independent of butchers, bakers and grocers, our only outside wants were met by the little girl who brought us butter and eggs, and by the Indians, who occasionally "swapped" bear meat and venison. We provided ourselves abundantly with ducks, geese, prairie chickens and trout. Best gift of freedom, there was the absence of the Irish Biddy! As to our stable, the ponies we rode from the railway station were retained for daily service, and when not in use were turned loose to get a good living with the herd. As they were neither shod nor curried, we could dispense with farriers and grooms.

Time never hung heavily on our hands, although society, with the exception of our guests, was limited. We were amused without the luxuries of lectures, theatres or concerts, and on Sundays we always attended the little Mormon meeting, where gathered the settlers of the neighborhood.

People become liberal in a country where the very mountains and rocks teach them that every thing gives thanks unto the Lord who will not refuse the sincere offerings of any men that he has made. Even our Congregational parson realized this sentiment when he accepted an invitation to preach. He told the bishop that there was plenty of religion on which we could all agree. The latter replied, " Give us some of that, then. You can't use it all up on one Sunday."

Sometimes we "want a carriage." Then we hire a farm wagon and drive where there is a road ; where there is none, through the sagebrush, carrying our guns on the way to visit the Sulphur Lake, the Swan Lake, Formation Springs, the Devil's Icehouse, and other sights within the radius of a few miles.

Sulphur Lake is a sheet of water an acre in extent, many times stronger of mineral than the springs of Sharon and Richfield, and bubbling over its whole surface with escaping gas, whose noise is heard a mile away. Behind it is a mountain of sulphur. Its shore last year was a yellow sulphur beach, now black as charcoal. A few months before our visit, some curious persons, anxious to know what a literal lake of fire and brimstone was like, visited the place one dark evening. They dropped their matches on the beach, and in a moment found their most vivid anticipations realized. The lurid flames circled the mad, fuming waters, and threw their light on the crags, and thus these amateur artists painted a horrible picture, which absolutely scared them as they looked from fire to lake and from lake to mountains, and then at the unearthly faces of each other. The venturous souls carried away a most vivid realization of the awful significance of the Scripture allegory whose representation they had produced.

A few miles beyond is Swan Lake, a most pleasing contrast to this infernal pool. Lying on the top of a high hill, it occupies what must have been the crater of a volcano. Its waters are so exquisitely transparent that the bottom can be seen at the distance of sixty feet, but their alkaline action has coated the rocks and fallen trees with a white covering, and as one looks over its edge at any part of its circumference of three hundred yards, he sees that he stands on a crust; for the water, or its predecessor the fire, has eaten away the rock hundreds of feet under the shores. This is wonderful and grand ; but a prettier sight is the escape of the water as it seems loth to run down to the plains, but leaps in silver cascades from one moss-crowned basin to another in lovely embellishments, the sight of which would reward a landscape gardener for his journey.

The Formation Springs are courses of water constantly changing their currents, leaving deposits, petrifying trees and bushes, and creating substances like the brittle coral of the sea. They have hollowed out large caves, frescoing their walls with festoons of white drapery, and then, finding a subterranean outlet, have disappeared beneath the surface, how deep no one can tell, until three miles below the darkened stream rushes up again to the light of day, and runs sparkling to the river.

Down the valley in another direction is the old volcano. It is more easily climbed than Vesuvius, and its ashes have been blown away or have consolidated themselves during the ages since the crater emitted its fires, but far around lie the huge blocks of lava, and the earth is ploughed into gigantic furrows of stone.

What we have named "the Devil's Icehouse," was but lately discovered. Some young men on a hunting excursion found a deep cave where snow and ice could be seen at the bottom. We went up to visit the place, and our party was the first to explore it. There we found hundreds of tons of pure ice, from which we brought home a supply. It is a permanent icehouse, not affected by the upper air, which marked eighty-five degrees, while in the cavern the glass stood at twenty-nine.

Compare such wonders as these with the sights and curiosities of a German spa! I do not mean to be enthusiastic, but take all the famous watering-places of Europe, with the little that nature and the much that art has done for them—combine them all, and you will find that this wild sanitarium of the Idaho Mountains will send you back to your home with better health and more interesting recollections when your summer is ended.

The most convenient way to reach Soda Springs from the East is by the Union Pacific to its terminus at Ogden, where the "Utah and Northern" narrow gauge railroad branches north to Montana, at the same point whence the Utah Central runs in an opposite direction to Salt Lake City.

This Utah and Northern Railroad, commenced by a company whose capital soon became exhausted, was seized by those terrible monopolists, Sidney Dillon and Jay Gould, and by them started into new life and a prospective career of prosperity. In the estimation of Mr. Kearney this was probably unjustifiable. The enterprise should have remained passive until labor could have completed it without the aid of money. The new company has made it an important auxiliary to the Union Pacific line, to which it will largely contribute from the traffic with Idaho and Montana.

Indeed the unexpected success of the main trunk road from

the Eastern States to the Pacific is attributable to such enterprises as these. It is no more than justice to the present managers to say that by their energy and capital they have brought it to a position not attainable by any other means. The road would have been bankrupt long ago but for the business they have made along its line, in the lateral branches, which, unlike the branches of a tree, bring nourishment to it instead of taking it away.

The Utah and Northern line was already in operation one hundred and twenty-seven miles in a north-west direction from Ogden to its temporary terminus at Oneida. That is the nearest point from which Soda Springs may be reached over a wagon road of thirty-two miles. It is possible, if the recent gold discoveries at Cariboo are as productive as is anticipated, that at an early period a branch may be built from Oneida. This, moreover, would be the easiest way of reaching the Yellowstone Park.

At present that magnificent national domain is almost inaccessible. I am no advocate of subsidies for the benefit of individuals or corporations, but in this instance it may be suggested that a vast pleasure-ground like the Yellowstone is of little use to the people unless the donor adds to the gift the opportunity of approaching it. The Utah and Northern Railroad takes us to Oneida in the direction of the Park, and then goes about its business to the North-west. The settlers of Idaho and Montana hail with joy every rail that is laid down for their benefit. They have been too long condemned to journeys of from three to five hundred miles in stage-coaches, and to the payment of enormous and slow wagon freights, not to realize the benefit conferred upon them. Already the track is advanced forty miles beyond Oneida through the Bannock Reservation, and soon the new terminus will be beyond it.

Oneida is an itinerant town. It journeys onward as the road progresses. Hotels, houses, stores, saloons, stables and all other buildings are put up in sections marked and numbered. When the active Superintendent Mr. Dunn gives the order, the whole town is taken to pieces in two days, packed on the train, and with all its inhabitants moved to the next stopping place.

New streets are then laid out, and a new city, formed of the old materials, springs into life, flourishing until fifty miles more of railroad is completed. Then it moves again. Thus it will continue to move till the travelling municipality is mergéd in the permanent city of Virginia or Helena, at whichever of them the road may terminate.

Oneida seemed to us full of life and vigor. As we came out from our tent-covered hotel in the morning, horses, wagons and teamsters were camped far and near. The men were turning out, rubbing their eyes, accounting for the infernal racket of music and dancing we had heard in the night, when saloons and faro tables were doing a profitable business.

The train had come in loaded with freight of all kinds of merchandise and agricultural tools. Twenty-six wagons with their four-horse teams were drawn up at the station waiting to reload and begin their long journey of three hundred miles, and the coaches were off already with their passengers. Their owners and drivers will doubtless regret every shortening of fifty miles, but the owners of the goods and the tired travellers will rejoice. Many more wagons with their downward freights of bullion, and ores of silver, copper and lead, were discharging their loads, and our hotel was filled with jaded, dusty passengers, who congratulated themselves on the comfort in store for them in the easy motion and rapid transit of a railroad car. Each of the coaches that had arrived carried three of Wells, Fargo & Co.'s messengers, with double-barrelled guns, loaded with buckshot, and they were preceded by forerunners on horseback armed in the same way. This is the habitual style of travelling in these territories, and do you wonder if the new style is a welcome improvement?

When I had occasion to visit Oneida three weeks afterwards, it had taken a short jump of twenty-two miles. Its last situation was on the eastern border of the Bannock Reservation, and it was intended by the railroad company that it should make a flying leap across the forbidden ground to the banks of the Snake River. But as this was not practicable before the winter might set in, a compromise was made with the Indian Agency, whereby no liquor was to be sold, and so the town was permitted to make a temporary stand on this nominal ground of the Redskins. Of course, there were no "saloons," for what is a saloon without whiskey, and what is a railroad town or any other town in this western country without both?

All the noise, bustle, snap crack and devil-may-care exhilaration that pervaded Oneida by night and day were consequently wanting in this new settlement of Black Rock. The coaches and wagons were drawn up at the station to receive their passengers and freight. They earned their money, but it seemed to afford no pleasure, for they came and went like funeral processions, mourning because whiskey was not. Nevertheless, I apprehend that the real business of the country did not suffer by the deprivation. Every mile gained in the direction of Montana is a step leading to the comfort of individuals and the prosperity of the nation.

The extension through Marsh valley winds along on a level surface smoothed out by nature among great bowlders of lava, which, if continuous, would have defied engineering science, giant powder and money. Before we came to this slightly downward slope we ascended the grade until we passed through a narrow gate-way, whose buttresses of encircling mountains stand perpendicular but a few feet from either side of the track.

In remote ages this must have been the northern boundary of the Great Salt Lake, which has now receded more than a hundred miles south. Precisely in this gate-way the water-springs now divide, part of them trickling down to Snake River, and thence through the Columbia to the Pacific in the channel forced by the disruption, and the others seeking the level of Salt Lake.

The "bench marks" easily traced through all the valleys to Southern Utah showing the former flow of the water, begin at these enormous gate-posts, and keep their exact line of altitude for four hundred miles. Repeatedly in journeying across the country we traced these indications, and it is absolutely demonstrable that what is now called the Great Salt Lake, was once an inland sea not less than four hundred miles from north to south, and two hundred from east to west, more than twice the size of Lake Superior. The long chain of the Wasatch Mountains was its eastern barrier, while it spread itself over a great part of Utah and Nevada in the west, and of Idaho at the north. Its recession has left bare the Cache and Salt Lake valley and their connections, as well as what is called the Great American Desert, through which the Central Pacific road is built.

Probably there is no area on the continent more barren in its natural state than this old lake bottom, and none that has been made so productive by irrigation. The Utah and Northern, the Utah Central, and the Utah Southern Railroads traverse it lengthwise, and their branches spread across it, so that if, as some persons think possible from a recent rise of the lake, this whole ground should be again submerged for a few centuries and then become dry, the people of a future age may wonder who dropped this big gridiron in the basin.

Yet our eastern friends seem to know as little about these great railroad enterprises of the West as may come to the knowledge of our imaginary descendants. Their stock and bonds are not for sale in the gambling market, but are owned chiefly by the Mormons, who manage their property economically and profitably to themselves, in opening up this great agricultural and mining country.

A few miles beyond the little station of Black Rock, the Marsh Valley opens upon the rich and extensive plains of Snake River. Here is an unlimited range of pasturage, and for a hundred miles the road will run through what is to some extent a farming land of the Indians. When it is stolen from them after its value is ascertained, it will speedily be peopled by settlers. Almost on the line too are the new gold mines of Lost River, to which a large emigration is predicted.

The especial object of my visit to Black Rock was to find Mr. Danilson, the Indian agent. While at Soda Springs, we had seen many of the Indians who are scattered in the summer season through the region bordering on their reservation, to which they generally return in the winter to live upon the crumbs from the government table.

Now, it is a fact, attribute it to what cause we may, that there is not the slightest danger to life or property from Indians in Mormon settlements. Gentiles say that this safety arises from the joint hatred of Mormons and Indians to the government. Mormons say—and I believe them, for I am a witness of its truth—that it is because their people never cheat the Indians and never refuse them food. At any rate, I felt perfectly safe, even when mounted on a good horse and with a good gun—most desirable of all property—among the many Indians we met miles away from the village. These Bannocks, whose tribe was on the war-path at the north, never molested us. They came to our door with game, fish and skins, for which we "swapped" with them, if we had occasion for such things. If not, we gave them bread, meat and coffee. We never locked our doors against Indians, but we slept at night with loaded guns by our bedsides, in anticipation of possible visits from white "road agents."

From the Bannocks who could speak English we heard the same universal tale of woe. How I wish that one eloquent old man whom we heard could have some useless politician's half hour on the floor of Congress! He did not talk from a rostrum or a pulpit in fine periods of rhetoric, but mounted on a sorry pony, whose drooping head seemed to be bowed down in sympathy with his master's grief, he told of the wrongs of his people.

"Indian kill 'em two white men 'cause white men steal 'em squaw. Spose Indian steal white man squaw? White man no kill Indian? So white man clean 'em out all Indian! steal 'em land, steal 'em squaw, steal 'em horse, cheat 'em Indian, starve 'em Indian, kill 'em Indian! All right; Indian die!" And suiting the action to the word the old man rolled off upon the ground, folded his arms across his breast in imitation of death as he added, "Heap happy now!"

The Bannocks were loud in their complaints against the Indian agent, and many of the settlers seemed to think they had cause. They said that in winter they had scanty food on the reservation, and in summer were driven off to get their own subsistence without powder or shot. It was intimated that the agent drew their rations in the mean time for his own profit. When I came to call upon Mr. Danilson I frankly told him what was said of him by the Indians and by the settlers.

"It is not the first time that I have heard these stories," said he, "and I am sorry to say that there is some truth in them, only they unfortunately accuse the wrong party. It is Congress that is to blame for making insufficient appropriations."

In a long conversation with Mr. Danilson, some curious developments came out touching the philanthropic policy of the government, which acts like a mother-in-law in her attempt to make people happy in her own way. The religious welfare of the Indians is impartially cared for by allotting the reservations among the different sects.

The Shoshones and Bannocks, of whom there are one thousand of the former, and six hundred of the latter, are turned over to the Methodists, the agent forcibly remarking that he "would be d——d if anybody but a Methodist should preach to them, for it was the order." At the same time he observed that an Indian had no idea of religion, anyway, and government didn't do this with the expectation of converting them, it was only to keep the churches from quarrelling.

In a temporal way it desires to civilize the wild Bannock, and the ingenious plan it adopts to make him a farmer, is this: when the spring opens, every Indian who will work on the land has his rations continued—that is, the ratio of the rations that the agent has been able to serve out. Then, those Indians who do not choose to be farmers, are turned loose to hunt upon the reservation, whence all the game has been killed off by the emigrant and cattle trains, or to search for it where they can. And this hunting is to be done without powder or shot! To sell ammunition to them is a penal offense. This is simply turning them over to the charity of the settlers, who are themselves poor, but who are prompted by policy, as well as humanity, to see that they do not suffer for want of food.

POLICY OF THE GOVERNMENT.

"In fact," said Mr. Danilson, "the amount of rations allowed by government is so miserably small, that most of the Indians must be driven off for the greater part of the year, or all of them would starve. If I divided equally what I have, it would not amount in value to five cents per head daily." By dint of teaching Indians in this novel way to become farmers, one hundred and twenty-five families have been forced to cultivate some of the bottom lands on the Snake River ; but from all accounts the product of their farms does not exceed the government stipend of five cents per day to each individual working upon them.

Upon asking Mr. Danilson what he thought of the proposition to turn the management of the Indians over to the army, he replied that while the Indian agents were the best civilizers, the officers of the army could undoubtedly maintain better order, and might entirely prevent war and raiding, if they were allowed to feed and clothe the Indians comfortably, but that neither civilian nor soldier could keep them quiet in any other way.

I am more than ever convinced by this interview that the civilization and conversion of savages is of small account, even if practicable, in comparison with full stomachs for them, and the safety to white men that would result from placing all these tribes under the absolute control of the army, which should be sustained in its duties by sufficient appropriations.

CHAPTER XXX.

TRAVELS AMONG THE MORMONS—THE PROLIFIC PATRIARCH—
THE LEGEND OF BEAR LAKE—BROTHER COOK AND HIS
FAMILY—VICARIOUS BAPTISM—A MORMON COURT—A PROS-
PEROUS CONVERT—BLACKSMITH'S FORK CAÑON—RETURN TO
THE LINE OF THE UNION PACIFIC.

Our equipage was what my facetious friend "Sunset" Cox once called a similar outfit—"a horse and a half." The half in this instance was the best part of the whole, for the patient mule was more enduring, whereas the horse advanced, as the Dutchman expressed it, "mit a yerk." Stopping was his favorite gait, which whip and spurs induced him to change occasionally. Both animals delighted in straying. Even when hoppled at night they strayed miles away, and all the walking I required was obtained in hunting them up in the morning. But they were of great service for daily use at Soda Springs, or rather they were indispensable luxuries.

Taking a farewell glass at Nature's great soda fountain, the animals were packed for the journey with valise, saddlebags, fishing rods and gun, and about noon we mounted them and took our way south-easterly, for the Bear Lake region.

We followed the banks of the Bear River for eight miles, to

the most practicable ford, and wading its rapid current, crossed a divide which brought us into the Nounan Valley, a grassy meadow where the cattle and sheep of Bishop Merrill were grazing. After travelling nineteen miles, we arrived at the Episcopal mansion, a log house of one story, but a home where we were kindly entertained by the hospitable prelate and his wives. Some twenty children were running about the premises, and several of them dined with us. A leg of good mutton was upon the table, but the fresh butter and rich cream were the chief attractions.

Again mounting our animals we left this quiet little valley. Still following up the Bear River, and leaving on our left the towns of Bennington and Montpelier—names that reminded us of those Green Mountains nearer home—and travelling twenty miles further we came in sight of Paris at sunset. No Arc de Triomphe shone in the distance, no Dome des Invalides or Column of Vendôme, nor did we approach the city through inviting suburbs. Descending into a valley just covered by the dark shadow of the western mountains, and extending over it to the foot of the still sunny range of hills at the east, there lay before us a Mormon village of less than a thousand inhabitants, scarcely one of whom was to be seen. We reached the house of Mr. Rich, who had kindly offered us his hospitalities while at Soda Springs.

" Is your father at home ? " I asked of a youngster who proved to be a brother of our friend.

" Yes, sir, I guess so," he replied. " He must be in one of his houses."

" But isn't this his house ? "

" Oh ! no ; this is my brother Joe's, who is expecting you. Father's got five houses, because he's got five wives."

"And how many brothers and sisters have you?"

"Well, I had about sixty once, but there ain't more'n forty of us alive now."

Mr. Joseph Rich gave us a cordial welcome, and in the evening we were introduced to the patriarch, a hearty-looking man of sixty-five, who from his jollity one would have supposed a bachelor, rather than a five-fold husband. He is a high dignitary, the president of this district, having the supervision of all the bishops of the neighborhood. He "gives counsel." This means that if his advice is followed in secular affairs, persons to whom it is given are absolved from responsibility in their dealings with their neighbors.

Having obeyed the divine command to increase and multiply to such an extent, an extra degree of holiness is attached to him, and he seems very fond of his superiority in this respect. Lately there was a gathering of the Rich family at Cape Cod, where it is supposed to have originated. Our venerable friend was present as a full representative, and on that occasion he astonished his relatives by the time he occupied in reciting the names of his children. Cape Cod and all "down east" were forced to yield the palm of productiveness to the representative from Idaho.

In the evening he talked very freely about family matters, in which he took a numerical rather than an ancestral pride. We were surrounded by a dozen or two of his children of all ages, from babyhood to manhood. One of them, a sprightly young woman, the mother of children older than some of her brothers and sisters, told us that she had failed in the task of counting her relations.

"Say, father," she asked, "isn't Eliza the oldest of 'em all?"

"Well," answered the prolific parent, "I believe she does come somewhere among the first."

"Now look here, old man," she exclaimed, "this kind o' thing has been well enough for you, but I don't mean my husband shall be bothered as you are in taking count. He shan't have nobody's young ones to count over but just mine. Let me catch him gettin' sealed in this world; he may get sealed for eternity as much as he likes, but nary a seal shall he have down here—not if I know it!"

In saying this she gave expression to the almost universal sentiment of the younger Mormons of both sexes. It is now useless for the church to preach polygamy, holding up Abraham, Isaac, Jacob, David and Solomon as examples. A woman of the present day is contented with no fraction of a man, be he prophet, priest, or king. She wants an individual whole.

There was the usual morning exercise in hunting for the horse and mule. Both had been hoppled, but the former was attracted by a passing drove, and was found consorting with them three miles out upon the plains; and the latter, who with his legs tied could jump a four rail fence as easily as a convict can scale the walls of Sing Sing, was discovered helping himself to the oats of a neighboring farmer.

In the mean time, while a dozen boys were looking for them we were breakfasting with Bishop Budge. Our kind entertainer was a Scotchman, converted many years ago from Presbyterianism, as he said, to "a saving knowledge of the truth." His notion of the truth has gradually been enlarged until he reached his present dignity, and lest there should be any mistake in his obeying the Scriptural command, that a person of his order shall be "the husband of one wife," he has provided himself with a relay of two more, so that in the case of the death of No. 1, he may not be disobedient for a moment.

"Ah, well," said he, "they think ill of me at home for changing my religion ; but there was my brother Aleck who took it most to heart. He was on his way last year to California, and turned off the road a bit to see me, and to try to bring me back into the fold. When he got here he spent the whole evening in lecturing me, and then went to bed. In the morning I gave him the best breakfast the country would afford—coffee and rolls, trout, beef and venison steak, and such like. Poor Aleck! he looked all over the table, and then turned upon me his sorrowful face, blurting out, 'Oh, Jamie, mon! Jamie, mon! did I ever think it would come to this. I could hae forgi'en ye a' yer poleegamy, *but hae ye gien up yer parritch?*'"

As the dwellings occupied by No. 1 and No. 2 were undergoing repairs, we were welcomed in his smallest house by No. 3, a young Danish woman, of neat appearance and pleasing address, who informed us that she accepted her present situation when she was only fifteen years old. When a No. 1 is married, she generally speaks of herself as a married woman. Later wives, although pretending to be married, speak of their change of state as the time when they "went into polygamy."

We had an excellent breakfast, and Brother Budge gave us a very flattering account of the spiritual and temporal condition of his flock.

"Paris," he said, "is the principal town of that part of Oneida county called the Bear Lake district, which as you go south you will find to be the most fertile of any part of Idaho that you have seen. We raise an abundance of wheat, oats, vegetables of all kinds, and the small fruits. Our people are industrious and thriving. They have a rich soil, a great deal of which requires no irrigation, and produces freely forty or fifty bushels to the acre. The climate is healthy, and the scenery of the lake and the mountain cañons is unsurpassed for beauty and grandeur. The people are virtuous, as a class, and consequently happy."

What we saw afterwards, justified the truth of his encomium.

The large Mormon majority of this district is due to the fact that when it was settled, the territorial line of Utah was supposed to include it, but the new survey placed the inhabitants on the outside of that line, and as they had already brought the land under cultivation, and were unmolested by their fellow-citizens, with whom they are on amicable terms, they preferred to remain in the enjoyment of their possessions.

On the morning of our departure a very funny incident occurred. The old patriarch had discovered, on the evening before, that one of his sons was becoming weak in the faith and intended to abjure his religion. Moreover—and with a family of fifty it will not seem strange—he had forgotten to baptize this one black sheep. Accordingly, *vi et armis*, he dragged the young man from his bed and put him under the cold waters of the neighboring creek before breakfast.

At noon the horse and mule were saddled, and bidding adieu to our hosts, who as usual declined all offers of money, we passed on to St. Charles, the next settlement, where at the distance of eight miles from Paris we came upon the shores of Bear Lake, at its northern extremity. Our road lay through great fields of wheat, in the harvesting of which the whole population, men, women and children, were busily engaged. The farms extended to the borders of the lake, now spread before us in all the beauty of pleasing contrasts of the yellow wheat-fields and blue waters, darkening to the lofty range of gray mountains that extended along the eastern shore.

Skirting the western bank we came to the small village of Fish Haven, where we stopped to lunch with Mr. Stock. The lady of the house told us that she and her husband heard the glad tidings of salvation at Port Natal, beyond the Cape of Good Hope, and on embracing the faith they sold out all their possessions, and sought the Lord in these "his holy mountains." Thus the Mormon missionaries penetrate the remotest corners of the earth, even "carrying the war into Africa."

But they are not solicitous about the negroes. They consider them to be the descendants of Ham, "cursed with a curse." They are rather pro-slavery in their notions, the negro in their estimation being doomed by the Almighty to be a "servant of servants" forever. They admit that he has a soul, but although he may have a place in heaven, he never can be "exalted." He is sometimes baptized, but is not admitted to the priesthood, that is, he is not permitted to "talk in meeting," a privilege the negro is always ambitious to secure, and consequently seldom embraces "the faith delivered to the saints."

There were several Mistresses Stock, and each one had a stock of children. Beds, cribs and cradles constituted the furniture of the house. We took lunch under difficulties, and then rode five miles further down the lake to Swan Creek, the first settlement within the boundaries of Utah territory, where we had been commended by Bishop Budge to the hospitalities of Mr., Mrs. and another Mrs. Cook.

Two or three rude cabins, a sawmill and gristmill constitute the settlement of Swan Creek, and all these are the property of our host, Mr. Cook. All around the borders of the lake were his fields of wheat and corn, and the green meadows where his cattle feed extend far and near. When this part of the country becomes better known, tourists will frequent Bear Lake, hotels will stand upon its banks, and steamboats will stir its waters. But now only a passing stranger visits it. Here and there may be found a hamlet on its shores, and perhaps the only navigable craft upon it are the little skiffs, in one of which we paddled out on its deep waters and beheld the bottom, many fathoms beneath, as clearly as the blue sky over our heads. It abounds in salmon trout and fish of various other kinds, and has a romantic reputation.

No Indian was ever known to launch his canoe upon it, to bathe in it, or even to fish from its banks. They believe it to be sacred to the monsters of its depths, and dare not pollute its waters, or take from them a single fish put there for the food of the dreaded proprietors.

The legend is that centuries ago, when the Sioux and Bannocks were at war, a chief of the former tribe became enamoured of a dusky Bannock maiden. The course of true love, which never did run smooth, led them over mountains and cañons in their escape from the pursuit of the hostile tribes, whose members were for the time in league for mutual vengeance.

At last, like the Highlander with Lord Ullin's daughter, they came to the shores of the lake, their angry relatives close behind. There was no gallant old ferryman willing to risk his life for the "winsome ladye," and so they plunged into the waves to become targets for arrows and tomahawks.

But suddenly the Great Spirit transformed them into two enormous serpents. Rearing their heads from the water they shot from their mouths a volley of beach stones on their paralyzed foes, but few of whom escaped to hand down to succeeding generations the warning to beware of this enchanted lake.

Aside from all such superstition as this, there really is good reason to believe that the lake is inhabited by some abnormal water animals. We conversed with seven persons, among them our friend, the bishop, who at different times had seen them, and they told us that many other individuals could verify their report.

The length of these monsters varies from thirty to eighty feet, and their bodies are covered with fur like that of a seal. The head is described like that of an alligator. In one instance the animal came close to the shore, and was entangled in the rushes, where he squirmed and splashed, and made a horrible noise like the roaring of a bull.

It is true the Mormons are a very credulous people. They believe in all sorts of revelations and appearances, angelic and diabolical. Some allowance should therefore be made for this tendency of their minds, but with all that considered, it cannot be possible for so many people to be utterly mistaken. There are unquestionably in Bear Lake some fish larger than the ordinary salmon trout. Whatever they may be, they did not exhibit themselves for our benefit.

We remained three days with the kind people on whom we had been quartered. Mr. Cook was an elderly man. His family consisted of two wives and twenty children, ranging from manhood to infancy, and a sister who had just left her husband in the east, to join the church. I have not been slow to criticise the bad features of polygamy, but, with a disposition to do the institution whatever justice it may be entitled to, I readily admit that this was in every respect a happy family. The utmost conjugal, parental and fraternal affection prevailed among them all.

The head of the establishment was a sincerely religious man. His devotions, morning and evening, and before every meal, breathed the spirit of earnest love for all mankind, and of desire for their conversion to what he believed to be the truth. He had implicit faith in every dogma of his church, and oh how he did wrestle with the Lord for the strangers under his roof, and how he did urge upon us the duty of entering the fold!

Like all Mormons, he believed in "baptism for the dead." He said he had been baptized in one day two hundred and forty times for his dead relatives and friends. He seemed to wish that I might die before him, in order that he might be baptized for me: and in case his wish for my early death was not gratified, and he should pass first through the dark valley, he enjoined it upon his sons to go into the water for me. So all the male members of the Cook family are enlisted for my salvation. Good, kind-hearted old enthusiast, far be it from me to ridicule your faith!

Jane and Adeline, the two wives, were equally interested in the eternal welfare of my wife. If either of them survives her, whenever her death is announced, baptism by proxy will be performed for her, and if their death precedes hers, as, with all due regard for these excellent ladies, I hope may be the case, then one of the girls is to take the mother's place in the ceremony.

The elderly Mrs. Jewett had the zeal of a new convert in complying with all the formalities of Mormonism. She must now be "sealed" to some other man. She remarked: "This troubles me more than any thing else. I don't see who they can get for me. At my age I am not very marketable, and then I was always so neat and particular. Folks out here are most of 'em dreadful dirty. To be sure it will be celestial marriage, and I needn't stay with 'em on earth without I've a mind to: but I wouldn't like dirty folks even in heaven!"

Mr. Cook proposed to seal himself "celestially" to any unmarried ladies of our acquaintance, and we gave him a list of several who have passed beyond matrimonial chances in this life, and who are probably now, without their knowledge, the brides of Mr. Cook for the future world. Poor man, he little knows what hard bargains he has made!

I have no space to write about all his revelations, manifestations, and various extravagances. According to his belief, the garden of Eden was in Ohio, and the ark was built in Missouri. He produced the Bible to prove that it could easily have drifted to Ararat in seven months. As this could not be denied, he claimed for himself the full force of his argument.

Such were some of the wild notions of this curious family; and yet with all their religious insanity they attended most industriously to their farm and their mills. Their house was scrupulously neat, and their table loaded with substantial food.

Before leaving Swan Creek we attended an ecclesiastical court. It is the practice of the Mormons to settle all disputes with each other by referring them to a tribunal of their own, rather than to encourage litigation and employ lawyers. Mr. Cook had "jumped" an adjoining tract of land which a brother Mormon had pre-empted five years before, but never occupied. In strict conformity to the laws of the United States—and this was not disputed—Cook had gone upon the land last year, put up fences and raised a crop of wheat. Finding the land had now become valuable, the original pre-emptor came back and took possession. This was the case before the tribunal.

The court was held in a log cabin fifteen feet square. At one end was a chair for the president, and on extemporized benches sat the council of twelve, six on each side. The plaintiff, defendant and witnesses were between the two rows of councillors. This is the regular form. The court was opened with prayer, and then the parties to the suit each told his own story, producing his own witnesses. They both agreed to let the question be settled by the council, reserving the right of appeal to the head of the church at Salt Lake, but in no case to the law courts of the land.

When the evidence was all in, and the arguments had been concluded, which occupied two hours, the president gave his decision, subject to objection from any of the council. There was no opposition to it, beyond some slight modifications. The verdict was that the original pre-emptor should retain the property, but that he should pay brother Cook for all the expense he had put upon it.

As Cook wanted the land more than the money, he took an appeal. Then everybody shook hands all round, and the court was closed with an invocation of the divine blessing. The farmers harnessed their teams and went home satisfied with the reflection that, if they had done no good, they had certainly done no harm, and—a consolation that no lawyer ever feels—that they had put nobody to the expense of a dollar.

Leaving Swan Creek we rode along the lake for seven miles, under the shade of a natural avenue of cottonwood and willows, forgetting our curiosity to see the "lake monsters" in the beauties of water, sky and mountain, that needed no legends or aid of imagination to make them attractive. Then our road led us around the foot of a mountain to a town fitly named Meadowville. Fording a stream called Duck Creek, fifteen miles from the house of Mr. Cook, we came to the ranche of Mr. Kerl, a Mormon of a different stamp. Whatever religious bigotry he had, he kept to himself; and if in the neighboring houses we had not seen two young women and a crowd of children who evidently belonged to him, we should not have surmised that the family who entertained us were other than ordinary Gentiles. Mrs. Kerl is an Englishwoman, who, as she frankly confessed, had been at service in her youth, when her husband was a gamekeeper's boy in the "New Forest." It is their only boast of Mormonism that it has been the means of elevating them from their former condition to the proprietorship of this valuable ranche. Here they have great droves of cattle, flocks of sheep, and herds of horses ranging the slopes of mountain pastures, and three hundred acres of land, producing full crops of wheat and oats. Here they make tons of butter and cheese, and live literally on the "fat of the land;" while, if there is any poetry in their souls, their notions must be enlarged with their estate. When Goldsmith mourned over his deserted village of the plain, could his eye have rested on a scene like this, where man becomes his own master under Nature's smiles, and fed by her teeming abundance, he would not have deplored the fate of "Sweet Auburn" in his plaintive verse.

Did the sun shine brighter, were the meadows more green, the mountains more purple, the stacks of yellow grain more abundant, or was there not, besides all these, something in the quiet contentment of the people around us that caused us so fully to enjoy the day spent in this happy valley?

Very opportunely Mr. Kerl was intending on the next day to go down in his wagon through the cañons towards Logan, a distance of fifty miles, and we took advantage of this to ease our animals of their heavy packs of luggage. After a morning of successful shooting on the meadows we left the ranche, in company with its owner. Passing the first divide we obtained a farewell view of Bear Lake, and after that our path wound through a labyrinth of mountains, up and down wild cañons, by the side of their streams, the scenery ever changing; green slopes, perpendicular crags, lovely valleys, succeeding each other so rapidly that only a confused memory of beauties was left upon our minds.

In this way we passed over twenty-seven miles, and at evening came to "Blacksmith Forks," where the cañon of that name begins its descent to Logan, and the Ogden Cañon branches off to the left. We camped on the banks of the head-waters of Logan River. Having hoppled our saddle beasts, and tied the others to the wagon wheels, we built a fire and cooked some grouse and ducks shot on the way, and then, after a social game of euchre by the light of the camp fire, made our preparations for the night.

Mr. Kerl kindly gave up his bed by stepping out of his wagon, where we lay down upon the hay with a glorious blue canopy spangled with stars over our heads, and although the frost was so severe at this altitude of seven thousand feet that our breath froze upon the blankets, we passed a night of luxurious sleep unknown to those who lie upon "downy beds of ease."

The morning was excessively cold, but we were soon comforted by a good fire and an excellent breakfast like our supper of the evening before; and then, at sunrise, we saddled and harnessed our beasts and resumed our journey.

The remaining twenty-five miles was a continual descent, and an uninterrupted scene of grandeur until, emerging from the cañon, we came down on the plains of Cache Valley, and then, beautiful as were the meadows and the harvest of grain, how tame every thing appeared compared with the remembrance of all that we had left behind! The atmosphere had lost its elasticity, and for the time we experienced a depression of spirits which led us to look back regretfully upon the mountains, and to sigh for a breath of their pure air. Unmindful of the fatigue, we would fain have turned and retraced our steps.

We arrived at Logan soon after noon and there took the train for Ogden, after returning our animals to their owners. Appreciating their many good qualities their faults were freely forgiven, and the mule's rider thought that she detected a tear in his eye when she bade him an affectionate farewell.

CHAPTER XXXI.

THE UNION PACIFIC RAILROAD—THE ROCKY MOUNTAINS—
EASY-GOING EMIGRANTS—GREELEY, ON THE ROAD TO DENVER.

On leaving California, after crossing the Sierras Nevadas, the traveller is carried over an elevated plateau, as before described, until by a somewhat gradual descent he comes to the valley of the Great Salt Lake, the lowest level between the Sierras and the Rocky Mountains. From Ogden begins the ascent of the great range through the Weber and Echo Cañons, amidst the wildest scenery of the route.

The Sierras, sooner traversed, may leave more pleasant memories of thickly wooded valleys which offset the ruggedness of their peaks. These bare and lonely mountains, with their sharp outlines of adamantine rocks, impress us with ideas of stern sublimity, in which not a single thought of beauty enters.

We rise to a grade 1125 feet higher than any on the Central Pacific Road, and among innumerable buttes and glacier-worn crags are carried on towards the breezy plains of Laramie.

The Union Pacific Railroad is coming to be considered a frequented avenue leading out of New York. It is well known in the courts and in the halls of Congress, where it is annually made the object of attack, and its present stockholders subjected to punishment for the Credit Mobilier transactions and the crookedness of old contractors. It will be a happy day for them and for the public when all disputes are finally settled, and this great work, constructed for the relief of the country in its dire necessity, shall have free scope to develop its peaceful industries.

Aided by nature, whose obstacles its first mission was to overcome, it is already opening vast fields of mineral wealth. When the road was begun, the presence of gold and silver ore on this side of the Pacific slope was almost unknown. Now its feeders from Utah, Idaho, Montana, Wyoming, Dakota and Colorado bring thousands of tons to its depôts.

Of coal, then absolutely undiscovered, its own mines in Wyoming alone last year produced 276,000 tons, and the best iron in the continent has been found abundantly on its route, where foundries and works have been established. Besides these metals, vast deposits of sulphur, soda and oil-bearing rock are now being exploited.

Not the least of its resources are the ever multiplying herds of cattle and flocks of sheep that roam the fertile plains. These old homes of the buffalo and antelope have been captured by them; for the inexorable laws of nature dictate " the survival of the fittest," in an invariable line of progress. Useless animals are superseded by those that are necessary to man, as useless men, Indians, greasers and negroes are being swept away by those lords of creation born of the Anglo-Saxon race. It is a high title, but they have assumed it, though all of them do not bear the stamp of nobility.

When Mr. Greeley advised the young man to "go west," a compliance with his counsel was a literal obedience. The young man went. He was not carried; he went, either on a solitary march with gun and pickaxe over his shoulders, or walked by the side of slow moving oxen drawing all his worldly goods. Among them, and first of his articles of necessity, was his youthful bride, who, leaving the comforts of her eastern home, fitted herself on the long tramp to become his helpmate and not his expensive toy.

Emigrants of this style are not yet extinct. On the prairies we often passed them taking their weary road that had its advantages in reconciling them to their new home. At one of the stations on the plains west of Cheyenne, while other passengers were at their meal, we strayed away to look at a temporary housekeeping arrangement not far from the train.

The horse and cow were grazing at a little distance from the empty wagon, from which the top had been removed and converted into a tent. Out of doors a rosy cheeked young woman was preparing the dinner upon a miniature cooking-stove while the husband was engaged in an employment that would not have suggested itself to us—beating into flat slabs the tin cans that he had picked up on his journey. These, he said, were to cover his roof when he built a house somewhere.

"Somewhere? And where is that?" we asked.

"Well now, mister," he replied, "you are too much for me there. I suppose we must stop somewhere by and by, but the further we go, the less we want to. I like to keep going this way. My wife, she likes it; and the baby in there seems to like it too, for she grows like a weed. We are none of us sick; we always have plenty to eat, and so we don't see the use of stopping. But one of these days I suppose we shall get to the Pacific, and then we shall have to stop. In the mean time, if we strike a good place we may build a house to live in for a spell, but for the present we are well enough off."

The shrill whistle hurried us back to the train, whence from the windows of our car we looked back with a feeling almost of envy upon the happy vagrants.

That young man was not the one the Tribune philosopher had in mind when he gave his memorable direction. From present appearances, he will not contribute much to build up the waste places, although from a selfish point of view he is happier than the pioneer, whose object it is, first of all things, to make himself rich.

Mr. Greeley was a man of ideas, some of them, as many people think, erroneous, but he was undeniably right in wishing, for the good of the nation and of the individual, to send the poor laborer away from the crowded city to the new soil of the great West.

Approaching Denver, after branching off at Cheyenne, the road passes through a town called by the name of the philosopher, founded two years before his death, and intended to realize his favorite scheme of communistic labor. Had he lived, he might have rejoiced over the success of this experiment on a small scale, and had he lived many years more he must have discovered what almost everybody anticipates, that the plan would fail when carried out on a large scale.

Greeley is very like a Mormon town. About two thousand people of advanced ideas gathered here and established a common home, tilling the land, pasturing flocks and herds for mutual support and profit. They have co-operative mills and stores, and possibly will live together, so long as their number is small, in happiness and peace. Unlike the Mormons, however, who in many of their towns have adopted this system, they are divided into different religious sects, thus lacking a common bond of union which might presage a more assured success.

CHAPTER XXXII.

THE CITY OF DENVER—SUNDAY—CLIMATE—RAILROADS—ENTHUSIASTIC MCALLISTER—COLORADO SPRINGS—COLORADO CITY—MANITOU—"GARDEN OF THE GODS" AND CANONS.

On the morning after our arrival at Denver, we started on a tour of observation, guided by a citizen who reckoned himself among the "oldest inhabitants." We were shown the wide streets on whose borders some little cottonwood trees were struggling for life and promising a future shade in return for the labor of irrigation. The hotels were in number and capacity sufficient to accommodate the whole population. There were houses in various gradations, from the elegant residences of the rich to the wretched dens of the Italians and Chinese.

The stores—in the relative proportion of one to each dwelling—were all open, for it was Sunday, and Sunday is the busy day of Denver. It is the day when the miners pour into the town to supply themselves with provisions, and the farmers bring in produce to exchange for their wants. The bar rooms, billiard halls, sample rooms and saloons were reaping their richest harvest of the week; all was life, bustle and confusion. What a busy place it is, we thought! If the exuberance of trade can only find vent by encroaching thus upon the Sabbath, what must it be upon weekdays!

Mingling with the uproar of trade, the church bells chimed in from all quarters, calling upon the people to divide the service of Mammon with God, by giving him at least one hour of the day. It is fair to the Denverites to say that they are willing to make this compromise. They generally close their stores, and some of them are even willing to vacate the bar rooms, at 11 o'clock. After service, our guide took us to view the antiquities, pointing with all the pride of an Italian cicerone to a log cabin built in the almost forgotten past of twenty years ago; for in the great West decades and even single years are centuries.

The settlement of Denver was begun in 1859. For the first nine years of its existence it was a mere mining camp, or rather a deposit of stores for miners. Then it lingered along, its population barely increasing to the number of four thousand, until railroads, the great pioneers of civilization, brought to it a sudden accession of inhabitants and wealth. Then it was the point to which the roads from Kansas and from Cheyenne approached. Now it has become the centre from which new railroads diverge. Southerly the Denver and Rio Grande has advanced far on its way to Mexico, forming connections on the line, with the Atchison, Topeka and Santa Fe joining it from the east. South-westerly the Colorado Central has grasped the oldest mineral regions. Westerly the Denver and South Park is looking steadily towards Salt Lake City, 450 miles to the west. From all these, lateral branches fertilize the productive capital of this new State of the Union, as the streams from its irrigating canals permeate its soil.

With gold and silver in its depths, corn and fruits upon its surface, tens of thousands of cattle and sheep roaming upon its hills and plains; above all, with health wafted in every breath of its invigorating air, it needs no prophet to predict the future of Colorado.

The stormy season of Denver is when it seldom rains. It would have been a pleasure to close our umbrellas on those October days and to welcome a deluge upon our heads. A duststorm such as we experienced would have been harder upon the animals under the care of Noah than the great flood. Forty days' dust like this would have effectually killed every man, beast and creeping thing within, as well as without, the ark. It penetrated the houses so that the color of the carpets was a uniform gray; it mixed with the food and was inhaled by the throat and lungs till the mucous membrane became like sandpaper and the voice between sneezes was like the caw of a raven. Nor was it common dust. It was alkaline, as universal redness of the eyes testified in addition to all the other miseries it inflicted.

The Denver optimists said that it was a special occasion. They never knew any thing like it before, and it would probably never happen again. The pessimists, and there are always some of them everywhere, said "that was just the way of it all the year round."

One should remain here a year in order to give a candid weather report. As we had not that time to spare, we are obliged to rely upon the mean of the metereological reports and statements of the people. From these it appears that it is sometimes very hot in midsummer, the mercury attaining occasionally 100 degrees in the shade, and it is sometimes very cold in winter, the glass showing 30 degrees below zero. But as these extremes are seldom reached, summer may be rated at 75 and winter at 40 degrees.

Rain falls freely at the opening and the close of summer, but seldom, almost never, from October to May, although snow is not infrequent. This condition of things will suit those who desire a "dry climate." But all the advantage derived from this dryness would seem to be counterbalanced by the dust storms.

Despite this almost intolerable nuisance, thousands of invalids make Denver a winter resort. Over five thousand feet above the sea level, the air is bracing and pure, dust always excepted, and this requisite for people with lung diseases, combined with the comforts of civilization afforded by hotels, stores and society, induce those who place, as we think, too much dependence upon such home luxuries, to settle themselves here to live or die.

We left Denver one morning for the south, on the Denver and Rio Grande Railroad, a cheaply constructed "narrow gauge," but a profitable investment for the present, and of well founded expectations for the future. The grade is of easy ascent for fifty-two miles to the "divide," along the banks of the South Platte, overlooking a valley on the right made fertile by canals which everywhere draw water from higher levels for irrigation. On the left was a wide stretch of pasture land, unbroken by forest or hill as far as the eastern horizon. In the valley the settlers grow their corn and grass, and on these boundless uplands they pasture their cattle which divide the grass with herds of antelope. These were so abundant and unsuspicious of evil intent that hundreds of them came down almost within pistol shot from the train.

At the "divide" there is a pretty lake of two or three acres, supplied by living springs in its centre. It has two outlets, one at its northern and the other at its southern border. The former meanders down into the Platte, the latter into the Arkansas, and after travelling thousands of miles apart in far different directions meet again in the Mississippi, and journey in each other's embrace to the Gulf of Mexico.

Passing numerous hamlets and ranches we arrived soon after noon at Colorado Springs, seventy-five miles south of Denver. This misnomer, for it has no springs, is a tastefully laid out settlement of between three or four thousand inhabitants, with good hotels, numerous churches, shops, banks, a high school, an incipient university, a deaf and dumb asylum, and all the concomitants of an advanced civilization. As a place of residence it is every way superior to Denver, and for invalids has incomparable advantages. Though 5986 feet above the sea level, the climate is far more equable, and its neighborhood to the springs from which it takes its name gives it a sanitary pre-eminence. It is the centre of trade for the large agricultural districts, and derives much of its prosperity from the mines, which it supplies with merchandise and provisions paid for in gold and silver.

The first attempt at mining was made in 1858, by a few straggling bands from the east and west, who had heard of the marvellous richness of the region about Pike's Peak. That fever soon abated, but new discoveries drew greater multitudes; and when the Kansas Pacific Railroad was completed ten years later, mining was a regular and increasing industry. Until lately the mines on the Colorado Central Railroad have furnished most of the supply, as that part of the territory was settled at an earlier date, and was easily accessible from Denver. For the same reason, stock raising and farming have made more advance in this region. Yet this is but a small portion of the 106,000 square miles comprising the State, which until the last twelve years was absolutely unexplored.

In 1873 some adventurous miners penetrated beyond the "snowy range" that divides the sources of the waters running into the Pacific and the Atlantic, returning with almost incredible stories of the wealth of those mountains. This produced as wild an excitement as lately prevailed about the Black Hills of Dakota, and it was complicated with similar difficulties. The western part of Colorado had been kept as a reservation for the Ute Indians, and it was much more valuable to them for agricultural purposes than the bleak mountains of the Sioux could possibly be to them. Fortunately the Utes were more tractable, and they wisely accepted from the government a fair price for the right of miners to occupy that part of the reservation suitable for mining, while the Indians still enjoy all that is of use to them for cultivation.

This new mining region is the famous San Juan country, which is expected to eclipse all previous discoveries. It is one hundred and seventy-five miles long from north to south, and one hundred miles wide, lying chiefly in Lake and La Plata counties. Major McAllister, a prominent citizen of Colorado Springs, to whom I am indebted for much valuable information, has investigated the facts connected with San Juan, so far as they have been reported, and is very enthusiastic in his belief of their just foundation.

"Gold and silver, sir!" he exclaimed, "there are mountains, yes, solid mountains of it; you absolutely stumble over rocks of solid silver. No other mineral country approaches it in value! To my certain knowledge there is enough of the precious metal in sight to pay the national debts of the whole world. You do not dig for it as elsewhere. It is all over the surface in every direction, in ridges of rock a hundred feet wide and many miles in length. I have seen a specimen weighing more pounds than I could lift, knocked off from one of these surface rocks!"

With proper allowance, the general idea obtained from Major

McAllister was that the whole of that country is traversed in every direction by seams of silver ore, in number practically unlimited, in width from two feet to three hundred, and in richness from fifty dollars to five thousand dollars to the ton.

We took the stage for Manitou, the real fountain of the mineral waters of Colorado, distant six miles from these nominal "springs." Half way, we passed through the old city of Colorado, built nineteen years ago for the capital of the territory. But misfortune or mismanagement followed it from its birth. The capital was removed by political adroitness to Denver, and when the railroad was contemplated the new colony at the "Springs" offered superior inducements for changing its line from a direct course. The city of Colorado was built on the piles of false expectations, and is now crumbling into the dust of oblivion. Large hotels were erected for guests, who never occupied their rooms, stores were built for goods they never received, banks for the deposit of money never entrusted to their vaults, and churches for swallows only to nestle under their eaves. It wears the melancholy air of Pisa without its magnificence.

Hidden under a lofty range of mountains, looking majestically down upon it from the west, with the towering summit of Pike's Peak standing sentry over the lesser giants of the air, is the little village of Manitou, the real Colorado Springs. It has been called the Chamounix of America, but Chamounix might be proud to be styled the Manitou of Switzerland.

Here is a land of lights and shadows. The morning sun streams through the valley by which we approach, and warms it at noon with its kindly but not overpowering heat, which the freshness of the air always tempers; and the evening sun setting behind these overtopping cliffs, projects their shadows upon the brighter scenes with a softness and beauty indescribable.

It were far better if those who come here to regain their health were compelled to live out of doors or in tents, but the more than comfortable hotels offer inducements not to be resisted. Three of these are of the first class, equalling the great Saratoga caravanseries in luxury, while second-class hotels and boarding-houses are open for people of moderate means.

The springs have already acquired a world-wide reputation. They are not unlike the fountains of Vichy or Kissingen ; the waters cool and sparkling with gas, holding in solution a strong body of soda and iron. Dr. Solly, an English physician of high repute, has recently published a pamphlet analysis of the waters. Many of his countrymen have settled in Colorado, who have come here to invest their capital in loans, which they can readily do at a high rate of interest, securing a far better income than they can get from their three per cent. consols at home. They are captivated with a genuine country life, which they can enjoy only on a small scale in their little island. Here they establish themselves on ranches, roaming wherever they please the vast plains abounding with game, and occasionally looking after their investments which yearly roll up into fortunes, while in the mean time they live in the enjoyment of a healthy and pleasurable existence. Some of them are the owners of neat cottages in and near Manitou, tastefully built and surrounded by green lawns, enclosed with rustic fences.

Nothing is more pleasing to an Englishman than to imagine himself " lord of the manor." Everywhere among the mountains there are natural parks, far surpassing in beauty and magnificence any that belong to the British nobility and gentry in their own kingdom.

Here the Englishman of moderate means at once becomes an aristocrat. He builds for himself a log cabin, set with taste and an eye to the picturesque, on some sheltered spot on one of the vast domains "taken up" by him without cost. Here he establishes himself as lord of all he surveys; buys cattle and sheep, and commences a business in which a "gentleman" can engage without a feeling of self-abasement, getting out of his employment, pleasure and a profit to be added to his accruing interest. He gradually becomes Americanized by adding manhood to his gentility, and in course of time proves a valuable citizen of the great republic. If he can gather a little settlement about him and become the patron of a tiny Episcopal church, with a rector who will dine with him on Sundays, he is supremely happy, comparing himself to the proudest duke or prince of his native land; for with his broad acres, his horses, his dogs, gun and parson, what can an Englishman ask more!

This settlement of Manitou was founded under the auspices of the "Colorado Springs Improvement Co." They acquired possession of the whole valley by taking up, pre-emption and purchase of claims, at little or no cost. They have laid out roads and shady walks, and in other respects adorned what nature had already beautified. They either own shares in the hotels or have sold the land on which to build them. Thus they have made a profitable investment for themselves, and have become entitled to the gratitude of the ever increasing crowd of visitors.

About five hundred strangers, not only from other points in the State, but from all directions, settle here during the season. The fame of the springs has gone out through all the world. In our estimation they rank next to the soda springs of Idaho. In four days they can be reached from Boston, New York, Philadelphia or Washington, a less time than was formerly occupied in travelling to Saratoga from either of these cities; and when Manitou is once reached, the object desired by invalids and true pleasure seekers is attained. Even Europeans, having heard its fame, are willing to tempt the dangers of the seas, and instead of resorting to the sleepy spas of Germany, come to Colorado to view its glorious scenery, to breathe its life-giving atmosphere, and to drink its health-bestowing waters.

After having tried all the resources of the pharmacopia, the nostrums of quacks, the reputed virtue of Bourbon whiskey, the climate of Florida and Nassau, and experiencing relief from none of these expedients, attenuated consumptives come to Colorado. Alas, they too often come to die. For it is certain that in the last stages of the disease the stimulating temperature of this region almost invariably proves fatal. The true physician is he who unselfishly counsels the afflicted, in the first stages of the disease, to abandon drugs, business, and home, and fly at once to the high plains and mountains of the west. The wisest invalids are those who come here with something to do as well as to be and to suffer. Occupation distracts the mind from self, and offers the best prospects of relief. The man with consumptive tendencies should sell out his possessions in the east and remove for life to Colorado. Here let him establish himself in business, and the best business he can find will be on the open plains or among the mountains, where he must daily ride to look after his cattle and sheep.

No one has described this region with more enthusiasm than Mrs. Lippincott (Grace Greenwood). She has done for the beauties what Major Powell has done for the sublimities, and is credible while he is almost incredible. I mean that while allowing for certain female poetic tendencies of embellishment, with a pencil dipped in *couleur de rose*, Grace is to be generally believed, as she would scarcely draw the long bow, when others are so constantly hunting over the same ground. On the contrary, the gallant major has told such fearful stories of hair-breadth escapes, that no one, at least until his Munchausenism is forgotten, will be likely to follow in his tracks. Mrs. Lippincott has proved her sincerity by building for herself a "love of a cottage," shaded by cottonwoods, entwined with clematis, on the banks of Fountain Creek, the rapid little stream whose ceaseless music is her daily and nightly serenade.

Two miles below the town, the "Garden of the Gods" is approached from a turn of the road leading over a rough path to the "Gates of Paradise," which form high battlements at the entrance. Why this area of curious sandstone formation should have received its title is not apparent. The name is calculated to raise different expectations from those eventually realized. There are hundreds of acres of hard red soil, with here and there patches of wild grass, disappointing our anticipations of shaded walks and beds of flowers. But the tall fantastic columns, turned by the lathe of glaciers thousands of years ago, are impressive monuments of the unknown past. These tower above our heads hundreds of feet and are of endless variety, of grotesque shape and outline.

The cañons in the neighborhood of Manitou, particularly that of Cheyenne, are grand and beautiful. An unending variety of walks and rides lead upward to the mountain peaks. All around Manitou within an afternoon's ride are scenes like these approached by gallops over the "Mesa" or high plains, where the fresh air and distant views add delight to the continual surprises of the road.

CHAPTER XXXIII.

ASCENT OF PIKE'S PEAK—THE HERMIT OF THE MOUNTAIN—
THE SIGNAL STATION—A HUNTING EXPEDITION—ON THE
DENVER AND RIO GRANDE RAILROAD.

There are two ways of making the ascent of Pike's Peak from Manitou. One is by following an ill-defined bridle path over a very rough country to the "timber line," where vegetation ceases, and then scrambling up an almost perpendicular slope of about eighteen hundred feet to the summit. Although the rocks are broken and slippery the enterprise would be a matter of small account, if the start were to be made at this point from a sea level. But it must be considered that the end of the "timber line" is already between twelve and thirteen thousand feet high, and every step is more fatiguing than a hundred on the plains.

The longer but more easy method is by the government trail, following the signal telegraph wire. Nor is the length to be regretted, for that route is vastly more picturesque than the short and painful one.

The ladies, for once, were willing to allow men to precede them, but they accompanied us about half the distance through the prettiest part of the scenery. Leaving the hotel at early morning we rode rapidly in the cool air over the Mesa of six miles, between Manitou and the mouth of Bear Creek Cañon. Here the wagon track comes to an end and a tortuous trail begins, crossing and re-crossing the stream continually, over rocks and through dense underbrush, beneath overhanging cliffs and through forests of cedar and pine.

The roar of tumbling cascades subsides into the rippling of comparative levels, and alternates with noisy uproar like the varying melody of the organ in its dulcet tones and deep diapason. We wound along for miles until we came to a zig-zag path cut in the sides of a high mountain descending to meet its opposite neighbor abruptly in the stream.

To those of us who first arrived at the dizzy height it was a curious sight to behold the long straggling line of our companions, creeping up the winding trail, clinging like flies to the sides of a wall. A light snow had fallen the night before, feathering the pines and frosting the rocks, adding greatly to the picture, but somewhat endangering the foothold of our animals in places where the road was but three feet wide, and they might fall by a misstep a thousand feet. It was better not to touch the reins, for to the unaccustomed it was a risk even to look down. Leaving the beasts to their instincts, Excelsior was now the watch-word.

The danger past, a lovely scene opened before us. As the Hudson spreads above the Palisades into the Tappan Zee, and contracts again towards the Catskills, so here the pass had scooped a plain out of the surrounding hills, and left a natural park for miles of comparative level. Such spots as these are often selected for cattle and sheep ranches.

But the owner of the park had squatted here, pre-empted and purchased the whole of it for a different purpose. His only desire was for a "lodge in some vast wilderness," where he might seclude himself from the world and never see any more of his numerous relations, whose names are Jones.

By actual measurement the lodge of Mr. Jones is 10,080 feet in the air. He has perched himself there for summer and winter, dwelling alone in a neat log cabin with windows of the largest plate glass, from which he can look boldly out upon the world while the world cannot look in upon him. Evidently Mr. Jones is a peculiar man. We were sorry that he was not at home, but were glad that, in accordance with the universal practice of rancheros, he had no lock upon his door, for by this time, although the air was clear and the sun bright, the ample fire-place of his mansion offered inducements not to be resisted. We made ourselves at home, kindling a roaring fire from the abundance of cedar logs at hand, giving out an odor like a hecatomb of lead-pencils. In the silent blessings which it is hoped our grateful hearts bestowed upon our luncheon, we did not fail to remember the hermit, who in the attempt to hide himself from his fellow-creatures had made a few of them so happy.

We were ten miles on our way, one half the distance to the Peak, and now sending back the ladies with an escort, three of us continued our upward journey. At the farther end of the park, the mountains drew together and enclosed us in their grasp until, as we emerged from the dense shrubbery, they opened once more and exposed to view on either side and beyond a scene of utter desolation.

Many years ago, ere the foot of the explorer had crossed the wilderness, a wide spread conflagration had raged. The Indian camp fires or the lightnings of heaven might have kindled it, but it was a melancholy sight, whatever may have been the cause. Tens of thousands of acres of a once living forest were reduced to an area of blackened stumps, and the fallen timber lay thickly as far as the eye could reach. Through five miles of this wretched field of desolation, we ascended to the Lake House, a log cabin erected for the convenience of tourists and the supply of the Government corps stationed at the Peak. A clear, transparent basin of water of twelve acres is here a perpetual spring, from which the streams flow down into the plains. We were told that the water is so cold that even trout cannot live within it, but as that useful experiment had never been tried, we scarcely credited the information. If the keeper of the shanty had been sufficiently enterprising to stock the lake with fish, he could with much less cost to himself have provided us with something better than fried ham, for which we angled in a sea of grease.

Here our ponies, who are as accustomed to the route as camels to the desert, exercised the same forethought. They knew that they would get no more oats or water until the next day, and accordingly ate and drank their fill. As we started onward we passed through a green timber line not reached by the great fire, encircling the summit like a garland. While crossing this belt a covey of mountain grouse whirred overhead, giving each of us a successful shot. Tying the game to our saddles we were happy in having secured a breakfast for the morning.

Then we came to the limit of the "timber-line," and by a scarcely perceptible trail wound our way among huge rocks for the rest of the journey. Colder grew the air as the day drew to a close, and we urged our tired beasts along that we might reach the Peak before darkness should come upon us. Our arrival could not have been at a more favorable moment, for as we stood upon the summit, the last rays of the sun were streaming upward from the Utah mountains, more than a hundred miles away in the west, gilding their clearly outlined summits, and reflecting changing colors from their snowy ranges to the skies. Then evening drew its gray shades over the vast panorama, and we stood alone upon the mountain with a world below us sleeping in the silent night.

We were cordially welcomed at their little stone shanty by Lieut. Brown and his comrade of the U. S. Signal Corps. They warned us not to approach the stove hastily, in coming in from a temperature of eight degrees below the freezing point, as others who had neglected this precaution had been attacked by apoplexy, endangering their lives.

Our first business was to carry some faggots to the brow of the peak overhanging the settlement of Manitou, and to kindle a bonfire by which our friends, 10,000 feet below, were assured of our safe arrival ; and then we gradually accustomed ourselves to the heat within doors. The peak is 14,216 feet above the level of the ocean, and Lieut. Brown said that next year it would be seventy feet higher by the new measurement which, having already elevated the plains, will push the mountain still further up. It was high enough for us without this complement.

We experienced some peculiar sensations difficult to relate or even to remember. A little walk, if walk it could be called, where we stumbled over disjointed fragments of rocks, shortened our breath almost to suffocation, and when at night we endeavored to sleep, although we were told that the attempt would be useless on the first experiment, the hour of semi-wakeful dozing was as unpleasant as can be imagined.

Queer fancies took possession of our brains. Every thing, including ourselves, seemed to be afloat in the air. New York and Boston rose up and danced about in an altitude of immeasurable leagues, with sun, moon and stars all round them. When we gasped for air, as we were often obliged to do, our lungs and chests seemed like pliable India-rubber bellows, expanding to the size of the body of an elephant.

The officers stationed here at first experienced similar inconveniences and hallucinations, but had gradually become accustomed to the novelty and necessities of their condition. Fortunately their time is much occupied in noting and recording observations, and telegraphing them to Washington; otherwise existence would be intolerable.

Here might be a favorable place for the cure of intemperance, for the smallest draught of alcoholic liquor produces nausea at once, and gives a forcible hint in favor of total abstinence.

The exact latitude of the Peak is 38 degrees 48 minutes north, and longitude 104 degrees 59 minutes west of Greenwich, as determined by Lieut. Brown. His scientific instruments for ascertaining the velocity of the wind, humidity of the air, rain-fall, cold and heat, and other matters considered worthy of daily reports, were shown and explained, and we listened to an exceedingly interesting lecture, illustrated by charts and diagrams, explanatory of the theory of storms and probabilities, a synopsis of which is read in the daily papers by thousands who never give a thought to the wonderful agencies of science by which they are evolved. This service was commenced in 1868. Then "Old Probabilities" was in his infancy, and for lack of a thorough education committed many blunders. Possibilities would have been a better title for him, but now probabilities amount almost to certainties, and soon will become absolute truths. Every village newspaper chronicles a prophecy of invaluable worth to the farmer, and to all the millions who daily look to these records for calculations of business or pleasure, and what a debt of gratitude the seamen on our coasts and lakes owe to the storm signals of this faithful monitor!

THE SIGNAL STATION. 303

The highest temperature on the mountains last year was reached in June, when the mercury stood at 57 degrees above, and the lowest was in February, when it marked 37 degrees below zero. Cold, however, depends more upon the wind than upon the thermometer. Late in the evening of our visit the glass stood at twenty-two degrees; but as the air was calm we were not uncomfortable out of doors without overcoats, although when the wind is violent the piercing blast is unendurable.

Snow is scarcely a respecter of seasons, for on July fourth it fell to the depth of fifteen inches, whereas in the winter it is all blown away, excepting the provision caught among the rocks, which serves for the only supply of water all the year round to the hardy inhabitants of the hut. The velocity of the wind is occasionally one hundred miles an hour, and at such times no one would envy the signal corps the scanty pay they receive for the invaluable service they perform.

There was no signal corps in the days when it was said, "The wind bloweth where it listeth, and thou hearest the sound thereof, but canst not tell whence it cometh and whither it goeth." Now, the desert of the west is known to be the place of its birth, and science has traced its almost invariable course from west to east, with a precision equal to the knowledge of the ocean tides.

Although the cold was intense, the mercury being but little above zero, and the wind whistling fiercely around the corner of our stone cabin, we were up and out betimes to see the rising of the sun. As the dawn approached, the gray chaos of the world below shaped itself into lesser mountains and plains painted in the sombre colors of mingled day and night. Then light glimmered and brightened on the eastern horizon, the dark tints of early dawn came out in rapid and changing dashes of brightness over the snows of the mountains, the green forests of the cañons and the boundless russet plains. The sunset of the previous evening impressed us with majesty, but the darkness soon gathering tinged our admiration with melancholy. Far more glorious was this clear sunrise glowing with the promise of a perfect day.

All our anticipations were more than realized; and with many thanks to our kind entertainers, we began the descent. The famished animals, expectant of water and oats at the Lake House, skipped nimbly over the rocks and fallen logs, and when refreshed finished the journey with spirit, bringing us back to Manitou early in the afternoon.

I have not space to enumerate all the pleasant excursions taken from that delightful watering-place. The mountains are intersected by romantic cañons, through which leap the streams pouring at last into the Arkansas. One of the wildest of these is the Ute Pass, leading to some of the mining regions in the west.

By this cañon Manitou Park is approached, distant twenty miles on an elevated plain one thousand feet above the village. This is a property belonging to Dr. Bell, an English gentleman, who has erected a comfortable hotel for the accommodation of summer visitors. In the winter it is a place of occasional resort for sportsmen, deer and other game abounding in the surrounding mountains.

Having formed a hunting party, we took advantage of a wintry day of the autumn to visit it. The seasons are singularly changeable in these regions. At times in November and December the snow covers the ground in the valleys and the frost seals up the streams, every thing betokening a Siberian winter. On the very next day, perhaps, nature is freed from her icy fetters, and all is genial summer again. The days of cold are really the most enjoyable, for the effect of snow upon the mountains and of the icicles pendent from the trees is exceedingly beautiful.

Ascending the "Ute Pass" on horseback, our camp equipage and provisions followed in a wagon. We were fitted out for the capture of herds of deer and antelope, to say nothing of expected grouse and rabbits, and it may be mentioned in the outset that we were disappointed in our anticipations in this respect, our spoils, after three days' hunting, amounting to one deer, five jack rabbits and a black squirrel. Nevertheless, we had no reason to complain, as we were compensated for this small result in healthy exercise and the wonderful scenery.

Arriving at evening, a blazing fire of pine logs gave a cheerful air to the almost deserted hotel, or rather to the adjoining ranche-house, which is occupied by the family in the winter. Mr. Thornton, the superintendent of the property, is an Englishman, and as Englishmen always bring their habits with them, we were reminded of the hospitality of British country squires on Christmas holidays. An immense round of beef graced the table, and venison in various forms kept it goodly company. We were waited upon by English servants who asked us what we would "be pleased to 'ave," and altogether the combination of English style and American backwoods life formed a pretty picture, lighted as it was by the cheerful glow from the ample stone fireplace.

If we did not kill much game, we sang many songs, told many stories, cracked many jokes, and when we rolled into our blankets at night, we slept the sleep of the weary, more soundly than others slumber in cities on their beds of ease.

As Mr. Thornton carried on the farm upon an expensive as well as extensive scale, he had a numerous retinue of laborers to care for the cattle and crops. We all messed together, the landlord and his guests at the head of the long table, and a dozen of his dependants at the other end. We thought of Cedric the Saxon and his family, so graphically described in Ivanhoe, when England, like Colorado, was comparatively a new country, for there was a bonhommie and roughness in the men of those times like our own grade of civilization in the west.

By day we roamed the mountains for game, and at night came home to enjoy the ample repast and comforts of the enormous fireside. Let no future sportsman be discouraged, however, by our want of success. We were a month too early for the game, as the deer were still upon the mountains. By and by, we were told, they would come down to the park, and even to the plains about Manitou; moreover be it considered, we were all amateurs, and I verily believe that if some of us had seen a buck he would have stared us out of countenance.

Leaving Manitou as we journeyed south on the Denver and Rio Grande Railroad, the country appeared to be better watered, both naturally and artificially. Farm ranches with large fields that had apparently yielded abundant crops, joined each other for miles along the way, and here and there were to be seen collections of pretty white frame houses, not unlike New England villages. All this land is fertilized by various little streams, leisurely doing good on their way to the Arkansas.

Forty-three miles from our starting point, brought us to **Pueblo.**

CHAPTER XXXIV.

PUEBLO—THE DENVER AND RIO GRANDE, AND THE ATCHISON, TOPEKA AND SANTA FE RAILROADS—CANON CITY—THE GRAND CANON OF THE ARKANSAS—DENVER AGAIN—COLORADO CENTRAL RAILROAD—IDAHO SPRINGS—GEORGETOWN—GENERAL GRANT'S DRIVE—RETURN TO THE LINE OF THE UNION PACIFIC.

Pueblo was the first place of more than ephemeral existence we had entered. It claims an antiquity of a far greater boast than the two decades which are the longest measure of modern settlements.

It was a Mexican town, as its name indicates. When our countrymen obtained possession of the unknown regions ceded by the treaty of Guadalupe Hidalgo, the pioneers found on this spot a collection of adobe huts, a Catholic church and a pulperia, which are the elements of a Mexican town, as one or two frame buildings and a billiard saloon are of an American city. Why the name was not changed to Smithville or Brownopolis does not appear. For once we were out of names, and Pueblo was adopted into the family without a new christening. Its "greasers" became free and enlightened Americans by a stroke of a pen, as the negroes rose to that proud distinction by the fifteenth amendment, and, like them, they have since aided in making our laws, and assessing property-holders for taxes. Indians and Chinese will come into possession of the franchise next, if they can be calculated upon to vote for the party in power.

But Pueblo has been rescued from the hands of its original inhabitants. The Denver and Rio Grande Railway passes through it from the north, and the Atchison, Topeka and Santa Fe has reached it from the east. Already it is the second town of the State in number of inhabitants, and rivals in hope the settlement of Colorado Springs. Here too is established the Central Improvement Company, whose profits are invested in ditching, grading, laying out town lots, building school-houses, and making ready for the immense population expected to pour into it as soon as business is lively again.

When one of these western railroads commences its travels, no prophet can tell where it will bring up. It goes on its mission of civilization, comfort and wealth, stretching itself in length and ramifying right and left until it spreads like arteries and veins over the body of the land.

So this enterprising railroad company, hearing of coal mines to the west, have projected and completed a branch to Cañon City, along the banks of the Arkansas. As we turned off upon this road from Pueblo, our way through the cañon was a delightful contrast to the uninteresting road over the plains. Passing a few miles beyond the coal mines, which by means of this branch are made productive for the region round about, we arrived in the evening at Cañon City, and were quartered at a hotel which might have seemed comfortable if we had not been spoiled by the luxury at Manitou.

The bright sunlight of Colorado, where clouds and storms are rare, displayed in the morning a pretty little town nestled under the mountains at the outlet of the Great Cañon of the Arkansas.

Cañon City derives its name from this wonderful gorge in the cliffs, and owes its prosperity to its facilities for supplying the mines of the upper regions. Its mineral springs are not unlike those of Manitou, soda and iron being the chief ingredients; and it may be safely affirmed that they are good for all imaginary diseases.

When the country is more developed, and better hotels and lodging-houses are furnished, doubtless the advantages of Cañon City as a health resort will commend themselves. Behind the town the mountains rise abruptly, forbidding a further progress of the railroad over an insurmountable grade. But it has been estimated that the road could be continued through the Grand Cañon, eleven and a half miles, by being chiselled out of the rocks, at a cost a little short of $100,000 per mile.

The cost scarcely enters into consideration in view of the recent developments in Leadville, which almost justify the wildest dreams of the exuberant Major McAllister. Leadville is now the great objective point to which all the Colorado railroads are extending, each eager for its share of the prey. The Atchison, Topeka and Santa Fe, having leased the Cañon City branch of the Denver and Rio Grande road, are actually carrying it in through the pass, presently to be described.

In treating of Colorado, I realize the truth of a remark made by a friend who has just returned. "If one undertakes to show the exact situations of things there, he must print his sketches on the day they are written." A year ago we would have said that seven or eight million dollars would be its annual yield of silver and gold. As these pages are going to press, we have from a reliable source the following estimate of its prosperity.

"During the last few days estimates have been shown, made by old miners, of the gold and silver product of Colorado for 1879. The lowest is about as follows:—

Leadville and Ten Mile	$12,000,000
Silver Cliff, Rosita, &c.	5,000,000
Gilpin County	4,000,000
Clear Creek County	4,500,000
San Juan County	1,000,000
Park, Summit, and Boulder	1,500,000
Total	$28,000,000

"This would be more than three times the yield of any previous year. But so good an authority as Senator Chaffee is of the opinion that the output at Leadville alone, from the time that a railroad gets there, will reach $3,000,000 a month. Whatever the results of this year's mining shall be, depends more upon the milling and transportation facilities than any thing else. It is agreed upon all sides that the ease with which the carbonates are mined, and the wonderfully rich manner in which they are showing up, make it no exaggeration to expect a bullion output of all the way from $20,000,000 to $40,000,000 from Colorado this year."

We took a wagon to ascend by a zig-zag road to the top of the mountains, through which the Arkansas pours its waters from the plains nearly twelve miles above. To reach this eminence, whence the best view is obtained, is a labor lightened by varying glimpses of distant snow-capped mountains and passages through the natural parks with which the country abounds. These are the abodes of elk and deer in abundance, although the enterprising rancheros are encroaching on the wild domain for their own cattle and sheep. The side-hills abound in timber, and the levels are covered with luxuriant grass in summer, turning to standing hay in the winter, thus offering abundant pasturage all the year.

We made the ten miles in a little more than three hours, and came to the summit table-land. Between us and the plain beyond was a yawning chasm, of such fearful and precipitous depth that we were brought to a sudden stand, from which we stared into the gulf below, appalled at its immensity. To look down perpendicularly two thousand five hundred feet, was something to make the brain whirl with dizziness.

The Arkansas, no insignificant river as we found it when crossing it, threaded its way along like a narrow ribbon dropped from these ærial heights, and the tall trees, as the glass revealed them to be, swept down by the current and piled here and there on the rocks, were to our unaided vision like handspikes or walking-sticks. We rolled some of the largest rocks that all our appliances could bring to the edge of the cliff into the river. When they reached the water they dropped noiselessly as fine shot into a basin ; all things, and we ourselves more than all, lessening to nothing in our august surroundings.

We strayed from one point of observation to another for miles along the cliffs, catching the sunlight touches and the dark shadows on the winding walls of this wonderful gorge, and tracing the stream in its tortuous course, sometimes black as night and again glistening like a silver streak in the sunshine. There are photographs of the Grand Cañon of the Arkansas that may be purchased, but the photographs of art cannot overcome its perverse propensity to cheat in proportions. The photograph of the memory is distinct, clear and indelible, and such will ever be our recollection of this stupendous scene.

From Pueblo, the point of return on the route north to Denver, the railroad continues southerly through Trinidad, to which place the Atchison, Topeka and Santa Fe have extended their road from La Junta, proposing to go on toward the Rio Grande, looking, like it, for a terminus on the Pacific. The resources upon which it depends are the pastoral and farming lands of the new country, and the business that increasing immigration will bring.

These references to various railroad ramifications may perplex the tourist, but wherever he goes in Colorado he will soon find some railroad on which he can travel in any direction and for any distance.

First impressions of Denver were not favorable, for they were of dust in the air, dust on the floors, dust everywhere. Scarcely were they blown away when our second impressions were given in snow. Not a good healthy snow storm, such as in Vermont gives promise of the music of sleigh bells and warm comfort under buffalo robes ; but each flake brought with it a drop of water, and when they reached the ground they carpeted the streets and sidewalks with gray slushy mud, unpleasant to look at, and unhealthy to wade through. Yet Denver is the winter resort of invalids. It was the middle of November, and they were pouring in from the springs and ranches where they had passed the summer and autumn. Hotels and boarding-houses were full of them. Ghost-like they glided through the corridors and shivered in the parlors and at the dining tables. Waiters were seen on the staircases carrying meals to the rooms of those who would never leave them again, and the direful echos of hollow coughs resounded through the halls. On sunny days, pale men and women crept out upon the balconies, or were propped by tender hands in pillowed easy chairs to bask in the warm light.

Just then the slaughter-house cure was a favorite treatment at Denver. Every day the death of oxen and cows was anticipated as renewed life to men and women. When the doors of the slaughter-houses were opened, a throng rushed in ready to catch the ebbing life of the doomed animals. As the warm red current gushes forth, glasses were held to be filled from the stream by people who stood around like the habitués of Congress Spring, to have their tumblers replenished. The blood of beasts is thus better utilized than in ancient sacrifices, if indeed its virtue is not imaginary.

The Colorado Central was the first railroad to radiate from Denver after the Kansas Pacific had reached it from the east, and assured the development of the territory. To the Ames family of Boston belongs the inception of this undertaking, as to one of them, whose meritorious enterprise will be remembered after the unjust obloquy which has been attached to his name shall have passed away, may be attributed the most efficient promotion of the Great Union Pacific.

The Messrs. Ames carried their broad gauge track as far as it was feasible, to Golden City, and then as the only means of reaching the mineral district through Clear Creek Cañon, adopted the narrow gauge, which has since come into general use in the west. It was an imperative necessity, for it must pass over a grade of one hundred and twenty-five feet, and for a short distance of even two hundred and seventy-three feet to the mile. Moreover, it has been found that in point of cost and in the expense of working, only about one-half the outlay is required by the new system. No one can pass over its line without admiring the engineering skill of its construction, surmounting obstacles that many incredulous minds considered impossibilities.

The credit of this stupendous work is due to Mr. T. E. Sickels whose name ought to be identified with the enterprise carried through by his resolute skill.

It has already reached the apparently insurmountable barrier of the " Snowy Range," the eastern slope of the Rocky Mountains.

We left Denver in a driving snow storm, scarcely an object of interest visible from the windows of the railway carriage, and arriving at Golden, were transferred to the narrow gauge. As we passed upward through the narrow and precipitous cañon, the clouds broke and displayed a scene of wonders. The bare rocks stood out in bold relief from the sparkling snow, and the pines in their fleecy dress of winter were more than ever beautiful. Turning and twisting through rocks and ice-clad defiles for eighteen miles, we thought of the great power that had riven the cliffs asunder with only more admiration than we accorded to the daring engineers, who, lowered in ropes from the crags overhead, first surveyed the route, and ventured with their human skill to combat the forces of nature.

This cañon, twenty-five years since bordering smoothly the side of its stream, has been, for its fifty miles of length, picked and turned over to the bed rock and sifted for the precious deposits, until it is as rough as the overhanging crags. Along the railroad line are to be seen conduits, sluices and winches, used in the process of placer mining, or abandoned when they have served their purposes. A few miners of the ancient persuasion still pursue their labors, although the best pockets have been cleaned out, and the chances of nuggets are so small that average daily earnings are scarcely more than the miner's support. The great crowd have left the exhausted placers for the mountains, where, under the organized system of capitalists or corporations, there is either great wealth to be gained or disastrous failure to be experienced.

The poor man, instead of working for himself is a day-laborer for hire, and the rich man becomes either a millionaire or a bankrupt. This is the tendency of all business at the present day as conducted by "soulless corporations," and yet corporations have done a good work for the country. Without them railroads and telegraph lines could not have been built, and progress would have come to a stand-still.

A corporation might do something for Idaho Springs. It began its career as a mining camp, and now aspires to be a watering-place and sanitarium, like Manitou.

Here is also a fine climate, unusual seasons excepted. It is in the midst of romantic mountain scenery, 7,400 feet above the sea level. Its mineral springs, hot and cold, of iron and soda, are said to be wonderfully efficacious. It is of easy access, only thirty-six miles or three hours from Denver, but there is no "Improvement Company" to spend money in making it attractive. No pretty temples are built over its springs, which resemble unreclaimed cesspools. No shady walks with arbors of trained clematis are laid out, and there is no order or beauty in the buildings that straggle about in the uniformity of ugliness, still preserving the wretched characteristics of a mining camp.

Georgetown, fourteen miles beyond Idaho Springs, is the terminus of this branch of the Colorado Central.

In 1866 it was a mere "camp" in the first year of its existence, and the total value of its productions was only $500. It is now forced up against the abrupt precipices of the Rocky Mountains, the human current having flowed upwards to a level of 8,400 feet, and there spread itself into the streets of a city. Its people may well be proud of their enterprise and wealth. Before them they have bright anticipations reflected from the tons of solid ore, inexhaustible in the mountains around them.

Already they have churches of every denomination. Georgetown has its high school, its halls for theatrical representations, lectures and political gatherings, without which the mountain eagles would droop and die, if they could not pick at each other with their beaks. It has its fashionable Stewart's for ladies, and saloons and billiard rooms for gentlemen, hotels for genuine comfort, newspapers, libraries and museums for general entertainment, in fact, all that can make happy this little secluded world.

In wintry weather we could not visit with advantage the surroundings of Georgetown. Above it is "Green Lake," a favorite resort in summer, and then clear and transparent down to its emerald depths. The "Devil's Gate," the "Bridal Veil," and other resorts of fantastic names are in the list of show places, and beyond all rises the lofty summit of Gray's Peak, in summer as well as winter wrapped in perpetual snow. Even had it been practicable to climb to its top, we would have been satisfied with our ascent to Pike's Peak, of equal height, as adventure enough for one summer. Warned by the portentous snow clouds wreathing the mountains and creeping towards the cañon, we hastened back to Idaho Springs, where, sorely against inclination, we were blocked up by storms for nearly a week.

Central City is situated on the branch of Clear Creek, from which we diverged in ascending the railway. A ridge of the mountains known as "the divide" separates it from Idaho, six miles away. The summit of the pass is about equi-distant from the two towns, and the route between them, an equal transit up and down hill with an elevation of one thousand feet to be overcome, must be through Virginia Cañon on the Idaho side, and by Russel's Gulch from Central City. In many places the road is very steep and cut around sharp turns. It was on this mountain that Gen. Grant took his memorable drive.

"You see," said Opdyke, "this was how it was. I've been twitted about it because I'm a democrat, and folks said I wanted to kill him on that account—just as if I wanted to kill myself too! I hain't got enough political principle for that. It was all a mistake about our getting down so quick. After we got a little over the divide, and I was puttin' on 'em along tol'ble fast, the president says he, 'Bill, how long will it be before we get down?'

"'About twenty minutes, or it may be twenty-five,' says I.

"'Couldn't you make it twice as much?' says he.

"Now I understood him 'twice as quick,' and accordin' I slung out the silk to please him. Well, they did lick it, that's a fact! Why, sir, we come around some of the curves with both side wheels in the air for forty rods at a time, so that a fellow who come along a spell behind us said I drove down in a wheel-barrow.

"The general, he gripped on to the bars and clinched his teeth, and actooally bit his cigar in two, so it dropped out of his mouth, but he didn't say nothin' till I reined up at Beebe's just ten minutes from the time he spoke first, and them six horses stood smoking like six high pressure ingines. When we got off onto the stoop, the president drawed back, and showing his ha'r says he, 'Mr. William Opdyke, take my hat, you're the only man that ever scared me!'"

It was not in the power of Opdyke to frighten us with this style of driving, for the journey over the mountain from Idaho Springs to Central City was the work of a whole day. The snow had fallen to the depth of two feet, and in some places much more. As we toiled up the ascent with frequent stops that almost amounted to an habitual stand-still, we had abundant leisure to admire the charms of the wintry landscape, but the poetry of "Beautiful Snow" was not inspiring enough to overcome the weariness of slow progress, the biting nips of the frost, and the sweeps of the fierce nor'-wester that whirled its white wreaths around us.

As we came down the slope towards Central City there was no display of coach driving calculated to alarm timid outsiders, but the jaded beasts, urged on by an unsparing lash, barely succeeded in staggering to the door of the Teller House, the principal hotel of the place, and considering its first-class pretensions, realized only in its high prices, the most cheerless and uncomfortable house of entertainment we had yet seen in Colorado.

Central City was almost totally destroyed by fire a few years ago. It is now rebuilt and ready for another similar experience. Here where gold has been scooped up by the handfuls no use is made of it to make life comfortable or any thing more than endurable. The town is one vast mining gulch, with shapeless houses dumped here and there among the excavations, and clinging to the side hills.

Black Hawk, where the reduction works are chiefly in operation, so closely connected with Central City that it may be considered a part of the town, is at the terminus of the western fork of the railroad.

Silver is the great product of the East Creek Cañon. On this side of the ridge the mineral chiefly produced is gold. We were escorted by a guide for more than a mile under the mountains through the tunnel of the Bob-tail works, turning off at different points to inspect side galleries, steam engines and little colonies of people busy in the subterranean darkness, by the dim illumination of tallow candles.

It was Sunday, the day on which in quiet towns there is a hallowed rest from labor, the stillness of the air only broken by the music of church bells, and godliness and cleanliness sit down together for one-seventh of the week in peace. There is happiness without gold. Here is gold without happiness. Ever toiling, day and night, week-days and Sabbaths, in darkness, begrimed with dirt, amidst the clatter of machinery, under the drippings of shafts and tunnels, the pale-faced miner works for the yellow dust that blinds his eyes to the sweet enjoyment of life.

We descended the western branch of the railroad until we came to the point from which we had diverged on the upward track to Georgetown, and then through Clear Creek Cañon came out at the foot of the narrow gauge road in Golden City. This little place may be said to live from the gold and silver washes of the upper cañons, having its refineries and works for reducing both metals.

At Golden we come again to the broad gauge track, by which a direct connection is made with the Union Pacific five miles west of Cheyenne, distance 119 miles. One may return, if desirable, from Golden to Denver, 17 miles, and thence take the Kansas Pacific for the east.

From a more southern part of the State, the Atchison, Topeka and Santa Fe forms a straight line to St. Louis.

CHAPTER XXXV.

CHEYENNE—PROJECTED RAILROAD TO THE BLACK HILLS—
THE GREAT CATTLE RANGE—LIFE OF THE RANCHMAN—
SUGGESTIONS TO YOUNG MEN—NEBRASKA—OMAHA—THE
BRIDGE ACROSS THE MISSOURI—RAILROADS TO CHICAGO—
THE CHICAGO AND NORTH-WEST—A DINNER IN THE
HOTEL-CAR—CONTRAST OF MINING AND AGRICULTURE—
CONCLUSION.

Various points on the Union Pacific afford communication with the Black Hills, north of its line, in Dakota.

The measured distance from some of these places may be less than from Cheyenne, but after careful surveys for grade this has been found most suitable for the starting-point of a branch railroad. Moreover, the selection has been influenced by the connection here with Colorado. Accordingly, the construction of a narrow gauge has been determined to Deadwood, the chief mining camp of the Black Hills, this summer, the whole distance to be not far from two hundred miles.

The ore of the Black Hills, although of low grade, is abundant, and gold mining has been very profitable, notwithstanding the disadvantages of transportation. The "Homestake" and other mines have put up their machinery at excessive cost, and yet are able to declare large dividends upon their stock. As soon as the railroad reaches Deadwood, or by the time it has made any considerable advance, such a stimulus will be given to mining and the business connected with it, that the enterprise cannot fail to be successful. Already Cheyenne derives no small profit from this trade.

Before the gold discoveries, it was a large town centred in the best cattle district of the West. Whatever the success of miners, whether there may be exhaustion or new discoveries of mines, ranchmen will never be poor and cattle will multiply beyond calculation. These vast plains, watered by the Platte river and its branches, in summer covered with luxuriant grass converted to rich standing hay in winter, are capable of sustaining cattle, sheep and horses in numbers that I will not estimate for fear of being accused of exaggeration.

The life of a ranchman—at least of some ranchmen—doubtless has its hardships. Before undertaking it, a man should make his calculations. A trial balance should suggest itself to his mind. Ranch life is debtor to a total change of habits, to the loss of "society," theatres, lectures, clubs and churches, besides many bodily comforts and table luxuries. It is creditor by profitable business, out of door exercise, the society of nature instead of fellow-creatures, and above all, by health of body and of mind. With this account before his eyes, let a would-be ranchman sit down, calmly reflect and decide. Were I a young man looking about for a business in life, I should draw a balance in favor of Laramie plains.

It may be asked, "Would you take a wife to live with you on a ranch?"

Certainly I would not take the Miss Culture introduced in the early part of this narrative; I would not take there a woman who is merely a fine lady, but I would take a lady who is a true woman.

This is not poetry; it is not the sentimentality of "love in a cottage;" it is practical. It is not the whole solution of problems of financial depression, over-production, unequal divisions of property, vice and misery, but it is a skirmisher upon the flanks of those evils.

Ranch life is a return to first principles of living to patriarchal simplicity. When we talk of "sitting down in heaven with Abraham, Isaac and Jacob," let us begin by sitting down after their example on earth.

But young men must not be led to suppose that cattle raising is an invariable success. Even to those who thoroughly understand the business, there come years of failure, occasional severe winters, distemper among the herds, Indian raids, thefts by white men, dull markets, and many other discouragements.

Experience is more necessary than is generally supposed. Don't imagine that you may lay aside your walking cane, quit the Fifth avenue promenade, jump out of your faultless clothes, rig yourself out in blue woollen shirt and buckskin trousers, take the train for Laramie plains, buy a herd of cattle, mount a mustang and be an accomplished ranchman in a week.

You would be bucked from your horse in less than three minutes; you would lose your cattle in the first year by theft and your own ignorance, and then you would come home disgusted.

Abandon the city and all your old conventional habits. Go west to seek employment from some man who has been successful in the business. Get what wages you can for one or two years; work for nothing if you can get no pay, and if no one will employ you on these terms, pay for the privilege of working. Your father has probably paid ten times more for your useless Latin and Greek than it will now cost you to get the practical information you require. Remember that no log cabin is so rude that it cannot contain a library, and reading is never so well digested as when it is an accompaniment of work.

We are at Cheyenne, six thousand feet above the sea level, five hundred and sixteen miles west of Omaha, towards which we gradually descend over this great cattle range to the lower plains of Nebraska.

Here are the rich farming lands owned by Government and the Union Pacific railroad in alternate sections. They are fast coming under cultivation, so that in five years from this time there will scarcely be an untilled acre on the line of the road through the whole State.

"Oumahaw," on the west bank of the "Mizourah," as town and river are called in the vernacular, was once the capital and is still the most prosperous city of Nebraska.

Although it does not correspond with our Eastern ideas of municipal grandeur, it is a very respectable town of 20,000 inhabitants, well provided with saloons, churches and schools, of which the High School, set on its chief eminence as a proud monument to be seen by all travellers, boasts facilities for "giving a fellow all the learning worth having."

Wiser than the Knickerbockers, who did not foresee that the avenue they called Broadway would be in the future too narrow for traffic, the people of Omaha have laid out all their streets one hundred feet wide, so that when the day comes for rapid transit, they will not be blocked up by omnibuses while the question is debated.

That eccentric gentleman, George Francis Train, who has

cultivated many grains of sense with all his wild tares, had much to do with the development of Omaha. He fully appreciated its natural advantages, and earnestly advocated the construction of the Union Pacific Railroad which starts from this point.

This great work was begun in the latter part of 1865. It was then Train made the prophecy that it it would be completed in less than five years. He was called a crazy enthusiast for this speech, as well as for many other sayings and doings for which he merited the name. But when the road was actually completed in a little more than three years and a half, no one gave him the credit his prediction deserved. Train invested all his money in Omaha lands, but taxes and financial panics have been too much for him to bear while he had also on his hands the liberation of Ireland, the prospective Presidency of the United States, and the conversion of all mankind to his own skeptical philosophy.

The Union Pacific Railroad may well be proud of the great bridge that spans the river here.

A steamboat captain on the train, however, remarked that "the durned river ain't to be trusted; the channel changes so often that the bend that's here to-day may be ten mile off in a year or two, and then what's the good of this bridge?" He was opposed to railroads, as they had injured his business, and so he trumped up this charge against the river that refuses to support him any longer.

I suggested that, in case his anticipations were realized, the bridge could be removed to suit the convenience of the Missouri, to which he replied that "it might not fit." "Anyway," he said, "railroads are a perversion of nature; the Lord made rivers to raft and steamboat on, and if they ain't enough men could make canals, and He'd find water for 'em. He never meant that these corporations should take away the business of honest men."

After crossing the bridge there is a choice of three railroads from Council Bluffs to Chicago—the Chicago and North-West, the Rock Island and the Burlington and Quincy roads. They run on nearly parallel lines at sufficient distance apart to develop the resources of Iowa and Illinois, States excelled by none of the Union in soil adapted to wheat and corn.

These roads are all singularly profitable notwithstanding their close competition. Their trains leave at the same time and arrive in Chicago together to form a connection with the Lake Shore Railroad to Buffalo. Without disparaging the others on which we have sometimes travelled, we cannot too highly praise the management of the Chicago and North-West.

Rolling along upon its smooth track we reach Chicago in twenty-two hours. Not the least of our enjoyments is the luxurious hotel-car. We dispense at last with the lunch-basket which has been the stay of life along the line from San Francisco to Omaha.

The Government directors who annually travel over the Pacific roads, do them no more than justice in reporting that they are well built, kept in excellent repair, and intelligently managed. Yet the public has one favor to ask of them. Let them come without notice upon the sharks who furnish meals for other passengers along the route, and let them breakfast, dine and sup as ordinary mortals do for five days.

Passengers pay their dollars not complaining that ninety per cent. is the landlord's profit, but they find fault with reason because they cannot get decent and digestible food at any price.

Hasty perpendicular feeding is in a great measure the cause of what Germans call "the American complaint," dyspepsia.

I am not partial to the Continental cooking—to sauerkraut, sausages, raw ham, caviare, lager beer and sour wine, but I do commend the practice of their railroads in permitting passengers to sit down at well served tables in well ordered restaurants, where even incongruous articles may be placed in the stomach at such considerate distances that they are comparatively harmless.

What a change from the "twenty minutes for dinner!" when we were obliged to leave our rolling homes, often crossing over mud and snow to cheerless barracks where supercilious waiters dashed upon the table cold and repelling dishes of tough steak, floating bacon, pies and baked beans, and cups of coffee and tea, the steeped productions of home industry; and then to listen as we bolted the indigestible mass for the expected scream of the whistle. Now, the polite negro, yes, I will call him the colored man, if he pleases, and in the joy of the moment, my colored brother, politely hands us a bill-of-fare at which Delmonico need not sneer, lays a spotless cloth, and sets upon it warm plates, silver ware, goblets and wine glasses. Then follow in their regular order soup, fish, entrées, tender meats with succulent vegetables, dessert of ice cream and fruit ending with the best gift of Araby the blest, while sherry and champagne have moistened the abundant and comfortable repast.

All these roads make an uninterrupted progress through cultivated farms, and the green fields, or the harvest ripe and bending to the breeze, are in lovely contrast with the sterile mountains and plains of the uncultivated territories.

Happy farmers! we often exclaimed, as we saw them gathering in their golden treasures.

Poor devils! too, we sometimes called them when in one night the grasshoppers blasted their labor of a year, swept their green fields and left them desolated as by fire.

I have in my mind an indelible picture of an Iowa farmer leaning over his fence and surveying his stripped corn stalks, with an expression on his face of resignation, though a shade of it mingled with the query, "Is this the work of Providence or of the devil?" If the train had stopped long enough I would have tried to console him. I would have said, "My friend, we must all take our chances; mines peter out, cattle starve on the plains, ships are wrecked, merchants fail, tradesmen are unemployed; all these things happen, but they do not happen all the time, and it is equally true that the grasshopper does not always come in his might, and that he does not always come to the same place."

So, sons of the soil, take courage in the reflection that happiness and misery are mingled through the world, but the distribution of happiness is greater for you than for any of the rest. When you dream of rich deposits of gold and silver, imagining you may find them and help yourselves to unlimited stores like Aladdin or Monte Cristo, remember the comparison made by Governor Stanford, of the mining and agricultural industries of California, and see now how it has been justified by results up to the close of 1878. Take the mining interest in which I include Nevada, as the stocks of all the mines are quoted on the San Francisco Exchange. The total amount of dividends from California and Consolidated Virginia, the two great "Bonanzas," from the time of their first working has been—

	$71,180,000
Less assessments..	411,200
	$70,768,800

showing this net profit, nearly all of which was pocketed by four men, Flood, O'Brien, Mackay and Fair.

Per contra, the whole amount of assessments on the other 178 mines quoted on the list, has been—

	$71,253,040
Less dividends	45,039,500
Loss	$26,213,540

To this may be added the commissions and charges of brokers which, at a moderate estimate for all these years, may be computed to be $50,000,000.

If the stock list may be taken as a criterion it would appear that the whole people have lost more than a few men have gained. On the other hand, it is to be admitted that the laboring miners have gained a living, and that there are many other mines productive and unproductive not on the stock list where profits and losses cannot be estimated from reliable data.

My object was to make a comparison of the mining and agricultural resources of California, which should properly appear in a previous chapter. I had hoped to obtain the agricultural statistics of 1878, but as they are not yet forthcoming, I here introduce some figures kindly furnished for my purpose by Mr. Elmore H. Walker, of the New York Produce Exchange. It may be premised that the year 1877 was one of extraordinary drought.

The cereal crops of California in 1877 were—

Indian Corn .	1,550,000	bushels of the value of	$	1,472,500
Wheat	22,000,000	" " "		28,600,000
Oats	1,750,000	" " "		1,277,500
Barley . . .	7,800,000	" " "		7,020,000
Potatoes . . .	3,200,000	" " "		2,400,000
Hay	560,000	tons " "		8,400,000
Total value cereals, hay and potatoes . .				$49,170,000

In 1876 the California crops were as follows :—

Indian Corn.	1,600,000 bushels of the value of	$ 1,712,000
Wheat	30,000,000 " " "	34,200,000
Rye	78,000 " " "	74,100
Oats	2,450,000 " " "	1,813,000
Barley	11,800,000 " " "	8,142,000
Potatoes	4,000,000 " " "	3,320,000
Hay	850,000 tons " "	9,868,500

Total value cereals, potatoes and hay . . . $59,129,600

The wheat crop of California in 1878 was about as large as the crop of 1876, and is much larger than the crop of 1877. The barley crop of that State in 1878, was, it is believed, larger than the crop of 1876. Can any one doubt that the interest of California will be promoted by the encouragement of this more regular permanent and widely diffused industry, rather than by the development of mining, the source of speculation and gambling?

And now as we come so near the end of our journey among the farmers of the "Old West," the reports of their productions find an appropriate place following those of California.

CEREAL CROPS OF NEBRASKA.

	Bushels.	Acres.	Value.
Indian Corn	38,500,000	1,013,158	$6,930,000
Wheat	5,640,000	376,000	4,681,200
Rye	....	.....	....
Oats	5,400,000	135,000	810,000
Barley	520,000	21,667	140,400
Buckwheat	...	....	.....
Potatoes	1,500,000	14,286	600,000
Hay, tons	475,000	327,586	1,733,750
Total		1,887,697	$14,885,350

Cereal Crops of Iowa.

	Bushels.	Acres.	Value.
Indian Corn	156,000,000	4,800,000	$39,000,000
Wheat	37,810,000	2,607,584	32,894,700
Rye	....	....	....
Oats	42,000,000	1,105,263	8,400,000
Barley	5,300,000	230,435	2,120,000
Buckwheat	....	....	....
Potatoes	9,500,000	95,000	3,610,000
Hay, tons	2,550,000	1,961,568	12,112,500
Total		10,799,820	$98,137,200

Cereal Crops of Illinois.

	Bushels.	Acres.	Value.
Indian Corn	260,000,000	8,865,517	75,400,000
Wheat	33,000,000	2,000,090	34,320,000
Rye	2,844,000	158,000	1,422,000
Oats	59,200,000	1,600,000	13,024,000
Barley	2,760,000	120,000	2,152,800
Buckwheat	176,000	11,000	128,480
Potatoes	12,834,009	138,000	5,046,960
Hay, tons	3,936,000	2,466,006	23,104,320
Total		15,452,517	$155,198,560

The products of three great States whose industries are chiefly agricultural for one year amount to a value of $268,231,110. This has not been divided among a few men; its profits have been evenly distributed, and the aggregate loss falls upon none. Farmers, stick to your ploughs and thank God that you have inherited the curse upon Adam!

Arriving at Chicago we are so near to our homes that my readers will not care to be piloted over the well-known tracks that lead to the Atlantic coast. If they have been entertained I shall be pleased, and it will be a greater source of satisfaction if they have in any degree been instructed.

CONCLUSION.

We have travelled together over seas and mountains, beheld nature in her beauty and sublimity, and I hope that more practical observations have shown that, as a nation, we owe our wealth, number and power to what we produce, and are able by a great railroad system to transport from our rich and boundless acres. Manufactures and commerce, shackled as they are by tariff legislation, are small and of little account in comparison to this. Even agriculture feels the pressure of the burden imposed upon it by a monopoly that enhances the cost of the farmer's tools and household wants.

But notwithstanding all, with its natural advantages, it overcomes every obstacle that opposes its progress. With new and increasing appliances of machinery, guided by intelligent labor, it outrivals the old-world systems of tillage and harvesting, and insures us a lasting peace with the nations of Europe, for it brings them to our feet as suppliants for their daily bread.

www.ingramcontent.com/pod-product-compliance
Lightning Source LLC
Chambersburg PA
CBHW030321240426
43673CB00040B/1240